"A remarkable manual for discovering what really matters, then building a life around the answer, *How a Little Becomes a Lot* is loaded with practical advice for what to do next – but it's also one of those uncommon books that leaves you more deeply engaged with the world just by reading it."

Oliver Burkeman, author of *Four Thousand Weeks* and *Meditations for Mortals*

"If you've listened to his podcast, you know that Eric Zimmer is a deeply authentic and profound person. So, it's no surprise that now he has given us this deeply authentic and profound book. *How a Little Becomes a Lot* will teach you manageable ways to make meaningful changes in your life. And along the way, it will give you new understandings of the world – and of your very own self."

Susan Cain, author of *Quiet* and *Bittersweet*

"*How a Little Becomes a Lot* is a beautifully grounded guide to meaningful change. Eric Zimmer reminds us that transformation comes from the small, steady choices we make again and again – especially after our initial burst of motivation has faded. An entertaining, thoughtful companion for anyone learning to change from the inside out."

Kristin Neff, author of *Self-Compassion* and *Fierce Self-Compassion*

"*How a Little Becomes a Lot* is a powerful reminder that real change happens in small, consistent steps. Eric Zimmer shows us how tiny daily actions can rewire patterns, rebuild trust in ourselves, and create lasting transformation. Practical, encouraging, and deeply human – this is a guide for anyone ready to create the life they deserve."

Nicole LePera, author of *How to Do the Work* and *How to Be the Love You Seek*

"Chock-full of wit and wisdom, I finished this and instantly started it all over again, highlighter in hand. It's already brought me closer to the person I want to be. Everyone should read this book."
Catherine Gray, author of *The Unexpected Joy* series

"Eric Zimmer has traveled an extraordinary distance — from the chaos of addiction to a decade of intimate conversations with psychologists, philosophers, and spiritual teachers. In this book, he brings that journey together movingly. It's wise, compassionate, and will help lots of people."
Johann Hari, author of *Stolen Focus* and *Lost Connections*

"Eric Zimmer shows how real transformation doesn't come from willpower or grand gestures — but from small, intentional choices made consistently over time. Drawing on his own powerful story of recovery, he introduces a framework for aligning your actions and values, building momentum, and cultivating self-compassion."
Charles Duhigg, author of *Supercommunicators* and *The Power of Habit*

"*How a Little Becomes a Lot* is one of those rare books that seamlessly blends gripping stories, cutting-edge science and century-old philosophical wisdom to provide readers with a blueprint for navigating their lives more effectively. Eric Zimmer is a special person and this is a very special book. Required reading for anyone ready to make change in their lives."
Ethan Kross, author of *Shift* and *Chatter*

HOW A LITTLE BECOMES A LOT

THE ART
OF SMALL
CHANGES
FOR A MORE
MEANINGFUL
LIFE

ERIC ZIMMER

First published in Great Britain in 2026 by
DK RED, an imprint of
Dorling Kindersley Limited
20 Vauxhall Bridge Road,
London SW1V 2SA

The authorized representative in the EEA is
Dorling Kindersley Verlag GmbH. Arnulfstr. 124,
80636 Munich, Germany

Copyright © 2026 Dorling Kindersley Limited
A Penguin Random House Company
10 9 8 7 6 5 4 3 2 1
001–352014–April/2026
Text copyright © 2026 Eric Zimmer
Eric Zimmer has asserted his right to be identified
as the author of this work.

First published in the US in 2026 by HarperCollins Publishers

CALVIN AND HOBBES © 1995 Watterson. Reprinted with permission of
ANDREWS MCMEEL SYNDICATION. All rights reserved.

CALVIN AND HOBBES © 1988 Watterson. Reprinted with permission of
ANDREWS MCMEEL SYNDICATION. All rights reserved.

Cover design by Jordan Lambley

All rights reserved.
No part of this publication may be reproduced, stored in or introduced into a retrieval system, or transmitted, in any form, or by any means (electronic, mechanical, photocopying, recording, or otherwise), without the prior written permission of the copyright owner.
DK values and supports copyright. Thank you for respecting intellectual property laws by not reproducing, scanning or distributing any part of this publication by any means without permission. By purchasing an authorized edition, you are supporting writers and artists and enabling DK to continue to publish books that inform and inspire readers. No part of this publication may be used or reproduced in any manner for the purpose of training artificial intelligence technologies or systems. In accordance with Article 4(3) of the DSM Directive 2019/790, DK expressly reserves this work from the text and data mining exception.

A CIP catalogue record for this book
is available from the British Library.
HB ISBN: 978-0-2417-6714-6
TPB ISBN: 978-0-2417-6715-3
Printed and bound in the United Kingdom

www.dk.com

This book was made with Forest Stewardship Council™ certified paper – one small step in DK's commitment to a sustainable future.
Learn more at www.dk.com/uk/information/sustainability

To all those who still suffer

CONTENTS

INTRODUCTION — xi

PART I: BEGINNING

1. Little by Little — 3
2. What Is Worth Wanting? — 23
3. The Architecture of Change — 45
4. Moments of Action — 71

PART II: BECOMING

5. Be a Friend to Yourself — 97
6. We Don't See the World as It Is, We See It as We Are — 129
7. The Middle Way — 153
8. We Find Ourselves in Others — 177

PART III: BEING

9. Allowing Everything to Be Exactly as It Is — 217
10. The Gift of Presence — 245

CONCLUSION — 267
APPENDIX: END OF CHAPTER EXERCISES — 273
ACKNOWLEDGMENTS — 309
NOTES — 313
INDEX — 329

HOW
A LITTLE
BECOMES
A LOT

INTRODUCTION

IF YOU WERE WATCHING THE MOVIE OF MY LIFE, THE PIVOTAL SCENE WOULD show a dingy yellow room in what was once a tuberculosis hospital in Columbus, Ohio, in the winter of 1994. A counselor would be talking to a young man slumped in exhaustion, looking equal parts frightened and lost. Me.

I weighed one hundred pounds, my skin jaundiced from hepatitis C, with the shadow of fifty years in prison hanging over me. I was a homeless heroin addict at the end of his road, and even I could smell the despair on my own skin.

"Eric, you need to go to long-term treatment," the counselor told me.

"No, thank you," I said, summoning what little dignity I supposed I had left. Then I dragged myself up and slouched down the hall like the wounded animal I was.

Back in my room, I had what they call a "moment of clarity" as I looked out my clouded window at cold gray skies. It was a few days before Christmas. I realized with sudden, terrifying lucidity that my current path led only to death or prison. Dope sick, shaky, and afraid, I turned, walked back down the hall to that yellow room, and opened my mouth before I could change my mind. "Okay," I said, "I'll go to your treatment."

That would be the high-drama, dark-night-of-the-soul turning point in the movie of my life. And it was an important moment—but it's also anything but the full story. In getting from that wounded place to where I am today, that scene is not as monumental as it may seem. Deciding to enter treatment would be nothing without the countless tiny decisions I made day after day, year after year afterward: deciding not to take the route past that bar, calling my sponsor instead of my dealer, showing up to a meeting when every cell in my body wanted to stay home and hide.

When we think about life-changing events, we tend to think in the singular. The epiphany. The miracle. The watershed choice that will put us on a new trajectory for good. But that's not how real change happens for most people, most of the time. It happens little bit by little bit, with a thousand chances to do A or B, each choice a thread woven into the fabric of who we become.

The story of me getting sober in the movie would be a classic recovery montage—gritted teeth, a couple of shaky smiles at a support meeting, a swelling soundtrack as I turn down a dealer's offer. A few quick scenes and suddenly I'd be transformed.

But the reality can't be abbreviated, because it is what happened in the long stretches of time the camera would never capture: when it was just me and my questions about how to fill the next day, hour, or minute in any way that would keep me going.

This book is about all those other moments. The title of this book is inspired by a Tanzanian proverb that sums up their true power: *Little by little, a little becomes a lot*. Perhaps you've never had as dark a night of the soul as mine, but we all experience a million tiny opportunities for choice and change. The good news is that we can learn to live more wisely in each and every off-camera moment, making small choices that add up to something bigger and more dramatic.

• • •

Facing debilitating addiction at twenty-four caused me to become intensely interested in two things: how people change, and the pursuit of wisdom. There's not much mystery about why I was interested in the former. I needed to change to survive. But my questions went deeper than my own salvation. I watched friends die, people with brilliant minds and contagious laughter who wanted to live but couldn't break free from the grip of substances that were killing them—and I couldn't understand why. "Why do we get locked into patterns?" I asked the universe. "And why are only some of us lucky enough to make new ones?" Was it willpower? Was it chance? Was it something else entirely?

As my life improved and I began to have more "normal" concerns, like being successful at work, raising children, and keeping my cholesterol in check, these same issues of change kept coming up. Why was I able to work hard at specific points yet at other times procrastinate nearly endlessly? Why could I commit to positive behaviors at some times but not others?

If you're like most people, you've probably had the very same thing occur to you. You know what you want to do—you want to exercise more, eat better, stop procrastinating, be patient, or get around to this thing you've been putting on the back burner. And you do it occasionally! But follow-through? That's another story altogether.

For me, it never seemed possible to think about any one goal in isolation. The smallest wish for change (how can I stop being late all the time?) led to impossibly large thoughts (how should I be using my finite time on this planet?). Why we are here, what matters in life, how should we live—these questions were inescapably present beneath the surface of the everyday. And yet, for many of us, they are the kinds of questions we don't quite know how to carry. We tend to hand them over to religion, or else we gesture toward something we call "wisdom," unsure of whether it's something we're meant to study, practice, or simply hope will find us.

I had been searching for a compass for a long time. After my so-called moment of clarity, I found my way into a 12-step program. One thing about those programs—they don't hesitate to suggest a spiritual solution to what looks, on the surface, like a physical problem. I wasn't in a position to argue at the time, given that finding *some* solution was a life-or-death necessity. But as I found my footing, I also found that the search itself had taken hold of me. I became a lifelong seeker—not only of change, but of meaning.

I followed wherever that thread led—through the *Tao Te Ching* and the writings of Rainer Maria Rilke, through the insights of modern psychology, and even through the adventures of Calvin and Hobbes. I wasn't looking for one truth—I was learning how to recognize it in many forms.

Many years later I started my podcast, *The One You Feed*, to explore what makes life worth living. I interviewed scientists, psychologists, thought leaders, artists of all sorts, spiritual teachers, and public figures—often asking how we change, and how we make that change mean something. As the podcast grew and I built a coaching practice, two distinct threads emerged that captured my attention.

The first was how much overlap there was in the principles of the best ways to live a meaningful and happy life. All the major religions, the great philosophers, modern psychology, and iconic thinkers repeated many of the same things. The second was how rarely these realms of knowledge, which seemed to me pieces of a shared puzzle, were put in direct conversation with one another.

The field of modern behavioral science explained so much, and it was fascinating to recognize my own struggles reflected in study after study on the neuroscience of procrastination, habit change, "willpower." At the same time, I saw the insights of this science narrowly focused on certain behaviors: eating right, exercising, saving money, and increasing productivity.

Themes of personal and spiritual growth, meanwhile, resonated deeply with my listening community and coaching clients, but the most profound principles seemed hard to apply in a practical sense. It's one thing to recognize wisdom in the Buddha's teaching that the root of suffering is desire, but quite another to know what to do with that. Should we . . . just stop wanting things so much? Compassion and equanimity are always wise words, but like a moment of clarity, there's a long way between recognizing a good idea and actually living it.

I began to think about combining the two threads. Could the science of change be applied to achieving wisdom? Instead of using this knowledge just to upgrade a habit or two, could we use it to improve our character? Could we use it to loosen the grip of old conditioning, to soften our reflexive reactivity? Could it help us feel more calm, more grounded, more at home in our own lives?

Over the course of ten years and more than eight hundred conversations, I have become convinced that the answer to all these questions is *yes*. These are ways of creating and maintaining positive change that combine both *outer behaviors* that support our health and well-being, and *inner attitudes* that help us find more peace, meaningfulness, and ease in our lives.

I say this not as an expert in any one tradition or school of thought, but as the seeker I've always been, with the privilege to have followed my curiosity to many fresh perspectives, deep wells of learning, and, yes, field-leading experts. This book is the result of over a decade (really, a lifetime) of searching for the truth about how and why we change, and asking what role change ultimately serves in a meaning-filled life.

When we pair modern behavioral science with principles that have stood the test of millennia, what we get is something I call *wise habits*. They are the sum of our **habits of thought** and **habits of behavior**. To take just one (little) example: In the early days of my recovery, my sponsor used to insist that I walk around the room, shake everyone's hand, and introduce myself. I could barely think of anything I wanted to do less. But that simple act became a behavior that forced me out of isolation. Over time, that outward practice rewired my inner dialogue. Instead of thinking, "I'm broken and alone," I began to think, "I belong here." And the more my thinking about my connection to others changed, the easier it became to do the behavior.

Wise habits have worked for me, and I hope they work for you.

• • •

Living a good life is hard. It means answering, day in and day out, two questions I've been asking myself for a long time:

What do I want to do?
Who do I want to be?

If you're like most people I've coached (and probably most people, period), you've asked yourself some version of these questions before—often with a heavy dose of self-criticism. "Why can't I just do what I promise myself I will?" "Why am I acting like someone I don't want to be?" The voice in your head has likely been less than kind—not just about your failures, but about what those failures seem to mean about you.

From a certain angle, this book is two books in one. The first is a manual for outer change: for answering the question *What do I want to do?* and being able to follow through. It covers the art and science of habit formation, ways to bolster self-control, build resilience, and sustain change over the long term. If you stay focused on external goals—improving your sleep, moving your body, eating better, meditating more often, reading more—you'll come away with plenty.

You might also come to this book with the second question, *Who do I want to be?* On this path, this book is a program for changing your inner experience, helping you to feel more at ease, a greater sense of purpose, and less in conflict between your values, desires, and behaviors. The "wise habits" we'll explore, such as self-compassion and presence in the moment, will be revealed not only as agents of change, but as profound sources of meaning in themselves.

Whichever path you choose as a reader—whether you lead with *What do I want to do?* or *Who do I want to be?*—the big reveal is that they're just two lanes of the same road. Because in reality, our inner and outer lives are never separate. Working on one necessarily works on the other. The principles for developing a wiser inner life make it easier for you to change your outer life. And our behavior in the world affects our inner life to the same degree. At its deepest level, this book isn't about transforming any one aspect of yourself—it's about transforming how you relate to *you*, your struggles, and the process of change itself.

The chapters that follow tell the story of a wiser approach to change in three parts: Beginning, Becoming, and Being. Part I will lay out the mechanics: How to begin something new. It's about recognizing the tiny, essential building blocks of behavior and thought patterns that will become targets for consistent, iterative improvement. We'll go through setting intentions with values work, get into the science of decision-making with "cues" or "prompts," and talk about how to make consistent space for reflection through what I call "still points."

Part II is about the grand middle of change—the becoming. It's a set of inner practices and perspectives, ways to enter into wiser dialogue with ourselves, day in and day out, whether or not change is at the top of our minds at all. This is for the months after January, when our resolutions aren't so new, when we have neither the momentum of beginning nor the validation of some grand goal achieved. For many people, this is the hard part. We'll explore how to exercise self-compassion, perspective, a "middle-way" mindset, and the benefits of community.

Part III, Being, is the long tail of change, when a little has actually become "a lot." It's about what happens when we reach the horizon we've been aiming for, and we have to readjust to our new baseline. Perhaps we struggle with not immediately looking to a further horizon with greener grass. It's also about ensuring that change isn't the only prism through which we're viewing and valuing our lives. To truly be present to our lives as they are is often to realize, like Dorothy at the end of *The Wizard of Oz*, that we weren't so far from our destination to begin with.

I've often imagined having a conversation with the version of me who initially refused to go to treatment all those years ago. What exactly was that guy thinking? What did he have on the schedule that was important enough to say no to saving his own life, even temporarily?

Then I remember that that young man is no stranger to me, even now. Addiction aside, what I sought as a headstrong youth falling into heroin and alcohol—a sense of meaning, fulfillment, and connection beyond the everyday—I still seek. Just in far healthier, more sustainable ways. This a book about how to recognize what you're looking for in the behaviors that make up your day-to-day life, and how to attune yourself to finding them.

In the pages to come you'll learn more about my experience living and teaching this path to thousands of people, and hear from some of the many scientists, researchers, teachers, and spiritual leaders I've been privileged to learn from and through. There will be 12-step wisdom and Zen Buddhism, the two traditions that have changed my life most profoundly. There will be representatives of the pantheon of Western philosophy from Plato and Aristotle to William James, and Eastern luminaries from Confucius and Lao Tzu to a little Sun Tzu. Jung and Freud, Abraham Maslow and B. F. Skinner will show up to defend classical psychology, even as we'll see an evolution to cutting-edge research on behavioral change, neuroscience, and social psychology. Hemingway, Steinbeck, and friends stop in from the literature section. There will also be punk rock lyrics, Calvin and Hobbes, and at least one 1980s cop show.

With a question as big as "how do we change?" we need the full gamut of wisdom to answer it.

That said, one thing that is outside the scope of this book: serious addiction recovery. Recovery has been for me, in so many ways, a *little-by-little* process, and I carry with me the lived experience of how profound gradual, self-motivated change can be. That said, I'm not a professional addiction counselor, and if you're in the kind of situation I faced in my early twenties, the truth is that immediate, seismic change may be necessary just to start the long path upward. This book is about what comes after that turning point. And for those of you who've thankfully never needed to do a full U-turn with your life, it's about the little big changes we can all make without reinventing the wheel.

No matter where we find ourselves—whether life feels generous or stripped bare—there is always some small step available to us. Not always the one we want. Not always the one that changes everything. But something. A movement toward meaning. Some of us are given more room, more freedom, more choices; others, fewer. But even in the narrowest of places, a choice still waits. Small, positive steps worth taking, choices worth making.

A favorite motto of Roman emperors and grand dukes was *Festina lente*. Make haste, slowly. The genius, and the urgency, of this message is that it fits in. Right now. It fits in with your life, and how you want to live. *Festina lente* is how real change happens. Not the fake kind. This isn't a TV makeover. This is how we move forward. Take it from someone whose life was once about as static as can be in a dynamic universe.

Little by little, I came back to life.

Little by little, this book will work on you. And by the end, it won't feel very little at all.

Part I

BEGINNING

ONE

Little by Little

Little by little, a little becomes a lot.
—TANZANIAN PROVERB

DASHRATH MANJHI HAD A HAMMER, A CHISEL, AND A MOUNTAIN OF GRIEF.

His wife, Falguni, hadn't died because of the fall that injured her. She had died because the nearest doctor was ninety kilometers away by the one narrow, rocky path that wound its way around the steep ridge that divided their village in India from its neighbors. If he had only been able to travel straight across the ridge, Dashrath knew, he could have gotten her to the doctor in time. As it was, he had to live with the memory of Falguni leaving him on the way as he sped along the circuitous path for help.

In his grief, Dashrath could have chosen to do nothing. He did not. He walked up to the steep rock face of the ridge at the edge of town, through which no road ran, and started hammering.

"Lunatic!" people hissed and murmured and yelled straight at Dashrath. What did he think he was doing? Digging to Nepal?

Anything else would be a better use of his time. It's not like he could single-handedly make a path through a foothill of the Himalayas. He must be mad with grief.

Dashrath didn't mind. Every day he came back and hammered a few more centimeters. Weeks passed, then months. Then years. The people who had mocked him began bringing him food, buying him new tools when the old hammer and chisel wore out. Eventually, everyone understood what at first only he had seen.

Twenty-two years after he began hammering at a wall of rock, Dashrath had carved a path straight through it. His road was 110 meters long, 7.7 meters deep in places, and 9.1 meters wide. It shortened the distance to the next town from 55 to 15 kilometers and transformed the life of his village. He became famous across India as Mountain Man, and lived out his days knowing that the next time a loved one needed to get to the doctor quickly, they could.

Little by little, a man moved a mountain. And as incredible as his story is, he is far from alone.

. . .

If you remember one thing from this book, let this be it: *Little by little, a little becomes a lot.*

You've heard some version of the idea, likely many times—Rome wasn't built in a day. Slow and steady wins the race. You eat an elephant one bite at a time. And yet, when we attempt change in our own lives, we can't help hoping for faster results. The silver bullet, the epiphany, the makeover montage, the superhero glow-up: Rapid transformations make for high drama and good marketing. Get rich quick, slim down fast, change your life with one call today. Our natural desire for things to be easy nudges us toward these promises. And when they don't work, we tend to conclude that we can't change at all.

The good news is that we can change. All of us. And meaningful, lasting transformation doesn't take a lightning-strike miracle, or willpower of steel, or six free months to spend in a Buddhist monastery. What it takes is this simple idea, which turns out to be one of the key elements in modern behavioral science and that echoes through our great philosophical and spiritual traditions.

This whole book is a guide to little-by-little thinking. But step one is to explain exactly why this approach is so powerful. There's a big difference between hearing something wise and trusting it enough to let it change us.

Here's how a little actually becomes a lot.

THE APPROACH

When I say "little by little" in this book, I don't just mean it in a vague, proverbial sense. An easy critique of the approach is to conjure scenarios in which "a little" is not actually likely to do a lot. Picking up a piece of litter every now and then won't keep a park clean, a skeptic might say; sending a couple of holiday cards probably won't bridge a family estrangement. Fair enough. So before we go further, let's define what I actually mean by this path to change.

Here's what I mean by "little by little": *low-resistance actions, done consistently over time, in the same direction.* "Low-resistance" is all about choosing actions we'll actually do, while "consistently" is all about repetition. In the same direction means that all the little steps are headed toward the same thing. The implementation can look different, as we'll see—stringing together minor activities versus breaking bigger activities into smaller chunks, for example. In the following chapters we'll explore how to choose these actions and dig more deeply into why they work. But know first that these qualities, resistance and consistency, are at the heart of creating momentum and overcoming the roadblocks in our way.

"The little decisions you and I make every day are of infinite importance," C. S. Lewis wrote, making a comparison to compound interest. "The smallest good act today is the capture of a strategic point from which, a few months later, you may be able to go on to victories you never dreamed of." Let's prove him right.

CHANGE IS HARD

Why is it so hard to change?

One answer to this cosmic question lives in a single word: homeostasis. Any complex system will attempt to remain in a state of balance or equilibrium, as you may remember from high school science. An object at rest tends to stay at rest, and (in purely physical terms) for any action there will be an equal and opposite reaction. "What goes up must come down" is a law of gravity, but also an easy way to think of the principle that keeps the universe in balance.

In our bodies, homeostasis is a built-in "don't rock the boat" system. Our bodies attempt to regulate our temperature, directing us to shiver when we're cold and sweat when we're hot. If we inhale a doughnut, insulin is released to get our blood sugar back to what the body considers normal. Our brains regulate neurotransmitters, our immune systems balance pro-inflammatory and anti-inflammatory responses, and our chronobiology does its best to keep our sleep and waking cycles in check.

In major systems like ecology, an ecosystem tries to balance species diversity and population. In economics and finance, supply and demand counterweigh each other while our central banks try to balance recession versus inflation. Whatever the system, there are forces making small tweaks to keep it in balance.

This is all well and good when we're talking about avoiding a recession, or preserving biodiversity, or dodging a sugar coma. But by its very nature homeostasis affects our ability to make lasting change. It is our bodies and minds saying, "Whoa . . . not so fast!"

If you are trying to lose weight, at some point your body will begin to make you feel hungrier or slow down your metabolism in an attempt to keep your weight within a "set point" range. You might have lasted a couple days on green juice, but here come the massive cravings for Lion Cub's cookies (a chain in my hometown of Columbus, Ohio, that should be regulated in the same way crack is regulated).

Our minds get in on the act too. When you try to change your thoughts, emotions, or behaviors too fast, your brain is liable to get unsettled, tempting you to fall back into old ways of relating. You try to write another gratitude list and are suddenly gripped by a darkness that Leonard Cohen would envy. You get into bed on the early side but scroll social media for hours.

You might even swing dramatically into what I call (dramatically) the "fuck it"s: your goal of reading a book every evening devolving into watching every episode of the '80s cop drama *CHiPs*. Try to do too much too quickly, whatever your goals, and it's all too easy to derail.

Little by little will be our secret trick to outsmart homeostasis. By introducing change gradually and incrementally, we can avoid tripping our system's *not so fast!* alarm bells.

THE SCIENCE OF LITTLE BY LITTLE

I've been lucky to interview BJ Fogg, founder of the Behavior Design Lab at Stanford University, more than once about the psychology of change. In his book *Tiny Habits* and elsewhere, he offers a particularly clear and compelling explanation of the big potential of small actions. His basic model of human behavior is below:

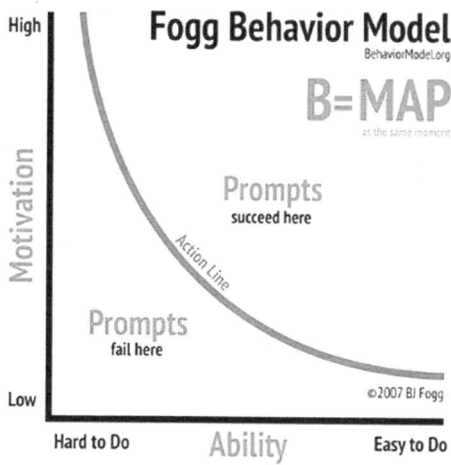

The model above shows three key variables that influence whether a behavior happens: **Motivation** (on the Y axis), **Ability** (on the X axis), and **Prompts** (which appear across the whole plane).

Motivation is what you'd expect: how much you want (or don't want) to do something. **Ability** refers to how easy the behavior is for you. That could mean skill level, energy required, or how logistically simple it is. **Prompts** are signals to do something.

According to the model, behavior happens *above* the action line. The harder something is to do, the more motivation we need. The easier it is, the less motivation we need to get started.

When we're stuck, it's usually because either motivation or ability isn't where it needs to be. Let's say a friend and I both want to cook healthy, tasty meals during the week. But I'm still mastering grilled cheese, and they're basically the Barefoot Contessa in shoes. Same motivation, wildly different ability levels. No surprise—I'm the one who ends up ordering takeout again. The difference in our ability levels doesn't mean that I can't join the Contessa in cooking more, but it does mean I'd have more work to do to cross that action line, even though our initial motivation was similar.

Or take the dishes: You and your partner may be equally capable of washing them, but if they find it calming and you find it soul draining, your motivation is lower—which makes it harder for you to get around to confronting a full sink.

We can think of the combined challenge posed by ability and motivation as our overall *resistance* to a given action.

Now, there are two ways to lower our resistance. The first is to raise our motivation level, which is easier said than done. This is where countless online seminars, cheesy YouTube videos with (allegedly) inspirational music, and all manner of Tony Robbins look-alikes live. But motivation is more a feeling than it is anything else, and feelings do not have levers that you can reach out and pull. How many times have we told ourselves we should feel differently than we do? And how often does that actually work? We can take steps to increase our motivation, as we will discuss in a moment, but we can't strong-arm our feelings.

The other way to get above the action line is to make the behavior easier. One solid way to do that? Make it smaller. If the action is smaller, it's easier. And if it's easier, we don't need as much motivation to tackle it. The full sink of dirty dishes might be too intimidating, but how about, for now, just washing one fork? One fork is definitively better than no forks.

If we are faced with a variable motivation level, which we always are, we can either spend a lot of time trying to psych ourselves up for some great effort or we can simply make the activity small enough (for that day, moment, or in general) that we have enough motivation to do it without hesitation.

Then, more often than not, something magical happens. When we achieve even the smallest goal we set for ourselves, it boosts our confidence—and our motivation rises with it. The better we feel about our chances of success, the more likely we'll keep succeeding.

Suddenly the dishes are done after all.

"It's really kind of amazing to see the power of it," Fogg told me. "As people take small steps and feel successful, it makes it easier to do and their motivation naturally goes up, which means, over time, they can do harder and harder things." This is the virtuous cycle of little by little: As we take small steps, behaviors become more manageable, and we can do harder things while feeling the same degree of difficulty. We can do more over time while staying above the action line.

I started this very morning with a case of floor-level motivation. I was groggily scrolling through *The New York Times* and Substack, wanting to do anything but ride my bike.

My brain and I were on the same page about this last night, when we had agreed on the many benefits of a bike ride first thing. Yet here I was dealing with mutiny. Instead of "Exercise is good for us!" my brain was now saying, "It's too hard," and of course, "Just another couple of articles."

The loop I was stuck in went something like this:

ME: Okay, it's time to do our one-hour ride.
BRAIN: Are you nuts? That takes ten units of energy [read Ability from above] and I, given my prone position on the couch, clearly only have one unit of energy.
ME: Come on, let's go.
BRAIN: Hey man, you're asking for ten units of energy when I only have one. Go pound sand.

Note: My brain is less of a mathematician than this, at least consciously; I'm translating a somewhat subconscious process. My actual conscious inner monologue, first thing in the morning, has all the eloquence of "ughhhh noooo . . ."

Anyway: What happens now? Very often we give in to the voice that tells us it's too hard, or we distract ourselves until it's too late and we have to get ready for work.

But today I took the approach of making the task much smaller. Instead of "Get on the bike and ride for an hour," I changed the task to "Just put on your bike shoes and clip into the bike." The new (barely conscious) conversation went more like this:

ME: Okay, let's just go put on our bike shoes.
BRAIN: Hmmm . . . well that takes one unit of energy and I have about that much.
ME: Come on, let's go.
BRAIN: Uh . . . okay, I guess I can do that. But just the shoes, right? Right, Eric?

And I got on the bike and started pedaling, at which point my brain finally remembered that this had been its idea in the first place. I lowered my resistance to the activity by shrinking the first step way down, thus allowing me to have enough motivation (even though I didn't have much) to get on the bike. At that point, the next step didn't seem so hard either.

We believe we get motivated and then act, but often it works the other way around. We act and motivation follows. Once I get moving, I feel like continuing to move. This, too, obeys the laws of homeostasis: Just like an object at rest stays at rest, an object in motion tends to stay in motion.

"Sometimes you can't think your way into right action," runs a common phrase in 12-step programs. "You have to act your way into right thinking."

• • •

BJ Fogg's model exemplifies the power of little by little, but he's far from its only expert corroborator. Another of the most widely cited theories of behavior change is the catchily named Transtheoretical Model of Behavior Change, often abbreviated as TTM. First developed in the late 1970s and '80s by scientists James O. Prochaska and Carlo DiClemente, the model is still recognized as the preeminent umbrella/synthesis of how we create change in our lives.

The TTM stresses that making change is so much more than just our actual behavior. It's a five-step process:

1. Precontemplation
2. Contemplation
3. Preparation
4. Action
5. Maintenance

Note that more than half of these stages occur before "action" has even been taken. This is another testament to the incremental, step-by-step nature of change: that the process involves not only thinking about what you want to do (contemplation, preparation), but even before that, *thinking* about thinking about it (precontemplation).

We'll return to the earlier stages of the TTM in later chapters, but for now let's skip ahead. Prochaska told me on my podcast that "the action stage isn't about starting with big changes. It's about starting smart—with attainable, realistic goals. It's about continuing to set small, achievable goals and celebrating each accomplishment along the way." These little wins add up, he writes. "They reinforce your determination and motivate you to keep going."

ARE WE JUST TALKING ABOUT HABITS?

Many of us have been seduced by the idea of optimizing our "habits," and for good reason. Under the scientific definition of what it means for something to be "habitual," we barely need to think about it again. It happens automatically. The problem with large behaviors is that they're rarely conducive to this "set it and forget it" goal. The bigger the change we want to make, the more likely it is that instead of habit what we should be seeking is *momentum*.

I will use the term "habits" throughout this book, but generally in a less exacting way than above. When I refer to *wise habits* I mean habits in the general sense of regular patterns of thought and behavior, whether or not they feel automatic. That said, there are two reasons I want to distinguish between the stricter definition of habits and "little by little" here.

One has to do with a question I have been asking podcast guests for a long time now: *Why is it still hard to make myself exercise?* If we follow basic reward theory, that we tend to want to do things that make us feel better, I should ALWAYS want to exercise. I have exercised pretty regularly for almost thirty years now, and EVERY SINGLE TIME I've done so, I thought afterward: "Boy am I glad I did that." Not once have I wished I had sat on the couch instead. And yet, I still so often go through the battle scenario described above, in which I have to trick my brain into getting me off the couch in the first place.

So why doesn't exercise feel like a habit? Because evolution has opinions, and unfortunately, most of them are: "Please lie down." It all comes back to *homeostasis*. Every organism—whether it's a gazelle or you—is wired to balance energy output with anticipated intake. That balancing act considers all sorts of variables: reproduction, daylight, food supply, the vague hope of not dying. And unless there's an urgent reason to do otherwise, the system defaults to "conserve energy like your life depends on it," because for most of history, our lives actually did.

The upshot is that given the major energy spend of exercise, its rewards have a high barrier to entry. Sure, toning our muscles might make us healthier and more desirable in the long term, but on any given day our systems don't recognize what will be so great about sweating into exhaustion.

The second reason not every "little by little" action is habit material is *context*. In the field of behavior change science, "context" refers to the whole host of situational, environmental, and social factors that influence our behavior. For an action to become a habit, we need to repeat it in the same way, the same place, and often at the same time. Change the context, and often what seemed habitual simply stops happening. (Have you ever struggled to get back in a groove after vacation?)

One study found that for a given behavior to reach a high degree of "automaticity," it needed to be done in the same context for around 18 days in the best case, 254 days in the worst case. That's all well and good if the behavior in question is buckling your seat belt, but less so for more complex goals.

Most of us in the modern world live with shifting contexts. We plan to work on our novel right after the kids are off to school, but today little Geraldo is home with a cough. And next week it is you who has the cough, and then your husband (who is usually the one to take the kids to school), and then Geraldo catches it all over again. Or maybe it's that Bark Twain has to go to the vet. Or your boss texts you about something that, apparently, the entire company's future hinges on being done this very second.

There are ways for us to work on maintaining a behavior in the face of life's unpredictability, as we will discuss in future chapters. For now it's enough to say that any action that requires a significant chunk of time or energy is unlikely to become truly habitual, however many steps you break it into.

A more realistic goal is to cultivate momentum. If you've ever ridden a bike, you know exactly what momentum feels like—or more precisely, what it feels like when you don't have it.

Those first few pedal strokes from a dead stop are brutal. Your muscles strain, the bike wobbles uncertainly, and progress feels glacial. Every rotation requires deliberate effort, a conscious decision to push down, then around, then down again. The temptation to give up looms large, but once you get moving momentum does a lot of the work. It's not so hard to pedal. You can even coast for a bit. As long as you keep the bike moving, you can reap the benefits of momentum.

It's always easier for me to get on the bike if I did so yesterday—or if I've been doing it regularly—than if I haven't been riding recently at all. Motivation will always be part of the equation, and there will always be some resistance to overcome. But we can still lower the threshold in a lasting way.

Consistency is also important. This is the other side of the little-by-little coin we started the chapter with: These actions need to be not just low-resistance, but repeated. If habits are defined by anything, it's repetition. Even if something never becomes truly second nature, consistency is what turns one-off efforts into long-term patterns.

Matt Wilpers, a highly sought-after trainer and Peloton coach, agrees. "For beginners," he writes, "training frequency is more important than both duration and intensity." He encourages athletes to first get consistent in their training before aiming for the level of Gatorade ads, where every workout ends with someone triumphantly collapsing like they just saved the world from an asteroid.

Before any heroics, Wilpers says, practice just showing up on the days that you decide to train. From there you can increase duration and intensity. In other words, step one is just getting on the bike, again and again.

A THOUSAND MILES

I learned the hard way about the importance of showing up long before I ever climbed on a Peloton.

"Rarely have we seen a person fail," is the beginning of a reading that happens at the start of nearly every AA meeting in the world. Early on in my recovery I went to at least one, if not two, AA meetings per day. So I heard the reading over and over, often feeling mocked by its confidence. I also heard the program's famous Twelve Steps read at nearly every meeting. And the Twelve Traditions. Let's just say there's enough repetition at a 12-step meeting to make a broken record jealous.

At first I gritted my teeth and zoned out to get through the readings. Then I made a game of memorizing them, which wasn't that hard to do as I heard them all twice a day.

On top of the recitation at regular meetings, we had to read the same 164 pages of the AA Big Book—the program bible written by founder Bill Wilson—at Big Book study meetings. Only one book and only the first 164 pages of it? I felt sure my brain would turn to sludge.

And the clichés, oh God, the clichés. "One day at a time." "Easy does it." "Keep coming back." It felt like an infinite loop of Chicken Soup for the Boring Soul.

And you know what? I got and stayed sober.

Was it in spite of or because of the repetition? I think it was largely because of the repetition, as I'll explain below. But we are faced with a quandary here. Repetition can lead to deeper insight and compounding growth, but it can also lead to stagnation, apathy, and a desire to quit. I was in danger of giving up on AA before I'd even scratched the surface—before I'd let the process do what it was designed to do.

What saved me was finding a way to appreciate just how meaningful, even spiritual, repetition can be.

• • •

Around the same time I'd discovered the joy of alcohol, at the age of eighteen, a high school teacher introduced me to Zen Buddhism. Although my understanding was weak, it spoke to me. The idea that something extraordinary could be hidden within the ordinary world resonated deeply with me, as did the belief that even in life's hardest moments, peace is waiting, if we can just allow ourselves to access it.

Six years and a lot of questionable choices later, tasked with finding a "spiritual solution" to aid my recovery but not drawn to the mainstream offerings of Columbus, Ohio (I found the concept of an interventionist Christian God hard to square with my situation), I remembered those books about Zen my teacher had given me.

I cracked them open again and quickly realized that the voices that spoke to me—Shunryu Suzuki, Mark Epstein, Jack Kornfield, Pema Chodron—all emphasized one thing above all: If you want to grow spiritually, you have to meditate. So I made it my mission to start a consistent practice.

And yet no matter how hard I tried I could not stick with it.

Most of my books said that I needed to meditate for thirty to forty-five minutes, so that was always my goal. I might do it for a day, a week, maybe a month one time. And then I would just quit.

At the time I didn't know anything about, as BJ Fogg would put it to me years later, the "compensatory relationship" between ability and motivation. I just knew that meditation was really hard for me to do and I could not seem to keep at it.

I would sit down, close my eyes, and then it was like the dark circus came to town. The ever-efficient processor nestled in my head would say, "Marvelous, you're paying attention! Shall we begin with the classic hits—'Imposter Syndrome,' 'Catastrophizing,' and the chart-topping single 'Your Life Is Meaningless'? Or would you prefer some fresh material from my *Worst Case Scenarios* album?"

To use the scientific terminology, half an hour of meditation was too high on my ability axis. Despite believing that it was gravely important for me to do this, I couldn't keep my motivation high enough to make it a practice.

After many, *many* failed attempts, I finally decided that I would aim to meditate for just three minutes a day, but that I would do it every day. This was, of course, the solution. It was something easy enough that I always had enough motivation to do it. Eventually I was able to increase how long I meditated for, and over time, how well I could do it (less circus, more peace). And I reflected on the power of even the smallest repeated actions.

One of the most famous expressions of little by little comes from the *Tao Te Ching*: "A journey of a thousand miles starts under one's feet." The Buddhist tradition also emphasizes a gradual path to personal transformation. The Dhammapada, one of the core Buddhist scriptures, says: "Drop by drop is the water pot filled. Likewise, the wise person, gathering it little by little, fills themselves with good." Nirvana, or enlightenment, is most often described as the end point of a long journey, during which we gradually rid ourselves of the weight of earthly desires.

Yet there has also been a debate in spiritual circles forever about whether enlightenment is actually more of a lightning strike, something that comes to us all at once, if at all.

My own adopted tradition, Zen Buddhism, has a rich history of stories of sudden enlightenment. As a user on the r/Buddhism subreddit wrote, these stories all sound something like: "So-and-so worked in the monastery kitchen. One day Master such-and-such kicked him in the ass and suddenly he was enlightened." In one actual example, a student named Gensha stubs his toe and promptly cries, "This body does not exist!" There are also the meditative koans

("What is the sound of one hand clapping?") which are sometimes described as tools for "direct pointing," or prompts to trigger an immediate, epiphanic experience of spiritual awareness.

To see only sudden enlightenment in these stories and practices, however, is to miss the forest for the bodhi trees. The moments of revelation come after long periods of practice and studies. Gensha the toe stubber practiced an ascetic life in the mountains for years, thinking about the ephemeral nature of things like pain, before his holy stumble. Even the hypothetical monastery kitchen worker put in his time before the rewards of that work were revealed in a glorious instant.

The modern spiritual marketplace is filled with promises of a shortcut to enlightenment. The logic is something along the lines of "everything you need to awaken is right here and is always right here and all you have to do is see it directly." Which is like telling a Little Leaguer, "All you need to hit a home run in the major leagues is to watch the ball come in, swing at the right time, and let the ball do all the work." Slightly more often than a chimpanzee types a novel the kid will hit a home run, but they are far more likely to end up with a traumatic brain injury.

Gurus of popular psychology sometimes make similar promises, with neat parables of "breakthrough" moments.

One thing my very gradual road to building a meditation practice did was to disabuse me of any and all such get-enlightened-quick dreams. If there is someone out there who could focus perfectly enough to access the secrets of the universe or his own psyche all at once, I'm not him. But I am someone who could practice sitting, listening, being present—three minutes by three minutes, day by day.

Another old Chinese proverb says: "Read a book for 100 times then the meaning will emerge." In my Zen practice, my teacher had me read the same 165-page book for six months. We chanted the same thing at the end of each meditation session and bowed, in the same way, each time.

Back in my early days of AA, reading the same 164 pages of the Big Book over and over, I would have been shocked to hear that the task I was rolling my eyes at was almost identical to something I would do happily in pursuit of Zen years later. And yet: Meaning did emerge in those early days of sobriety. I kept showing up to meetings, reading the readings, sitting down to at least try to meditate. My days without drinking added up. And eventually, "Rarely have we seen a person fail" came to seem less mocking than fortifying. "One day at a time" and "keep coming back" were still more clichés than koans, but they took on the weight of lived experience.

We all know the phrase "practice makes perfect," but it is more accurate to say that repetition breeds results. This is because the more we repeat a task or activity, the more comfortable and confident we become in our ability to do it. We become more efficient and effective as we become more familiar with the process.

We also trust the process more, even subconsciously. We see ads for the same products many times; politicians parrot the same messages on what feels like an endless loop. Why? Repetition breeds results. It seems like it should take more than repetition to make something persuasive, but scientific study after study shows that it really does work. This is due to something called the illusion of truth effect. People rate statements that have been repeated just once as more valid or true than things they've heard for the first time.

The key, I believe, is to be intentional in our repetition. We should pause and ask ourselves why we are doing this and what we hope to gain from it. We should strive to bring our full selves to the task. We should be aware of the potential for complacency and strive to remain curious and engaged in the process.

What I got from remaining curious and engaged in my journey toward sobriety was not only sobriety itself, but a lifelong interest in the ways each of us seek wisdom and meaning. I'm still somewhere on that journey of a thousand miles, grateful that I get the chance to continue.

THE FIRST STEP

In his book *The Quiet Before*, author Gal Beckerman makes the argument that even revolutions start gradually, with creative exchanges of ideas in small rooms and among limited networks. "We are gripped by the moment when the crowd coalesces on the street—the adrenaline, the tear gas, the deafening chants, a policeman on horseback chasing down a lone protester or a man standing up to a tank," Beckerman writes. But "change—the kind that topples social norms and uproots orthodoxies—happens slowly at first." The Civil Rights Movement, the women's suffrage movement, the LGBTQ+ rights movement: Behind each was a long path of (as the TTM would say) precontemplation, contemplation, preparation, action, and maintenance that made their eventual public actions undeniable.

For every "Eureka" moment there's a thousand dusty chalkboards. Years of failed attempts preceded the Wright Brothers' first successful flight. Even with famous lightning-strike discoveries, there's more to the story: After Alexander Fleming accidentally discovered a bacteria-killing mold called penicillin, it took fourteen years and the careful work of a number of other scientists before a patient was treated with the world's first antibiotic.

"If I have looked far," Isaac Newton said, "it is because I've stood on the shoulders of giants." But of course those "giants" were standing on shoulders too. In creating his physical laws Newton drew on the laws of planetary motion developed by Johannes Kepler, who in turn relied on the work of astronomer Tycho Brahe . . . who spent twenty years of his life watching the sky every single night, making meticulous maps of the movements of heavenly bodies governed by a force no one had yet called gravity.

The story that gets passed down is an apple to the head and a flash of genius. But the real story is one of thousands of little steps, thousands of nights spent watching the stars.

The first step in any thousand-mile journey is deciding where we want to go. Your first-choice destination might be enlightenment, or it might be getting around to using the stairs a little more often. Regardless, in the next chapter we'll cover setting intentions for change.

If you have the time to keep reading now, let's go, but if not that's fine too—just make a plan to come back soon. A little bit of something is always better than a lot of nothing.

ONE LITTLE THING YOU CAN DO RIGHT NOW

> Choose something you've been putting off and commit to doing it for exactly two minutes. Set a timer. When it goes off, you can stop—no guilt, no pushing through. You're not changing your life overnight—you're just proving that beginning doesn't have to be overwhelming.

TWO

What Is Worth Wanting?

> My mind's got a mind of its own.
>
> —JIMMIE DALE GILMORE

AS A SEVERE EPILEPTIC, TWENTY-SEVEN-YEAR-OLD KAREN BYRNE THOUGHT she knew what it was to be at war with herself. But when she woke up after brain surgery for her condition, she realized she'd had no idea.

"Karen, what are you doing?" her doctor said. "Your hand's undressing you." She looked down to discover that her left hand had been unbuttoning her shirt. She began rebuttoning the shirt with her right hand, but as soon as she stopped, her left hand started unbuttoning once more.

"You've got to get here right away," her doctor said to a colleague he'd already called. "We've got a problem."

The surgery had cured Karen's epilepsy but had left her with a rare disorder known as alien hand syndrome, in which one or more limbs literally behave as though they have a mind of their own. Triggered by damage to the tissue connecting the brain's two hemispheres, the condition has helped scientists study the extent to which different parts of the brain govern distinct areas of behavior and thought. In 1981 Roger Sperry won a Nobel Prize for his work with "split brain" patients, showing in experiments that a man with AHS could put together a puzzle with his left hand (controlled by the brain's right hemisphere, more often linked to spatial awareness and pattern recognition), but that when asked to continue the puzzle with his right hand (controlled by the brain's left hemisphere, which is more linked to language processing), he had no idea what to do.

In cognitive terms, AHS amounts to a failure of communication—the right hand literally doesn't know what the left is doing. But the science still doesn't quite explain the syndrome's most frustrating aspect: that for many sufferers, their alien hand seems intent on picking a fight. People with AHS have reported being slapped and choked by their estranged hands. While one hand tries to turn a page, the other tries to close the book. A concert pianist found herself fighting to practice a sonata while one hand wrestled the other away from the keys. The condition has been nicknamed "Dr. Strangelove syndrome" after Peter Sellers's character in the movie *Dr. Strangelove*, who scrambles to keep his right arm from saluting the Nazis.

Karen Byrne found herself in a constant battle with her left hand. "I'd light a cigarette, balance it on an ashtray, and then my left hand would reach forward and stub it out. It would take things out of my handbag and I wouldn't realize so I would walk away. I lost a lot of things before I realized what was going on." She began to wonder: What did her hand *want*? Why did it seem to have a different agenda than the rest of her body and mind?

Now in her fifties, Karen has decided that there is a method to her left hand's madness. In trying to do things like get her to put the cigarette down, she thinks her hand embodies the part of her mind that knows better. She aspires "not to smoke and not to curse and to be nicer to others," but she also knows she isn't always great at following through. That's when her left hand starts up.

"It's such a pain in the rear end, it really is," she told the hosts of the podcast *Invisibilia*, laughing. But she is convinced that "it's trying to make me a better person."

• • •

Karen Byrne's left hand may or may not be her own personal Jiminy Cricket, reminding her of her better angels even when she'd rather forget them. Jimmy Dale Gilmore has a song called "My Mind's Got a Mind of Its Own"; Karen lives that out more literally than Gilmore probably meant it. But her experience reveals a truth that applies far beyond those with alien hand syndrome: that we often want more than one thing at once. More than that, what part of us wants—a cigarette, say—can be in direct conflict with what another part of us wants—in Karen's case, to stay healthy and smoke-free.

On the path to lasting change, the first step is to know where you want to go. But because we're often pulled in more than one direction by the many priorities of our bodies and minds, our duties and pleasures, our fleeting impulses and long-term dreams, setting goals for the kind of steady, incremental change introduced in chapter 1 is rarely simple. In this chapter we'll discuss how to get in touch with what we value most, and how to aim our plans for change in that direction—without feeling like we're constantly at war with ourselves. No alien helping hand required.

MOTIVATIONAL COMPLEXITY

As far back as we have records, people have had opinions about what we want and what we should want. Maybe even before we had records.

I bet at least one guy in the Stone Age was tired of hearing, "You should put down the cave paint, Zog, and focus on getting a wife." (Or just as likely, "The hunt's not for you, Ugg, come back here and have babies.")

Religion, psychology, and philosophy have all made countless claims about the big picture of human motivation. Taoists stress that we should seek unity with the principle of balance that is the Tao, while Christians believe that one finds true fulfillment and purpose by aligning one's life with God's will. In Islam the primary human motivation is to live in submission to the will of Allah (Islam itself means "submission").

Among philosophers, Epicurus might go down the easiest, with his conviction that we live by the simple desire to seek pleasure and avoid pain, so we should live it up while we can. Friedrich Nietzsche preferred a world in which nothing matters but the human drive for superiority and imposing one's will on everyone else. (Yikes.)

Sigmund Freud found a treasure trove of human motivations in his trio of the superego (what society says we should do), the ego (what our "reason" says we should do), and the id (what our inner Tasmanian Devils of appetite and emotion say we should do). The pioneer of psychoanalysis was also convinced that all women envy penises and all men harbor a latent desire to kill their fathers and seduce their mothers, so it's fair to say he wasn't batting a thousand.

Merits of their ideas aside, I think we can agree on which of these guys would be fun to hang out with.

All of the above provide interesting lenses on what fundamentally drives us, or at least interesting history lessons on how generations before us have wrestled with the same timeless questions. But none of these theories strikes me as complete. It is easy to see in all of us that we are motivated by things beyond pleasure, or power, or dreaming about killing our dads (hopefully). On any given day we want things on every scale of significance: a delicious meal, fulfilling work, someone to love and be loved by. Just this week I have wanted to see Belle and Sebastian in concert again, to go to Cedar Point to ride the newest rollercoaster with my friend Chris, and to drive to Dayton to support my friend Jon, who is having a hard time caring for his parents. I've wanted to write this book. I've wanted to watch a basketball game at the time I set aside to write this book. I've wanted to spend a year in Europe. I've wanted the pain in my neck to go away. Any of us could create our own list of what's driving us at any given moment and probably extend it for pages and pages.

Psychology often describes motivation in the neutral language of "needs"—what we need, or think we do, to thrive and grow. Psychologist Abraham Maslow pioneered this line of thinking with his famous "hierarchy of needs," which ranged from the baseline of physical well-being to more cognitive and emotional goals. A more recent macro theory frames our needs as a trio: autonomy, competence, and relatedness. I find parts of these theories relatable in my own life and in the experiences of my listeners and clients, but still unanswered is the question that comes up when I think of Karen Byrne's combative left hand: What do we do when the things we want conflict with each other—when our desire is literally pulled in opposing directions?

When I think of motivation, I don't think first of a neat hierarchy or checklist. I think of a soup. When making a soup you start out with a set of ingredients that, over time, break down and blend together. We likewise have a complex interplay of needs, wants, beliefs, and values swirling inside us, and as they go into this soup they start to dissolve into one another. The flavor we get, aka our final impetus to act, is a combination of these ingredients that becomes almost impossible to reverse engineer. We might be able to tell the broth is salty, but is that because we added salt, soy sauce, or a bullion cube? In the same way, I know I want to go on the new rollercoaster with Chris, but is that primarily because I value investing time in our relationship, or because it would mean an afternoon off from writing this book (which, let me tell you, challenges my sense of competence)? Both? Or neither—am I just an Epicurean who finds it fun to be upside down going really fast?

I like the term motivational complexity as a shorthand for this soup of competing priorities. At any time, the ingredients can either combine to point us in one direction (rollercoaster!) or leave us in indecision, like a cartoon character with a devil on one shoulder and an angel on the other. Add to this that many of our motivations are working at levels below consciousness (who knows what that bay leaf, or that preverbal relationship with our mother, is adding), and we have a recipe for sometimes feeling like strangers to ourselves.

The parable of the Two Wolves, from which I take the title of my podcast, is all about this very thing. In the parable there's a grandparent who's talking with their grandchild, and they say, "In life, there are two wolves inside of us that are always at battle. One is a good wolf, which represents things like kindness and bravery and love, and the other is a bad wolf, which represents things like greed and hatred and fear."

The grandchild stops, thinks about it for a second, and looks at their grandparent and says, "Well, which one wins?"

And the grandparent says, "The one you feed."

VALUES AND DESIRES

You might be thinking that "good wolf versus bad wolf" sounds a little black and white to describe motivational complexity. But to me the parable is less about some clear separation of "good" versus "bad" within us, and more about the image of an ongoing battle, unseen but felt: all those competing ingredients, all those competing sources of motivation. We have a lot of wolves inside us. The essential truth is that we have power to choose what in ourselves to encourage and *what to leave unfed*.

I find it useful to think about our many sources of motivation in two basic camps: **values** and **desires**. The more clinical language of "needs" recognizes how much of what we want is shaped by biology and conditioning, often outside our conscious control. But this book is about what we *can* control. It's about choosing what we want our lives to look like, and then actually being able to move in that direction, little by little. Framing our wants as either values or desires can help bring the unconscious into the light—so we can have real agency over which parts of ourselves we're feeding.

I don't want to draw the line between these terms in permanent marker. As we'll see, the borders can get blurry. But in general, when I say *values*, I mean the things we've decided are worth wanting. *Desires*, on the other hand, are what we want whether we like it or not. Values are motivations we choose to cultivate: the goals, morals, and ideals we'd etch into a family crest (honor, loyalty, wisdom!) or name a Victorian child after (Prudence?). Desires are our instinctive, in-the-moment cravings—even the ones that stick around. (I'm guessing no Victorian child was named after lust or chocolate.) Values are what we want *most*, while desires are what we want *now*.

You can probably see one motivational conflict coming: when desires and values clash. We might value being healthy, but we might also desire to pull out the Juul we haven't quite been able to get rid of. We might value civility, but we might also desire to lean on the horn in stop-and-go traffic. We might value prioritizing time with our children or partner, but we might also desire to keep scrolling

TikTok for just another thirty seconds . . . minutes . . . wait, what time is it? And why am I watching someone demonstrate how to peel a banana using only their elbows?

In each of these cases, the behavioral goal is pretty straightforward: to sort out whether we're acting from desire or from value, and then to use that awareness to help us choose what we want *most* over what we want *right now*. It's exactly the role Karen Byrne feels her left hand plays—to remind her of her values when her desires point in a different direction. Without that kind of intervention (or even with it), overcoming an unhelpful desire in the moment is easier said than done, and we'll get deeper into strategies for doing so in the following chapters.

First, though, there's another kind of motivational conflict to talk about: values versus values.

When you encounter a conflict between values, the resolution is rarely simple. You might value the creative pursuit of finishing your novel, but also the security your current job provides. When I started *The One You Feed*, I had to weigh the stability of a successful software career against the creative and emotional fulfillment of a project that hadn't yet proven itself as a viable path. The list goes on: You might value freedom and spontaneity, but also want to start a family. You might care deeply about nurturing your friendships, but still wonder if it's okay to leave the party early because you're really trying to get better sleep.

Value-based conflicts can create motivational tension not just in the big, life-direction kind of way—*When do you want to start a family?*—but just as often in the day-to-day—*Are you going to leave early or not?* And unlike desire versus value clashes, they can't be resolved in the moment. The only way to lessen how often and how severely you find your values in conflict is to get greater clarity about what you actually, really want most of all.

That's what the rest of this chapter is about.

MIMETIC DESIRE AND HAVE-TO HASSLE: THE CALL IS COMING FROM OUTSIDE THE HOUSE

From the time we're born we are inundated with value messaging. Our parents are our first influences, for better or worse, but soon the rest of what Freud called the "superego" comes in: friends, school, popular culture, politics, religious traditions, and every other resident of the existential peanut gallery, some louder and more insistent than others.

At some point as we grow to adulthood, we decide which of these sources of value we actually believe in. Or do we? I've talked extensively with author Luke Burgis about "mimetic desire," which is how he describes the pervasive phenomenon of wanting things because we see others wanting them. As I write this I am in Atlanta working from my favorite library, which I get to by driving down a lovely, tree-lined road through a neighborhood called Buckhead. Through the trees, it's hard to miss the road's other signature feature: staggeringly large and expensive homes. I mean jaw-dropping wealth. I've seen these houses countless times and they still amaze me.

This morning, like many times before, I began to envy that sort of wealth and feel bad about myself that I don't have it. That is a mimetic experience: seeing the product of someone else's desire, or values, and suddenly feeling the need to reexamine your priorities. Burgis calls this "social contagion," the idea that we all, often without even realizing it, catch other people's emotions and other people's behaviors (and their taste in houses).

At the same time my real estate envy kicked in, I happened to tune back into the music playing in my car. It was a band I love called The Gaslight Anthem—kind of punk rock, I suppose. The values I've picked up from punk rock are about authenticity, realness, generosity.

Not chasing what society says you should want, but finding your own way. I started laughing at myself. Here I was, salivating over mansions while listening to a soundtrack about not caring what anyone else thinks—as the houses faded into the rearview mirror.

I love this example because it illustrates in miniature a process that we all go through regularly. We are exposed to images of better, brighter, and shinier lives than the ones we have, and we often begin to feel envy. We get these on TV, on social media, or driving down the road, you name it. The increasingly targeted nature of this type of consumerism makes it tough to avoid. And it pulls us away from what is most important to us.

There is nuance in all of this. Sometimes we see something that really does resonate with us, and our unexpected desire for it points to undiscovered or unacknowledged values. Perhaps you started out volunteering for the social cachet, but you've since come to care deeply about the benefits that can come from using your time this way. Maybe you started out following your partner to the gym, but you discover your love of the boulder wall all on your own.

Some values you've borrowed, however, might only be borrowed after all.

Susan David, a leading management thinker and Harvard psychologist, distinguishes between "want-to" and "have-to" goals. "Want-to goals," as the name suggests, can feel motivated by desire (what David calls "intrinsic interest"), or by an awareness that the goal aligns with the values we feel are core to our identity (what she calls "integrated interest"), or both. The key is that we feel we're pursuing the goal because we're actively choosing to do so.

"Have-to" goals, on the other hand, are driven by external factors. They're what gives the word "should" a bad name, driven as they are by feelings of obligation or shame, even if we're the ones doing the shaming. Maybe it's our parents we hear say "Get a real job!" Or maybe it's just the thought of their voices, perfectly preserved on the tape recorder in our minds. "Have-to" goals might technically line up with our values, but as long as we're framing them as obligations, our motivation to act on them tends to drop. In her book *Emotional Agility*, David writes,

> *Want-to motivation is associated with lower automatic attraction toward the stimuli that are going to trip you up—the old flame, the glimmer of a martini passing by on a waiter's tray—and instead draws you toward behaviors that can actually help you achieve your goals. Have-to motivation, on the other hand, actually ramps up temptation because it makes you feel constricted or deprived. In this way, pursuing a goal for have-to reasons can actually undermine your self-control and make you more vulnerable to doing what you supposedly don't want to do.*

When the mother of my partner, Ginny, started suffering from Alzheimer's and needed more intensive care, caring for her often felt like a "have-to" situation. We made the eight-hour trip every two weeks, to help someone who was not, as the disease progressed, exactly easy to be around. She was repetitive and prone to lashing out, and Ginny had the impossible task of grieving the person her mother had been while staying present with her body and ailing mind through their final struggles. What helped us face it all was knowing that when we looked back on this situation, we wanted to look back on ourselves as people who didn't shy away from the work of caring for others.

"Living according to your values isn't all it's cracked up to be," we joked at the beginning or end of a particularly exhausting day. But by saying that, we were actually reminding ourselves of a beautiful truth: that we didn't just *have* to be there for Ginny's mother, we *wanted* to be. And in that intentional, want-to headspace, we were surprised how many moments of joy found all three of us.

• • •

One of humanity's greatest skills is our ability to do many things automatically: We can dress ourselves without having to stop and ponder every aspect of it (until you are going on a job interview or a big date), we can drive home without having to think about every signal and turn (though maybe we should), we can create to-do lists without thinking about the reasons behind every little errand and email. We could not live day-to-day if this wasn't the case. You would be completely exhausted by the time you finished breakfast if the mundane tasks of living weren't somewhat automatic.

But as many of us have discovered, there is a downside to running our lives on "have-to" autopilot. Socrates famously warned us that the unexamined life is not worth living. Jean-Paul Sartre, a leading figure in existential philosophy, introduced the concept of "bad faith" (*mauvaise foi*) to describe the self-betrayal of passively living out the roles and responsibilities of life without thinking about them. According to Sartre, we have the freedom to create our own essence through the choices we make, but often reject this by living inauthentically.

"The more we can reflect on" our values, Susan David told me, "the much better chance we have of not being on autopilot." A simple example she gave was that you might "value family, you value presence and connectedness, and yet you've got this habit and the habit is you always bring your cell phone to the table. And this is a precious opportunity with your family, but you are squandering it through a habit that you might not even have reflected on." By surfacing an awareness that our behavior is in conflict with our values, we might be inclined to set the phone aside.

I start my podcast with the same quote every week: "It takes conscious, consistent, and creative effort to make a life worth living." Identifying our values is about the "conscious" in that statement.

Let's get off autopilot and take the controls.

NAMING YOUR VALUES

What is the meaning of life? What makes a life worth living? What does it mean to be successful?

If this was a spirituality-first book, I could just hand you a set of values to live by—the ones that have helped guide me, and so many others, toward a wiser, more fulfilling life. Values like patience, perspective, and acceptance. And I *will* sing the praises of those principles in the chapters to come. But for now, I want to invite you to turn inward—to reconnect with the good ideas you already have about who you want to be in the world.

Values work is long and hard and ongoing, but as with everything else, there's a little-by-little way to go about it. Below is the first of several exercises designed to help us step back from everyday motivational complexity and discern deeper kinds of wanting. (The rest, as with most exercises going forward, can be found in the appendix.)

They're meant to take *some* time, but not a lot: thirty minutes here and there is enough. And if that still feels unrealistic, give yourself ten.

• • •

What makes me happiest, proudest, and most fulfilled?

This exercise emerges from concepts in humanistic psychology like Abraham Maslow's work on self-actualization and peak experiences.

Take some time to reflect on the following questions. You may want to write down your thoughts as you go.

STEP 1: *Identify three times when you were happiest.*

Think back on moments, days, or periods in your life when you felt a deep sense of happiness, joy, or contentment. What was happening? Who were you with? What were you doing? Describe these experiences in detail.

STEP 2: *Identify three times when you were most proud.*

Recall situations where you felt a profound sense of pride, achievement, or self-respect. What had you accomplished? What challenges had you overcome? What principles or standards were you upholding? Describe these experiences.

STEP 3: *Identify three times when you were most fulfilled and satisfied.*

Consider the periods when you felt a strong sense of fulfillment, satisfaction, or sense of purpose. What needs were being met? What were you contributing to? How were you growing or expressing your potential? Describe these experiences.

STEP 4: *Determine your top values, based on your experiences of happiness, pride, and fulfillment.*

Once you have done this, look back over the experiences you described. What themes emerge? What qualities, principles, or motivators seem to be sources of happiness, pride, and fulfillment for you? This will give you an idea of some of the things you value.

· · ·

I recently checked in with my own values through this very exercise.

The question "What makes me happiest?" led me straight to a value I call adventure. I realized that I feel most alive—most like myself—when I'm exploring. Whether it's stepping into a place I've never been, lying on a surfboard waiting for the next wave, or gripping the side of a rock face, there's something about seeking the unknown that fills me up. It's not just about doing things I haven't done before; it's about the sense that the world is bigger than I thought, and I get to step into it.

What makes me proudest is almost always something to do with being kind or giving. I'm proud of my son, but I can trace that back to a value of really giving myself to being his parent. I'm proud of all the people I sponsored in 12-step meetings. I deeply value my friendships and relationships. And if you asked the people who know me well, most would probably name kindness as one of my core qualities. So I gathered all that under a single word: kindness.

When I thought about what makes me feel most fulfilled, what came to mind was the satisfaction I feel when I'm learning something or being challenged. But I also noticed a spark of excitement and possibility whenever I walked into a library or a bookstore. So it wasn't just the learning itself—there was something more. Eventually, I was able to bring all that together into a single value: curiosity.

Reflecting on what other things matter to me, I realized the ongoing importance of my sobriety and my emotional health. My emotional health, in turn, is strongly influenced by my physical health, and my physical health allows me to be kinder, more adventurous, and more curious. So I added that to the list.

Finally, I felt the presence of Buddhism and Taoism in the way I view the world. There is a line from the Stephen Mitchell translation of the *Tao Te Ching* that says: "When you realize there is nothing lacking, the whole world belongs to you." I recognized this as a deep truth and something that continues to inspire me, which I was able to call contentment.

Kindness, adventure, curiosity, contentment, and health. I came out of reflecting on my values with five strong points of orientation.

Now I want to make a few points about this process. First, it's something that's evolved over time for me. It's the result of lots of thinking about values. Not in some impossibly intense silent retreat spent puzzling at my inner makeup—just in asking the right type of questions multiple times (little by little).

Second, there wasn't one magical exercise that answered everything. I looked at the facts of my life—both inner and outer—from a few different angles and chose what made the most sense to me. There are plenty of things I care about that didn't make the final list. I value tolerance, fairness, humor, and more. But we have to limit our values in some way, and this list was short enough to memorize and keep in mind in the scrum of daily decision-making. As we used to say in project management, "If everything is a priority, nothing is."

My values won't be everyone's, and that's fine—there isn't a right or wrong answer to this or any exercise. But for each of us, there are answers that are more true.

Beginning to think critically about values is a necessary stage in setting your compass for any kind of lasting change. At the end of the chapter you'll find several more thought exercises, each designed to open a subtly different window for contemplation. If doing multiple exercises seems daunting, try just one to start, and if you're balking at the idea of diagramming your entire value system, focus on holding in mind just *one* value you want to live toward.

If you want to create your own family crest, however, by all means go ahead.

ANOTHER WORD ON DESIRE

Our values may be the defining base of our motivational soup, but our desires shouldn't be ignored as ingredients either.

Desire is not a bad thing, in and of itself. It gets a bad rap thanks to millennia of strict spiritual and ethical codes, and because it's so easily "hijacked" by sources that want our time, attention, and resources (think of any ad you've ever seen), and because, well, it's got a mind of its own. But a life spent ignoring desire would be the life of a joyless martyr.

A wiser life is a life in which you feel that what you want to do is aligned with who you want to be—and desire is part of that. Which is to say that ideally, your values will be aligned with your desires more often than not. If you're getting a finance degree but you keep hanging out in art classes, your first thought shouldn't be that you're slacking on your major. It should be to get curious about the value(s) behind your desire to prioritize art class. Or if you're on maternity leave and find yourself daydreaming about leaving it all behind for a cross-country motorcycle adventure, your first thought shouldn't be to repress those feelings. It should be to notice that your sense of adventure is still with you, and to honor that. Maybe the cross-country trip will look a little different when it happens, but that's a matter of logistics. You can plan it all out while reminding yourself that for now you're doing something else you want to do, by caring for your new little person.

Even negative stimuli, the things we find ourselves pushed away from, can be helpful in orienting us toward an alignment of values and desires. If you find yourself dragging your feet on getting in touch with a friend or colleague, ask yourself why. Maybe there's a feeling of guilt, behind which is often a feeling of care. We don't want to pick up the phone or write the email because there's just so much to say and never the time and emotional space to do it right . . . so then we haven't done it at all. Once we have that feeling of care front of mind, we at least know what we have to do—something rather than nothing.

Sometimes being mindful of desire means knowing when enough is enough. After the pandemic Ginny and I began to spend more time watching TV series on the various streaming platforms. And while this is something I really enjoy, too much of it makes me feel "yucky" inside.

At first, I chalked up that feeling to a conviction I held that watching TV was inherently "bad." I cobbled this value together from some punk rock ideals and a penchant for high-minded literary types. But when I started to really examine it, I realized I wasn't sure I actually believed it. Some of the shows I've loved most—*The Sopranos*, *Breaking Bad*, *The Crown*—have inspired and challenged me as much as any great novel or film.

And yet . . . the yucky feeling persisted.

So I had to look a little deeper. And what I found illustrates an idea in motivational theory of being "for or against" something. What is more motivating? To avoid something bad or to get something good? What is a better motivation for health? Avoiding a heart attack or having more energy? Economists and behaviorists will debate these points endlessly, but I think the answer, like many things, is "it depends." It depends on you. It depends on the activity or thing. Both work in different ways.

The answer to my question about TV was contained here. The reason it felt yucky wasn't because what I was doing was bad. It was simply that it took time away from doing things that were more in alignment with who I wanted to be. TV watching doesn't generally address my curiosity (documentaries aside) and desire for adventure. When I began to look at my watching habits through this lens, I was better able to make changes that felt less like sacrificing something I enjoy than like making time to feed other parts of me.

All of that said, desire often is something we need to resist in the moment, whether because it's been hijacked by external forces or because what we want now just isn't on the same page as what we want most. We'll move on to the art and science of acting wisely in the following chapters.

PUTTING VALUES INTO ACTION(S)

As you may recall from chapter 1, the five stages of change according to the TTM (Transtheoretical Model of Behavior Change) are precontemplation, contemplation, preparation, action, and maintenance. In this chapter we've been in those first two stages—doing the important work of deciding what direction we want to move in before we make any kind of plans for getting there, and letting our values (and desires) orient us before we take our first steps.

In the next chapter we'll move into the planning stage, by discussing how we can set ourselves up for success when it comes to taking action. To get there we need to do one last thing in this chapter: to move from articulating our values to identifying behaviors that embody them.

In one sense this is a leap, crossing the gap between *Who do I want to be?* and *What do I want to do?* But in another sense, the gap isn't very big. Values are so often made to sound abstract, as if they exist only in some platonic ether outside the realities of our lives. But to me values are best practices waiting to happen. Whatever you planned ahead of time to be doing in a given moment is likely a reflection of a core value. And each of the hundreds of decisions you make in a day is an opportunity to live either toward or against your values.

Brad Stulberg, author of *The Practice of Groundedness*, spoke to me about moving from values to behaviors. "You have a core value of love, really honorable, beautiful," he gave as an example. "But what does love mean? So then you spend some time, you dig, you think, and let's say that you define love as being fully present for the people in activities that you care about." This gets us closer to a game plan, but still isn't specific enough for Stulberg. "Are you going to be fully present always? What if there are competing priorities?"

Having read this chapter, we know there always are competing priorities. In what seems less a coincidence than a commentary on modern life, Stulberg used the same example as Susan David to illustrate the challenge of practicing loving presence: phone use. "So then it gets down to the practices, and that's where you turn love into I'm gonna put my phone in the glove compartment of my car from six to nine so I can have dinner with my family and watch a TV show with my partner before I get it out again."

It might seem mundane, to move from the lofty poetry of LOVE! to the pragmatic realities of a plan for getting off your phone for a while. But this is where the magic of little by little comes in. Stringing together day after day of making time to be present with the people you care about most looks like the height of love to me.

Focus on one of your strongest values. Now try identifying one behavior you think would help you live out this value in daily life. Here are a few guiding questions:

- Are there times or areas of your life in which you feel particularly disconnected from this value? What goals, habits, or changes could you implement to close the gap?

- What's something you could do today that would honor this value? What's something you could do right now, however small?

- If a friend or loved one asked for your advice in living out this value, what would you tell them to do?

You might have come into reading this book with a habit or two in mind already, and that's fine. What I would ask is that you then do the reverse of the above: Take that behavior and trace it back to a core value. If you find you can't do so—if your goals seem trivial all the way down—then choose something else. For example, if you have long held a goal of losing weight but with closer examination you see that it's all about how you look and what others think of you, and neither of those things are actual values of yours, then it's worth finding a goal that does tie to your core values.

• • •

Our motivations will always be complex. Even if our values remain relatively stable, the territory of life is always changing, and with it the many factors that can either have us acting in alignment with who we want to be or feeling like strangers to ourselves.

The goal of this chapter has been to offer a few tools for setting your internal compass and to convince you that it is always in your power to decide where to go next.

But if nothing else, I hope you're convinced that Freud was a little off.

ONE LITTLE THING YOU CAN DO RIGHT NOW

Write down—on paper!—one value and one microexpression of that value that you will practice today. If the value you choose is connection, for example, your microexpression might be "send one encouraging text to a friend." Tape your written commitment somewhere visible and follow through before bed.

When you're ready to go a little deeper, flip to the appendix for extra exercises—or download the companion worksheets anytime at oneyoufeed.net/resources.

THREE

The Architecture of Change

> The supreme art of war is to subdue the enemy without fighting.
>
> —SUN TZU, *THE ART OF WAR*

I HAD BEEN SOBER FOR ABOUT A WEEK. I HAD BEEN IN DETOX AND CAME HOME for Christmas. The game was over, the jig was up—I had told my parents and the people in my life I was an addict, and I was convinced that I wanted to be clean. As short a time as a week sounds, those first seven days are a big deal for any recovering addict, and that night I believed that it had been the first week of the rest of my clean and sober life. I went to a recovery meeting and came home. And then things took a small, disastrous turn.

There in the mail was a gift from my grandfather. Twenty-five dollars. At that time twenty-five dollars was the magic number (for a shot of heroin).

Instantly I felt an overwhelming craving to use. I didn't want to, and at the same time I did. To this day I don't know of a worse feeling than that sensation of being torn in two. One part of me screaming, "Don't do it!" and another part screaming, "I have to do it!"

I paged my dealer, and he agreed to meet me in one of our five or so shitty regular spots around Columbus.

I remember driving there. It was snowing, and I was sobbing in the car. "Dream On" by Aerosmith was playing on the radio. With every turn signal a fresh wave of shame broke over me, and yet it felt like an invisible, malevolent hand was steering the car down the road.

• • •

We can leave that particular story there. You know how it ends. And while you may never have experienced the particular self-disappointment of relapsing under the sickly yellow lights of a strip mall parking lot in Ohio, who among us doesn't know that torn-in-two feeling—and the feeling of watching yourself make exactly the wrong choice.

In his letter to the Romans, Paul the Apostle complained, "I do not understand my own actions. For I do not do what I want, but I do the very thing I hate. . . . For the desire to do the good lies close at hand, but not the ability."

Before Paul got to feeling bad about himself, Plato and Aristotle had described the same condition as *akrasia*, a Greek word meaning something like "lacking command" or "weakness": that maddening, universal capacity to act against our better judgment. Suffice to say that we've been disappointing ourselves for at least as long as there have been philosophers to give our failings a name.

In the previous chapter we explored motivational complexity, or the incurable human condition of wanting more than one thing at once. We then dove into the worthwhile task of articulating our values—the goals, ideals, or qualities we most want to embody. This is a crucial step in naming the change(s) we want to cultivate, little by little. We also talked about desires—our more immediate, impulsive wants—and how these can come into conflict with our values in the moment of action. Like, say, when twenty-five dollars lands in your lap and your sobriety is equal parts precious and fragile.

This chapter and the next are about the moment of truth, which we'll call a "choice point," when we actually decide how to behave. You might have a laminated list of your top five virtues hanging on the fridge. You might have tattooed *discipline* across your knuckles. But even then, you'll still have to contend with the siren song of whatever shiny, comfortable, low-effort thing you want *right now*.

For most of us this is likely (hopefully) less on the order of a hit of heroin than, say, to hit snooze yet again . . . or to open up Netflix instead of the book we've been "meaning to read" for a year . . . or to stay quiet when we know we'd rather have spoken up. Same principle, though: Knowing the right thing to do is great . . . until you actually have to do it.

There are two main ways to think about our odds of success at a choice point. One is the **internal component**, by which I mean our state of mind in the moment. Emotional volatility is a recipe for *akrasia*: Think of the proverbial "moment of weakness," "crime of passion," or "2 a.m. text I really should not have sent." In calmer times we tend to feel more of a sense of agency over our impulses—a capacity to do what we intend even when it feels hard. In behavioral literature this capacity is referred to as "self-regulation" or "self-control," which roughly corresponds to our common understanding of willpower.

I don't love "self-control" as a term, in part because it carries centuries of cultural baggage around notions of discipline and denial. It also seems to describe an interior life of perpetual antagonism, in which some law-enforcement part of our psyche reins in the rest, when I believe the real best-case scenario involves more inner harmony than coercion. But we'll work with it both because behavioral scientists use the term and because I have to admit it's an intuitive way to describe the feeling of, well, getting your shit together.

What just about everyone who studies self-regulation or self-control agrees on is this: We want to minimize how often we need to rely on it. Some researchers suggest that this is because our self-control can burn out, like an exhausted muscle. Others think we're more resilient than that, but still agree that willpower isn't exactly the most reliable tool in the box. Every time you stare down that chocolate cake in the fridge and decide not to indulge might be weakening your defenses a little further, bringing you that much closer to giving in; or your self-control might win on a coin flip each time you open the door. Either way, if that cake stays front and center, the odds of you scarfing it down are only going to go up over time.

You may have flagged a key phrase in that last sentence: *If that cake stays front and center.* That brings us to the other major piece of the self-control puzzle: the **external, or structural, component**, meaning all the factors outside us that influence our actions. Where we are, who we're with, whether we've eaten or slept recently, whatever is demanding the attention of our five senses—these details all influence our mental states in the moment, and by extension, how likely we are to exercise self-control.

More powerfully still, structural factors can affect whether self-control is even necessary. If when we see the chocolate cake in the fridge, we move it to a lower, less-visible shelf, it might just be out of sight, out of mind, next time we open the door. (Or we could get someone else in our household to take that delicious bullet for us, removing temptation entirely.)

The beautiful thing about the structural side of decision-making is that we can plan for it in advance. By identifying what's likely to trip us up—and thinking through how to avoid or navigate those challenges—we can set ourselves up for success *before* we ever reach a choice point. Having a clear plan, being specific about our goals, aligning our environment with those goals, and thinking ahead about how we'll handle the inevitable obstacles can make a huge difference in our chances of creating real, lasting change.

That's what the rest of this chapter is about. In the TTM (say it with me: The Transtheoretical Model of Behavior Change), we've reached the "preparation" stage. It might be tempting to just skip ahead to the next step, action, at this point—but as Sun Tzu suggests in the epigraph above, the wisest approach to war is first to avoid having to fight at all. Below we will cover a four-part method for optimizing the context in which we make decisions, from fine-tuning our behavioral goals, to identifying the "prompts" or "triggers" that spark action, to reshaping our environments for success, and, finally, to anticipating likely obstacles.

As wonky as that sounds, in practice it can just look like hiding a piece of cake. Or telling your grandpa hey, thanks, but could you hold off on the $25 birthday checks for a while? Wise habits, it turns out, start with wise logistics.

WHEN YOU SAY "STRUCTURE" . . .

For a punk rock lover like me, "structure" can sound almost like a dirty word. I value adventure and spontaneity; I know how it feels to fear a prison of routine. So let me say from the start that the kind of planning we'll be talking about in this chapter is very elastic, and what's right for you might not be right for me and vice versa.

That said, I've learned how liberating structure can be. The first nine months of my sobriety I was in tightly controlled circumstances. I spent over six months in a halfway house that was known for its military-esque culture, where I—a twenty-four-year-old who had spent years doing nothing but rebelling—could not leave without a "chaperone" for the first month, and then had to sign in and out;

where I was forced to attend every group session and meeting; where I shared the same strict schedule with every other resident.

I loved it (most of the time). It felt so good to just fall into the house's rhythms and not have to figure everything out. When I was released, this discipline became a little shakier, and I began a long process of trial and error in figuring out what exposures I could handle. Twenty-five dollars in hand? Not okay for a while. Driving past an old favorite bar? Also not recommended. A free evening? Eventually, more and more doable. I valued my new freedom, but I also never lost the lesson of those early halfway-house days: When done right, *structure liberates*. Even at its most regimented, I knew my life in recovery was infinitely less of a prison than my addiction.

There are some best structural practices that work for everybody. A basic one trades on the fact that how you treat your body affects your mind. Somewhere buried in the seven hundred–plus interviews I have done is a quote that I cannot find but that I've been paraphrasing for years: "If your body doesn't feel good, then your brain is going to feel like shit."

Snickers has made a whole campaign out of the idea that when we get too hungry, we turn into monsters. In one ad we see Godzilla flirting with a girl on a beach, playing Ping-Pong, and dancing at a party. We see one guy saying, "Godzilla is actually pretty cool," to which another guy replies, "Except when he's hungry." Then suddenly Godzilla is playing the hits: rampaging through a city, blowing fire out of his mouth, and torching a taxicab. He is thrown a Snickers bar, and we next see him waterskiing and flashing a thumbs-up sign.

Those of us who have had children might not need a Snickers commercial to imagine sweet creatures going feral. At a certain point, if I didn't get my young son to bed or down for a nap, I knew he would enter a state in which there was nothing I or his mom could say to calm or settle him. He would be completely overwhelmed by his tiredness (and so would we).

Most of us are not rampaging lizards or toddlers (if your mom is reading you this book, might I suggest *Curious George?*), but the point remains that when we don't feel good physically, it's harder to be the people we want to be. In AA I was told to watch out for HALT: being hungry, angry, lonely, or tired—otherwise known as the four horsemen of bad decision-making, and a gateway to wanting a drink. For the nonaddicts among us HALT can be an equally useful warning system, though the consequences might show up instead as a lack of patience, or anxiety or depression.

We can't separate feeling better from thinking better. I spoke to University of Michigan researcher Michelle Segar about what she calls "the self-care hierarchy":

> *The self-care hierarchy is the idea that we all have some fundamental self-care behavior that if we don't get, we are not going to have a good day. And many people may not be aware of what that is. I think for many people it is sleep, and they just don't know it. But for other people, like my husband, he's very clear that it's not sleep, it's physical activity, because he knows he feels terrible if he doesn't exercise, but he doesn't feel nearly as bad even if he doesn't get very much sleep.*

I have a tendency toward depression, and now that I'm lucky enough to have nonsubstance ways of coping, my preferred solution is exercise. There's a saying that "depression hates a moving target," and as much as therapy, SSRIs, and meditation (among other things) have been critical for me, the most important thing I do these days is take the idea of a "moving target" literally. I know that a day when I make the time to run or bike or even just walk around is a day I'll be more myself. Exercise seems to reset my body or my nervous system in such a way that my mind comes back from the flatline of a depressive episode.

In other words, exercise is not just something I like doing; it's part of my structural approach to feeling up to life's challenges. And I've learned the hard way that this kind of basic yet thoughtful planning has a high return on investment.

CHOOSING BEHAVIORS (CONTINUED)

As we shift from identifying our values to planning for change, I want to offer two big-picture thoughts on the kinds of behavioral goals I'd suggest focusing on. Ideally, changes should be:

Doable within your current context. Chapter 1 said plenty on this subject, but just to reiterate: If the change you're seeking requires joining Greenpeace, or becoming a monk, or even leaving your current job or partnership or city, it's beyond the scope of this book's "little by little" premise. You may be led to make a significant, life-altering choice somewhere along the road we're beginning together—and if so, wonderful. But we're focusing on small, consistent efforts, implementable not tomorrow but today.

The changes we'll be focusing on going forward are also *more positive than negative.* That is to say, we'll be talking more about cultivating positive new behaviors than about stopping behaviors you'd rather avoid.

Hold up, you may be saying. *I have a laundry list of bad habits I'm ready to kick.*

I hear you. And you can apply the methods discussed in this chapter and beyond for exactly that. But I also think you'll see that almost every bad habit to be undone is also a positive new behavior waiting to happen. "Eating more healthily" is "eating less junk food" by another name. "Going to bed on time" is the glass-half-full version of "stop staying up too late."

There is value in reframing unwise habits into their positive variations for a couple of reasons. First, approaching change this way—focusing on what you want to do *more* of, rather than what you want to stop—makes the process feel less like deprivation and more like an opportunity for growth. There is a significant difference between telling yourself "I'm giving up cookies" and "I'm giving myself the gift of good health." For starters, only one of those contains a reminder of the core value behind your actions.

In the previous chapter I realized that I didn't feel bad about watching a lot of TV because TV is inherently bad, but rather because there were other things I loved doing that were getting crowded out. By focusing on making more time for hiking and reading, I did end up watching less TV, but that change never felt like a punishment or sacrifice.

Another reason to think about behavior change from the positive side is that stopping a behavior almost always involves choosing a new behavior to replace it with—so you'll need to have a habit upgrade in mind anyway. To understand how and why this works, it's time to dig further into the science of choice points.

TRIGGERING CHANGE

In his bestselling book *The Power of Habit*, author Charles Duhigg popularized an idea that comes out of behavioral science and addiction research called a "habit loop." He described a three-step process: trigger, routine, and reward. The idea echoes across modern psychology, all the way back to B. F. Skinner's behavioral chain (which expanded on his controversial but influential theory that humans are driven by a simple binary of reward versus punishment) and the foundational idea in cognitive behavioral therapy of "antecedent-behavior-consequence" (ABC).

In each of these models there is an underlying stimulus, or something that prompts us to act. This stimulus is known by many names: stimulus, cue, trigger, antecedent, prompt. When the stimulus is neutral or positive, I tend to use "prompt"; when it's negative, I tend to use "trigger." The words are synonymous, but I find these uses most intuitive (in part because of my time in recovery—more on that soon) so that's what you'll see going forward in the book.

So, the habit loop: The stimulus/prompt/trigger step starts the loop or chain in motion.

After that we have a behavior or action taken—the "habit" or "routine." And then finally we have a "reward" or "consequence" that tells our brain this loop is worth doing again . . . and again, and again, as our neural pathways make deeper grooves each time we get the same result.

You might get stressed while playing with your kids: They just can't agree on whose turn it is with the thingamabob, and regardless of who wins you can already hear the wails of *unfaaair!* This unwelcome feeling is the trigger. Then you reach for your phone and start scrolling Instagram, which is the behavior/habit/routine. The reward is that your mind is now distracted from your stress and you feel (momentarily) better. Cue the vicious cycle.

If we want to change the loop, we have three options: (1) change the trigger, (2) change the behavior, or (3) change the reward. Research suggests that it's pretty tough to change how we respond to a given trigger (has "just don't worry about it" ever worked?), or to stop wanting the reward (imagine telling yourself you "just don't want that"). So without making bigger structural changes, like avoiding a trigger entirely, our first best option is to change the action we take to get to the reward our brains already want.

In the example above, it might be hard to avoid the trigger of feeling stressed, so we'll take that as a given, and once that stress hits you'll have a natural desire for the reward of not feeling stressed. But you might try substituting a more adaptive behavior in the middle. Before reaching for your phone you could choose to take five deep breaths. And maybe, just maybe, your pulse slows down enough to remind you that you don't actually want to tumble headfirst into the Instagram rabbit hole.

This is where we get back to the virtue of substituting a negative "stop doing x" goal with a positive "start doing x" goal. The old phrase *nature abhors a vacuum* applies here. If you simply try not to grab your phone, you haven't put anything else in its place. You'll have to just stew in your discomfort, relying on self-control and missing out on the perfectly reasonable reward of a little moment of peace.

You might resist the urge once or twice—but eventually you'll cave, because there's a gap in the loop. If your goal from the beginning is to "take five deep breaths when I feel stressed," however, or even to "take five deep breaths when I feel like grabbing my phone," you start out with the advantage of a built-in alternative.

The same principle applies to habits like staying up too late. Rather than simply trying to go to bed earlier, you could establish a calming pre-bed routine, such as reading a book, taking a warm bath, or practicing light stretching. This replaces the unhealthy behavior of staying up late with a series of positive actions that prepare your mind and body for rest.

This is a basic example of structural planning: recognizing that we tend to act a certain way in certain situations, and preparing healthier ways to meet our desire-having, reward-seeking selves.

But we can get even more ambitious. Deep breath: Here's how to set yourself up for success with any goal for behavioral change. In a word, get ready to SPAR.

THE SPAR METHOD

Boxing is a brutal sport. Once the contenders are in the ring, it's just two pairs of fists and the possibility of a knockout. But before a boxer meets their match, there's a lot they can do to improve their odds of success (and, ideally, staying conscious).

Namely? They SPAR.

In the (hopefully) much less violent world of our path to change, SPAR stands for **specificity, prompts, alignment, resilience**. Breaking down each step:

1. **SPECIFICITY:** This step is about fine-tuning the behavior you've chosen to start or change. It involves setting precise, measurable actions and defining exactly what success looks like.

2. **PROMPTS:** This step focuses on designing cues that remind you to engage in the desired behavior (for positive changes) or avoid the undesired behavior (for breaking bad habits). These prompts make the behavior as automatic and easy to initiate as possible.

3. **ALIGNMENT:** This step is about aligning your environment with your goals. It involves setting up your physical space, social context, and routines to support the behavior change. It's about making the desired behavior the path of least resistance.

4. **RESILIENCE:** This final step is about anticipating obstacles and developing strategies to overcome them. It's about proactively identifying what might derail your efforts and creating a plan to navigate these challenges. This step builds flexibility and prepares you for long-term success.

The SPAR Method addresses what I consider all the key structural components for lasting transformation: clear plans, environmental cues, a supportive context, and a plan for overcoming obstacles. In the rest of this chapter we'll expand on each element. Feel free to keep your chosen goal(s) in mind as you read.

Specificity

"Get in better shape." "Sleep more." "Work less." "Listen better." "Read more." Do any of these resolutions sound familiar? I've heard them all many times from coaching clients, not to mention from myself. And they're all A+ goals for directions of change. But as action plans? They get a D-. They're well intentioned, values oriented . . . and incredibly vague.

So you want to get in shape. Doing what kind of exercise? How many times a week? For how long? With whom? Have you paid the fees for a gym? Do you need to get equipment? Do you know how to use the equipment? Do you need childcare? Is your schedule reliably free when you're planning to go?

Sorry to go attack mode for a second there. But if you felt overwhelmed or quietly dissociated halfway through, that's making my point: The less specific your plan of action, the more you're setting yourself up for failure. It's not procrastination at that point; it's confusion wearing a motivational hat. You can't procrastinate on something if you don't even know what steps to take!

One key specification is to break your broader objective into benchmarks. Instead of "I want to get in shape," try starting with "I want to go for a twenty-minute walk three times per week," or "I want to do ten push-ups and ten squats every morning." These are discrete, measurable actions we can actually implement.

Another key is to separate decision from action. When we make a decision in advance about what we want to do, how we're going to do it, and when we're going to do it, we ease the mental friction. When the time comes to take action, we can focus all our energy on doing the thing, rather than getting stuck in a loop of trying to figure out what to do.

Let's go to a random morning when you wake up knowing you should exercise. Without a plan, your mind starts spinning: "Should I go to the gym? Maybe I should do yoga instead. Oh, but the weather's not great for a run. Let me check the yoga class schedule . . . nothing fits. I could go to the gym, but I have to start getting ready for work soon." Sound familiar? It's exhausting, and by the time your brain finishes auditioning all the options, your actual window to do anything has quietly drawn its curtains.

Imagine if you had decided the night before: "I'm going to the gym at seven for a thirty-minute workout." When you wake up, there's no decision to make. You just get up, lace up your sneakers, and go. All your energy is focused on the action, not the deliberation.

We can apply the same principle to work. Say you have an hour free between meetings, but no plan for how to use that time. Your brain kicks off a quick game of indecisive Ping-Pong: "Should I work on that report due in a few days? Nah, I don't feel like it. Maybe I should start on the slide deck for tomorrow's presentation. But I'm kind of tired and unfocused. I guess I could just catch up on email. That *technically* counts as work . . ." Once again, you're using precious time and energy on deciding what to do, rather than actually doing it.

The solution? Decide in advance. Before you wrap up work for the day, take a few minutes to plan out your tasks for the next day. Assign specific tasks to those openings in your calendar. That way, when a free moment comes up, you can jump right into action without wasting time on decision-making.

Ambiguity is one of the mothers of procrastination. William James said, "There is no more miserable human being than one in whom nothing is habitual but indecision. . . . Full half the time of such a man goes to the deciding, or regretting, of matters which ought to be so ingrained in him as practically not to exist for his consciousness at all."

Harsh, Will. But fair. More than once I've caught myself wasting hours of precious free time in a loop of grand ambitions for how to use that free time . . . only to realize that I've spent half of a beautiful Saturday playing solitaire on my computer. (Don't get me started on solitaire—talk about a habit loop.)

To get more specific about getting specific, for any behavioral goal, ask yourself:

- What?
- Where?
- When?
- How?

Let's take the goal of getting more sleep. **What** is "more sleep" to you: eight hours a night? six hours? The **where** is pretty obvious in this case, but the **when** needs planning. What time do you need to go to bed to get enough sleep? If you have to get up at 7 a.m., then eight hours of sleep takes us back to 11 p.m. Okay, so if you want to go to sleep at 11, when do you need to get in bed? This might lead you to discover some uncomfortable truths, like realizing you need to start getting ready for bed earlier. Or that the TV needs to go off at a specific time. And if falling asleep is a challenge, you might need to throw in a few *how*s: Do you need a sleep mask? A white-noise machine? A cease-and-desist letter to your neighbors?

The point here is not to walk you through every detail of bedtime, but to give you a sense of the type of questions that you'll want answered ahead of time. Remember, ambiguity is our enemy. Any eddy of uncertainty is a place where we can fall off track. There is a Finnish phrase, *Minkä taakseen jättää sen edestään löytää*, which translates to "What you leave behind you will find in front of you." If your plans are incomplete, you'll meet your missing steps later, dressed as obstacles. Often in the middle of the night, looking very smug.

• • •

One more reason to get specific with our goals for change takes us back to little by little. Recall that under BJ Fogg's behavioral model, action happens when "prompts," "motivation," and "ability" come together at the same time. Our goal should be to lower the combined resistance of motivation and ability when we encounter a given prompt, to minimize the need for self-control.

Which means: The smaller and easier the action, the better. In chapter 1 we took the example of a sink full of dirty dishes. If washing that whole sink presents too much of a motivational challenge, try lowering the goal to washing a single fork. More doable! Ideally, that one fork will create momentum and lower our resistance to doing more—but if not, at least we'll have done something rather than nothing.

One of the questions I get asked often is: How little do you mean? Should I start by trying to exercise for five minutes or thirty? There is no answer that I can give you to plug in and use, because everyone is different and everyone's capacity is different. We are trying to balance choosing something that is easy enough that we will do it and yet significant enough to matter.

That said, a good rule of thumb is to start smaller than you think you need to. You can always increase the difficulty of the task as time goes on, but as we have said, success and failure feed upon themselves. The name of the game is (re)calibration: Try something, see how it works, and tweak as necessary. I'd much rather have you succeed for a week and decide to do more than fail and give up. Our goal is to achieve consistency and build from there.

Prompts

At the recovery center during my early days of sobriety, we were often asked to make a list of things that triggered us to want to use.

Picture a bunch of twitchy, hollow-eyed people sitting in a circle, squinting into an abyss of (very) blurry memories. Was it boredom? Stress? That one song that always seemed to be playing whenever we made catastrophically bad choices? The idea was to map out all our personal landmines so we could tiptoe around them and stay on the straight and narrow.

What we were really doing, though no one put it quite this way, was identifying prompts: the cues that lead to specific behaviors. In recovery, we called them "triggers," and they usually had a negative spin. But in daily life, prompts can be good, bad, or completely neutral. I prefer "prompt" as a more flexible umbrella term, since "trigger" tends to carry heavier baggage, even outside addiction circles. Prompts can be external, like an object, a location, or a calendar alert. They can be internal, like a mood or thought. A yawn that leads to coffee. An alarm clock that wakes us up. A tailgater that leads to an elaborate imaginary argument involving hand gestures and swear words you didn't even know you knew. Prompts are the "if" in any "if-then" sequence of behavior—they're what put us at a choice point.

So far we've mostly talked about prompts or triggers that just happen to us (a stressful situation, seeing cake in the fridge, money in the mail), but we also use them intentionally all the time. Many are time-based prompts: Go to the dentist at 10 a.m. Thursday, and take Sam to soccer at 3:30. Our lives would be in chaos without them.

Prompts are such a critical and varied part of how behavior works that we'll return to them throughout the rest of the book. (Again, they are the *if* in every single *if-then*). Here, as part of SPAR, I want to focus on a specific, intentional-use case: positive prompts we can use to cue ourselves to do something. There are six of these:

- The first is the classic **time-based prompt**, which as said above is probably the one we're most aware of. We give ourselves reminders to do certain things at certain times. At 2 p.m. I will take five minutes to step outside and breathe deeply for three minutes.

- A second type of prompt is **location-based**. When you sit down in your car you buckle up; when you leave the bathroom you wash your hands. (Hopefully.) These are both behaviors on the habitual/automatic side, but why not add reminders to yourself to do things in other places? "Whenever I walk into the kitchen, I will…" or "Whenever I stop at a red light, I will…"

- A third type of prompt we can use is the **preceding-event prompt**. This is also referred to in behavioral science as an "anchoring" prompt. An activity that already happens consistently can serve to cue the behavior we want. "After I take the dogs out in the morning…" or "After the kids are in bed…"

- The fourth type of prompt is **other people**. Other people trigger us in many ways, but we can choose to add positive prompts to that mix. Someone stopping by your house as they head out on a walk is a great reminder for you to go walk. A text from a friend sharing good news could be a cue to inspire you to reflect on gratitude.

- The fifth type of prompt is what I refer to as **random**. The idea here is to use the technology that usually distracts us to remind us. There are a number of apps available that we can set to go off randomly throughout the day, and with each alert comes a message about the reflection or behavior we want to take. I've used this approach with great success in the Wise Habits program I teach (this book is largely based on what I teach in that program). A study published in the *Journal of Medical Internet Research* in 2020 found that participants who received daily social media messages encouraging physical activity exercised significantly more than a control group.

- Finally, there is the Holy Grail of intentional prompts: the **emotional state** prompt. "When I feel angry I will..." or "When I find myself ruminating I will..." The reason I think of this as the Holy Grail—something precious, transformative, and famously kind of hard to get to—is that it requires both deep awareness of our inner state and a clear intention around what we will do in those moments. It requires, in other words, wisdom. But it can also help us become wiser, in a virtuous cycle of becoming more attuned to our inner lives and how our actions affect them.

Alignment

In a nondescript laboratory cage, a rat faces a stark choice: plain water or a morphine-laced solution. With no other options for stimulation or interaction, the rat repeatedly chooses the drug. This bleak scenario, replicated in hundreds of addiction studies (and portrayed in many antidrug ads), seems to show the relentless grip of drug dependency.

But what if this rat's environment offered more than just a choice between isolation and intoxication? This question inspired Canadian psychologist Bruce Alexander's Rat Park experiments in the 1970s.

Alexander wondered if the rats' drug use was truly a function of the drug's irresistible allure, or if it might be influenced by the impoverished conditions of standard laboratory housing. To test this, he constructed Rat Park.

He painted the walls with scenes that mimicked the natural environment, he covered the ground in cedar shavings, put toys out to play with, and most importantly gave the rats lots of other rats to hang out and do rat things with.

The results were striking. Given a richer environment and social interaction, the rats in Rat Park largely avoided the morphine solution, preferring plain water and the company of their fellow rodents. Even some of the rats who had previously been confined to isolated cages and compelled to consume morphine chose to wean themselves off the drug when moved to the vibrant colony.

While changing any behavior pattern involves a complex interplay of factors that can't be reduced to a single cause, Alexander's work is a compelling demonstration of the profound influence of environment on how we choose to act. All the more so because the rats' transformation was driven not by removing the drug but by changing the conditions in which they lived.

None of us human beings live in laboratory conditions. We can't optimize every part of our lives to lessen the power of negative prompts and to support positive ones. But there is plenty each of us can do to align our environments with our behavioral goals, both in terms of what and who we choose to surround ourselves with. And even a little of this kind of planning can make a big difference.

There is an entire field called environmental psychology, and it studies the ways our environments affect our choices and responses. In *Atomic Habits*, author James Clear cites research in this area exploring how three key factors, **proximity**, **convenience**, and **salience**, can shape habits and decisions, often in ways that operate below conscious awareness (read: autopilot):

Proximity has to do with how close something is to us. A recent study showed that an individual's proximity to a fitness center significantly predicted their likelihood of engaging in regular exercise. The closer they were to a facility, the more likely they were to exercise.

Convenience has to do with how easy it is to do something. Emily Balcetis, a professor of psychology at New York University, shared with me her strategy for setting up her drums to encourage practice. She said, "We put [the drum kit] in a space that we walk by to get out the door. The number of times that I practiced increased because it's like waiting for my husband, waiting for my kid to get their shoes on. I can go down and play for the five or ten minutes that it's going to take before they come out the door." The drums were placed for maximum convenience to take advantage of the small chunks of time available to her.

Salience speaks to how prominent something is. Is our attention drawn to it? Balcetis also said that she ended up playing her drums more often because having the set right by the door was an "automatic visual cue." This kind of environmental reminder can also work at a much bigger scale. In 2011, students from Roskilde University handed out free caramels to pedestrians in Copenhagen. They counted the number of caramel wrappers that were littered on the streets and in garbage cans. They then placed green footprint stickers leading to the nearest garbage cans and repeated the experiment.

The green footprint resulted in a remarkable 46 percent decrease in littered caramel wrappers on the streets. The footprints made it easier for pedestrians to find and use the garbage bins, but they also reminded them of the option to use garbage bins.

In some ways, the modern world has made environment modification more difficult for the average person. I'm old enough to remember when I could tell a client "If you don't want to eat junk food, don't have any in the house." Then came Deliveroo, Uber Eats and all manner of delivery services. An app called Gopuff seems designed to cater to every stoner's dream. (The top choices are Chester's Flamin' Hot Fries, Cheetos, and Goldfish.) In many cities you can now get your weed delivered right to your door.

Temptation doesn't just knock anymore—it texts, rings the doorbell, and offers free delivery.

What this means is that we have to get more creative. A client of mine had an issue with online pornography. At night, after everyone went to sleep, he would log on. To him this felt like a moral failing, and he genuinely wanted to stop. As we walked through his behavior step-by-step, a pattern emerged: Before bed, he always left his laptop on and connected to the internet. So later at night all it took was a couple of clicks and he was doing something he didn't want to do. Our first move was simple: Have him log off before bed. That helped a bit, but it still wasn't enough—logging back on was still too easy. So we went further. He started putting his laptop in his car at night. That extra bit of distance, literal and psychological, turned out to be just enough friction to stop him from doing it.

We can also use the digital world's tools of convenience for our own ends, as with the random prompt. I often use a tool, the SelfControl app, to stop playing solitaire or wasting time online in other ways. This is one of many such apps geared toward helping us spend less time on social media, play fewer games, not order DoorDash, etc. It might feel like cheating to literally outsource self-control in this way, but it's not—it's fighting fire with fire.

The last key piece of environmental alignment, and part of the magic of Rat Park, is to think about *who* is on the journey of change with you. In whatever ways possible, surround yourself with people who support and encourage the changes you're trying to make. This could involve joining a support group, enlisting the help of a workout partner, or spending more time with friends who engage in healthy behaviors. A 2010 study published in *The Journal of Health Communication* found that participants in an online weight-loss program who were assigned to a social support group lost significantly more weight than those who participated alone, to take just one of many studies.

I'll be talking much more about the power of social support in an upcoming chapter. For now, consider the groundwork laid. There's a saying that holds true no matter what any of us are trying to do: If you want to go fast, go alone. But if you want to go far, go together.

Resilience

"The best-laid schemes o' mice an' men gang aft agley [go often awry]." I'm betting that part of that line sounds familiar, but maybe not the whole thing. A verse by the Scottish poet Robert Burns, the fact that we need only a couple words to evoke the line's full meaning tells us just how universal it is. *The best-laid plans of mice and men* . . . will do it for most of us, or even just *best-laid plans* . . . (Or if you're a Steinbeck fan, just the mice and men part.)

Which is to say: It's no secret that planning takes us only so far, and that reality often has other ideas.

Once I have worked with a client to create a plan that has the elements of specificity, has designed prompts, and works to make their environment suited to their goals, I ask a simple question. "What can go wrong? What are the ways that this plan is going to fail?" Not in a hellfire-and-locusts sense—just your usual array of chaos and minor emergencies.

If your plan is to meditate right after the kids get on the school bus, it's worth thinking about what's going to happen on days when they don't. What if they miss it and you have to drive them? What if one of them is home sick and you need to stay with them? These are not freak occurrences—they're things we *know* are going to happen. So we can plan for them in advance.

A simple format we can use is if-then. In psychology it's called implementation instructions, which just means plans for what we'll do when things go wrong. *If x happens, then I will do y*: This bare-bones set of instructions has proven extraordinarily powerful in helping people stay on target with their habits. (It's basically another way to use prompts, with the prompt being "when your plans fall through.")

Back to our meditation example: *If one of the kids is home from school sick, then I will plan to do a shorter meditation in the room they are in rather than going to my usual spot.*

A little bit of something is always better than a lot of nothing. When a commitment gets interrupted, the goal is to still do *some* version of the planned behavior—no matter how small. Say it's 5 p.m., and you have an art class planned at 5:30. You're packing up your bag, headed for the door, and your boss comes up to you and says, "Hey, real quick before you go could you just pull me the latest numbers on the Simpson case?"

Now you're stuck. The Simpson case business takes twenty minutes, and just like that, the art class is off the table. But instead of scrapping the evening entirely, you pivot. You take a short walk and snap five photos that could later become paintings. What this alternative does is to keep alive a commitment to the values underlying the behavior you had planned. The value wasn't just "go to art class"—it was to invest time and energy in your creativity. You can't always do exactly what you planned, but you *can* stay flexible enough to honor the value underneath it.

We cannot anticipate all the unplanned obstacles. But as new behaviors gain more momentum, we often get a little better at rolling with the punches.

AND YET . . .

And yet. Even in the most structured environment in the world, even when everything is going the way we expected, even when we're not overtired or hungry, even when we've set up just the right prompt . . . the time comes to take action, and we still do nothing. Or we do the wrong thing. *Akrasia* all over again.

The time has finally come to move past the planning stage and into the instant of *action*. In the next chapter we'll ask what exactly is going on in mind and body in that moment, in what I earlier called the "internal component" of decision-making. We'll ask why self-control works, and also why it fails.

Before we do, I want to leave you with a bookend to the story of the twenty-five dollars.

I had been picking them up for several months and hadn't even thought about it. I waited in line at the pharmacy, got the slim paper sack with its stapled prescription, and brought them to my mom. They rode in the passenger seat through the warm summer months. I carried them, light as they were, up to her apartment week after week.

Opiates? Yes, opiates. Oxycontin, to be specific. The good stuff.

Twenty-five years earlier I would likely have robbed you at gunpoint for them. Twenty-five years earlier I drove a different car, sobbing, to a drug deal after my first week of sobriety. Now I'm shepherding the same basic substance to my mom without thinking about using once. Without really having any emotional reaction at all. I glance at the passenger seat; the pills feel no more significant to me than a loaf of bread.

I don't tell you this story to brag or show off. I tell it because it shows just how much we can change, and because it shows that things can get not just better but *easier*. What feels insurmountable for us today can become second-nature reality down the line.

Sometimes our best-laid plans work out pretty well.

ONE LITTLE THING YOU CAN DO RIGHT NOW

Pick one habit you want to build and get microscopically specific about your next plan to practice it. Instead of "exercise more," decide exactly what you'll do (ten push-ups), where (next to your bed), and when (right after you brush your teeth). Write it down as: "When I finish brushing my teeth, I will do ten push-ups next to my bed."

When you're ready to go a little deeper, flip to the appendix for extra exercises—or download the companion worksheets anytime at oneyoufeed.net/resources.

FOUR

Moments of Action

> Do what you can, with what you've got, where you are.
> —BILL WIDENER

IN ERNEST HEMINGWAY'S NOVELLA *THE OLD MAN AND THE SEA*, AN OLD MAN faces off with, well, the sea. Specifically, in one climactic scene, he faces two hungry sharks who have followed the scent of blood to the giant marlin he has harpooned and that he is now struggling to haul home. The old man hasn't caught a fish for months; he's feeling his age. There's a lot riding on him bringing in this marlin, he feels sure—so much so that he has braved storm-tossed, shark-infested waters for three days to get this far.

But after an Ahab-like chase, after he has pulled in his thousand-pound prize catch and lashed it to the side of his skiff, there is this moment in the story: He is miles offshore, waves rocking his tiny, unstable boat, facing down the "wide, flattened, shovel-pointed heads" of two blood-crazed sharks. He has just punched one shark and wedged an oar in the mouth of the other, but he knows he's far from safe. He wishes for all the things that could help him in this moment. If only his arms and hands weren't so tired. If only his harpoon wasn't buried in the marlin. If only he had a stone to sharpen his dulled knife. But these are just wishes, he knows: He is alone.

And then, the old man says what has become one of Hemingway's most immortal lines: "Now is no time to think of what you do not have. Think of what you can do with what there is."

It is a turning point in the story. The old man seizes what he does have—the boat's tiller—and steers away from the sharks, saving his life. As he does so he begins to worry about the bites the sharks have taken out of his marlin, and the even wider trail of blood that will now be following the boat . . . but he stops himself again. "Don't think of that. Just rest and try to get your hands in shape to defend what is left." He even sees an upside in what has happened: "She's much lighter now," he reflects of his boat, thanks to her cargo being partially eaten. He'll be able to get home faster.

・ ・ ・

The old man has challenges left to face (by the time he gets home, his prize fish will be just a skeleton, prompting some soul-searching on the nature of success), but we'll leave him there on his journey, sailing away from the sharks that would have ended things before he ever got the chance to rethink his giant-fish-based values.

I tell this story not because I recommend life-endangering quests on the open sea (not a little-by-little approach to personal transformation), but because Hemingway is a master of exploring what this chapter is all about: the moment of action. What happens within us in the very instant we have to decide what to do? And how can we more often meet a choice point as a wiser version of ourselves, even when we feel like our best-laid plans—or our best harpoons—have deserted us?

In chapter 3 we discussed the many external factors that

influence our behavior, from our physical environment, to who we're with, to whether we're tired or hungry. In the moment, any of this context can affect how likely we are to act how we've hoped to or how we'll later wish we did. The upside of this is that we can plan ahead of time. But ultimately, to quote the title of Jon Kabat-Zinn's masterwork on everyday mindfulness: *Wherever You Go, There You Are*. Which is to say, you bring your inner strengths and challenges with you to each choice point, no matter how well you've stacked the deck.

This chapter is about what happens when you're in the thick of it. Whether you've done all the advance planning in the world, or you find yourself facing a shark empty-handed, it's *you* in that moment. You might know what you were hoping to do, but your brain still has to give the go sign to act.

When we do overcome internal resistance to action, behavioral scientists call this self-control, as introduced earlier. In this chapter we'll get into how self-control works, how we can see it less as a battle than as a negotiation (with an elephant), and how we can strengthen our ability to exercise it when necessary. With any luck, like Hemingway's old man, we'll realize we have the resources we need to navigate the day's currents after all.

SELF-CONTROL AND ITS LIMITS

There are a lot of cheerleaders for self-control—or willpower or discipline—out there, as there have been for millennia. In Islam, *sabr* (patience and self-restraint) is mentioned over ninety times in the Quran, while in Jewish thought *yetzer hara* (evil inclination) and *yetzer hatov* (good inclination) exist in an ongoing internal battle. Among secular philosophers, after Plato lamented *akrasia*, or acting against one's better judgment, Stoic philosophers like Epictetus and Seneca advocated for the mastery of desires and emotions as the path to contentment. In the Enlightenment era, Immanuel Kant viewed self-control as crucial to moral autonomy, arguing that freedom comes from acting according to reason rather than from impulse.

Skipping to the end of the timeline, for a modern example of our cultural obsession with self-discipline look no further than our fixations on the diet and fitness regimen behind the latest celebrity superhero transformation or post-baby swimsuit photo op. Or if you prefer, there's "hustle culture," "boot camp" experiences, being "on the grind"—one need only skim the surface of pop culture to find testimonies to a sort of bootstrapping grit as the key to success and fulfillment. If you're not getting what you want, these voices say cheerily, you must simply not want it bad enough.

But then there is the science of self-control, which paints a somewhat different picture.

What self-control *is* is a matter of great debate, but most researchers agree on its contours. It is associated with our executive functions—all the cognitive processes by which we decide how to behave—that in our brains seem to live in our prefrontal cortex, the site linked with bringing our internal goals into the behavioral conversation. Neuroscience has shown that people with higher self-control show relatively more activity in the prefrontal cortex and less activity in areas associated with processing immediate rewards (like, say, a sugar high or the rush of a temper tantrum).

This suggests a neural tug-of-war. On one side, we have the prefrontal cortex working to maintain focus on long-term goals (the value-driven kind—what we want *most*). On the other hand, we have reward centers pushing for immediate gratification (what we want *now*). In those with strong self-control, the prefrontal cortex more often wins this contest.

Some researchers describe this tug-of-war by distinguishing between "hot" and "cool" cognitive systems, which sound like they were named for the angel and devil on our shoulders. The hot system, impulsive and sensory, seeks satisfaction, while the cool system embodies rationality and long-term thinking. Self-control involves the cool system overriding the hot system's urges. While our hot instincts might urge us to reach for a cigarette or impulsively check social media, our cool resources analyze the long-term consequences of these actions and potentially override the automatic response. The drawback, researchers including Daniel Kahneman argue, is that the latter system requires effort and has limited capacity, which means that self-control may fail when we're tired, stressed, or thinking about many things at once.

For a closer look at this mental tax, we go to a tale of cookies versus radishes.

Imagine you're a college student. You enter the lab, expecting to answer some questionnaires about your childhood or maybe get your brain scanned while looking at pictures of kittens. Instead, you're confronted with a plate of cookies that smell like they were baked by the collective grandmothers of the world.

But there's a catch. (There's always a catch in psychology studies.) The researcher, somewhat cruelly, hands you a plate of radishes. "Eat these," they say, "and don't touch the cookies."

This is the infamous "radish experiment" conducted by Roy Baumeister and his colleagues in 1998. The idea is simple: Self-control is a limited resource. Use it too much and it weakens. Force someone to resist delicious cookies and they'll have less willpower left for other tasks. It's an intuitive idea—it's the "fuck-it"s we've talked about, the cake staring at you from the fridge, or the possibility of being less than patient with your spouse after a long day of gritting your teeth to politely deal with a difficult boss.

To actually test the existence of a drain on self-control, the researchers didn't stop at torturing students with vegetables. They then gave participants a difficult puzzle to solve. The hypothesis was that the radish eaters, having depleted their resources resisting cookies while crunching roughage, would give up on the puzzle more quickly than those who got to indulge.

That's exactly what happened. The radish group threw in the towel faster than a boxer realizing he accidentally stepped into the ring with a prime Mike Tyson. From this and other studies, Baumeister and his team came up with the strength model of self-control, which posits that it acts like a muscle: Use it too much and it will wear out.

Scientists still debate what exactly it is that gets depleted (the original idea was glucose, which later studies have seemed to contradict), or whether self-control is really any different from a number of other mental processes (what *doesn't* get a little impaired when we're tired or hungry?). Other research has focused on the potential for training our capacity for self-control, which we'll get to shortly.

In any case, it's clear that self-control isn't a magic bullet for making good decisions—rather it's something to rely on no more than necessary. If we gathered all the top behavioral scientists in one room, this might be the one thing they'd all actually agree on. Everything in chapter 3 was aimed at reducing the need to use self-control in the first place—and that will always be a winning first course of action. If Baumeister had offered his subjects only radishes, it might have defeated the purpose of the study, but it definitely would have been easier for them to say no to the (nonexistent) cookies.

And yet . . . sometimes we do need to lean on self-control. To maximize our chances of success when we do, and minimize our chances of throwing a puzzle out the window and storming off to see if there are any cookies left, let's take a closer look at what we might be feeling in the moment of choice.

THE EMOTIONAL ELEPHANT

Self-control is closely tied to another familiar term: motivation. If motivation is how much we feel like doing something, "feel" is the key word there. When self-control fails us, it is very often an emotional issue.

I don't mean it's an issue that emotion isn't involved in at all—though that's exactly how people often interpret the pursuit of self-control, as removing emotion from decision-making. Part of the reason I don't love the term "self-control" is because it evokes this image of cold domination: one orderly part of us policing some inherently less acceptable, unruly part. I'm okay with picturing a tug-of-war inside me, or even the "two wolves" of the parable duking it out, but I draw the line at imagining some kind of inner police state, where the goal is for cool-headed reason to prevail over hot-headed emotion whenever possible.

For one thing, this just isn't how we actually work. However much we might want to believe we are rational creatures who think through our options before making a logical decision, social scientists have observed that this is almost never entirely the case. Whether we're looking at how people choose political parties, or investment opportunities, or even something as seemingly objective as medical decisions, we see that how we *feel* in the moment of decision often influences our actions at least as much as factual evidence for one option or another.

In other words: Even with the observed distinction between hot and cold cognitive systems, the lines between logic and intuition, thought and mood, calculation and sentiment—insert your favorite objective versus subjective binary—will always be blurred within us. In order to act on our values, we need to accept that our emotions are riding shotgun, and learn to work with them rather than try for a feelings-free version of ourselves.

Along these lines, a better way to envision self-control than reason versus emotion is a metaphor Jonathan Haidt introduces in his book *The Happiness Hypothesis*: It's like riding an elephant.

In this analogy, the elephant represents our subconscious, emotional, instinctive side, while the rider symbolizes our conscious, rational, reflective side. You may think, as the one holding the reins, that you're calling the shots—just as you may think your conscious mind is in charge of your behavior. But let's face it, the elephant is way bigger and stronger. It's a powerful and sometimes unpredictable part of you. The elephant is always going to have a mind of its own (and it's the one carrying your baggage).

Remember "have-to" versus "want-to" motivation from chapter 2— how tasks and goals tend to feel more sustainable when we're aware of wanting to complete them rather than feeling driven by a sense of external obligation. (Even if, in the realm of self-control, the "have-to" voice is no one's but our own.) The ideal is to find a way to get the elephant to *want* to go in the direction we are pointing, or not to fight us, or at the very least to distract him long enough for us to do what we want to do.

Part of the nuance here is knowing that the best approach changes with every situation. Sometimes it makes sense to acknowledge our emotions and work with them, but other times it makes sense to suppress them in the service of our larger goals. I have been asking a version of this question on the podcast for a decade now, and I'm sorry to say there is no simple answer. Context (as always) plays a role. If we are in a meeting with the CEO of our company and we start to feel sad about our dog passing away last week, that might be a good moment to gently file those feelings under "To Be Processed Later." But at home that night on the couch, leaning into that grief is probably the best thing for us.

We each have tendencies to one end of the spectrum of emotional expression or the other, and coming to understand these tendencies is key in learning how to steer your inner elephant. We might be the sort of person who resists any show of vulnerability, even when allowing that it would help us connect with others or get honest with ourselves. Or maybe we are a person whose emotions tend to run the show, to the extent that we feel incapable of setting them aside to deal with an unexpected situation or to step outside our own perspective.

Neither of these extremes serves us. What we want is flexibility in working with our emotions. In Buddhism this is often called being "skillful or unskillful." I love this phrasing because it isn't about right or wrong, and it isn't even about "control," per se: It is about what helps us feel like our wiser, truer self in a moment of challenge.

I often find it best to blend the two approaches by acknowledging what I am feeling and then gently setting it aside to focus on the action. "I know you are feeling sad right now," we might say to ourselves in that hard moment at work, "and that makes it hard to finish this report. But we can come back to the sadness later. Right now let's get through the report." In this way we have avoided the extremes: We have not denied that we feel something and at the same time we have not let it rule us.

Another useful approach is to make the elephant define how it *really* feels about what you're asking it to do. When we're facing a task and we find the voice inside saying, "I don't want to," it's often less an expression of deep internal conflict than a surface-level reaction. If the protest is "I don't want to exercise" or "I don't want to study," the answer under that protest is that you do want to . . . you just don't feel like it right now. One of the quickest ways to move out of a place of internal battle is to simply change what we are saying to something like "I *do* want to exercise, I just don't feel like it."

This is ultimately the same approach as the above—we acknowledge how we're feeling, then we set it apart from our intent to act. Remember that if you have done the work up to now, you will know, deeply and truly, that you want to exercise, or study, or start chipping away at the Great American Novel—whatever everyday goal(s) you've identified as in line with the values by which you want to live.

For some reason, for myself and many people I have worked with, changing "don't want to" to "don't feel like it" helps to get us out of our own way surprisingly often. "Don't feel like it" is a passing thing: an emotional reaction but not the kind to bow to right now, when we have more important business to get done. "Yeah, yeah," we tell our whiny pachyderm, and move on down the road. As we grow more skillful, which is to say more in touch with our wiser, truer selves, our elephant will trust us to listen when it matters.

EVEN IF . . .

Even if perfect self-control were possible, I wouldn't want it.

Before we get further into strategies for improving our behavioral follow-through, another word on what we should be aiming for overall. In short: balance.

In a recent paper, behaviorists Daniela Becker and Katharina Bernecker argue that training our focus entirely on long-term goals can leave us unable to enjoy much of anything in the present. When we try to let go of the long-term plan and enjoy ourselves, intrusive thoughts about "wasting" time dampen our ability to feel pleasure in the experience at hand. If our single-minded focus continues, we may miss out on opportunities for connection or growth and find ourselves unable to relax even when we want to. This is something I personally have to watch out for. My need to always use time "well" leads my mind toward focusing on the future, thinking about what I "should" do next rather than letting myself fully appreciate the present.

Excessive self-control can also impact our relationships. It might show up as an inability to compromise, or as a rigid demeanor others find off-putting. We might place sticking with our routines as more important than time devoted to the relationship.

At worst we might experience excessive control as a serious pathology. A friend of mine who has recovered from anorexia describes the disease as feeling like a prison of her own making, in which part of her desperately wanted to eat the foods she had been denying herself, but another, stronger part, fueled by shame and fear of excess, continued to impose a regimen of deprivation. This was a personal experience of a complex disease, of which no two experiences are alike; but she found part of her healing to be a therapeutic engagement with self-control across all areas of her life. Little by little, she discovered that her personal balance of happiness and health had, if anything, less to do with control than with learning how and when to let go.

For all of us, the key lies in a middle ground—enough self-control to achieve our goals, but not so much that it leads to rigidity or emotional suppression. Flexibility, self-compassion, and the ability to occasionally let go are counterbalances to a firm hand on the reins. Plus, a life without present-tense pleasure and joy is just not the life I want to live.

TAKING THE REINS

All that said, there are powerful ways to work with, not against, ourselves to increase our chances of self-control (or elephant steering) at a choice point. Many of these rely on two cognitive tools: **attention** and **framing**.

Attention is what we choose to focus on; framing is how we think about what we're focusing on.

Think of it like a newspaper. Attention is the story the paper chooses to cover on page one, the headline our brain pulls from the flood of sensory input and internal chatter.

Framing is the perspective the paper takes in that front-page story, meaning how we interpret what's happening. Is today's breaking news good or bad? Discouraging or encouraging? Scary or exciting? Frustrating or funny?

Attention and framing work in tandem to shape our perceptions and, ultimately, our actions. Once we're aware of this, we can start making them work for us. When faced with a challenging task, narrowing our attention to the next small, manageable step instead of the overwhelming whole can help us to overcome procrastination and maintain motivation. And when dealing with cravings or temptations, redirecting our attention elsewhere can lower the intensity of desire.

By reframing situations, we can change our response to them, emotionally and otherwise. We might reframe a competitive situation at work as a challenge rather than as a threat, or view a difficult conversation as an opportunity for growth instead of a burden to grit our teeth through. The switch from "I don't want to" to "I don't feel like," above, is a reframing technique—perhaps the simplest possible. Whether subtle or dramatic, this kind of shifting of the lens, in which we rethink the story we're telling ourselves, can transform our ability to persist in challenging moments.

Both tools have their advantages. Attention strategies are easier to implement in real time; less cognitive effort is needed to redirect your gaze than to invent a whole new meaning for what you're seeing. But framing strategies, though more demanding and slower to execute, can lead to more profound and lasting changes in our thought and behavior patterns.

Just now the sound of the dryer caught my attention and pulled it away from my writing. (Dryer sounds may not bother you but I swear we turn ours on and it's the Battle of the Somme in there.) Using attention, my first reaction was to shut the door to my office, turn my eyes back to the white digital page, and tune out the now-muffled clanging. But if I found myself fixating, getting more and more frustrated (it's happened), then I could try reframing the situation. I could tell myself that this is good practice for working in even noisier conditions. Or I could look at it from a different angle: Remind myself that the sound means clean clothes are happening, that I'm lucky to have an in-unit washer and dryer at all. Maybe even remember that my sense of gratitude at the life I have is part of why I want to write this book in the first place.

At any point in the above I might find my irritation relaxed enough to get back to writing. But you can see the strategic differences: the quicker fix of attention (close the door, hope for the best) versus the more cognitively intense approach of rethinking dryers, the universe, and everything. Given that our mental resources are limited, it makes sense to start with attention and then move to framing. But sometimes, attention isn't enough—we have to change the story we're telling ourselves.

・・・

In the story that began this chapter, as Hemingway's Old Man faces off with hungry sharks, he uses both strategies to spur himself to action. First, he redirects his attention to the present, and to the tools most likely to get him out of this situation: "Now is no time to think of what you do not have. Think of what you can do with what there is." Later, as he steers away and finds himself in danger of getting lost in grief over his half-eaten fish, he reframes the situation: At least his boat is "much lighter now." When you're sailing for your life, that's undeniably useful.

With this overview in mind, we're now going to look at some of the most common challenges to self-control. I call them the Six Saboteurs: the autopilot pitfall, fatigue fallout, shortsighted stumble, emotional escapism, the self-doubt stalemate, and the insignificance trap. You could probably sacrifice the alliteration I clearly like so much and think of more, but these are the challenges

I've seen come up most often with everyone from friends and loved ones, to clients and students, to myself. To address them, we'll see how attention and framing can help us do our best with the tools at hand.

The Autopilot Pitfall: Cruise (Lack of) Control

I've spent considerable time deconstructing my own autopilot responses, for example, how my hand seems to confuse "time to open this work document" for "time to play solitaire again." I can trace a line between internal discomfort—be it frustration, doubt, or boredom—and the directions my autopilot takes me. But the defining element of this pitfall is that it unfolds below the threshold of conscious awareness. We don't actively choose to deviate from our intentions; we're off base before we even realize what's happening.

Imagine having a few chips while watching TV—and looking down as your hand scrapes the bottom of the bag. Or finding your phone in your hand for the tenth time in ten minutes. We've all been there. We do these things not because we've decided they're the best use of our time and energy, but because the part of us that would have chosen otherwise is out to lunch.

Tools to Overcome It

Attention is going to be our primary tool here. Often all it takes is enough awareness to see that we're making a choice—at which point we have the option to decide whether or not it's a choice we want to make. To cultivate this awareness, check in with yourself throughout the day: Just ask what you're doing and why you're doing it.

I have a program on my phone that activates whenever I click on my email app, prompting me to take a breath in and out and then select how long I want to use the app for. It does not block me from using the app, but it does make me aware of what's happening and forces me to consciously affirm that I do, in fact, want to check my email—which then usually leads me to reflect that I don't *want* to, I just *feel* like it. This simple prompt has reduced my sometimes-compulsive email checking by about 500 percent.

You might have clocked that setting up an app like this is really a job for the planning stage, not the action stage of behavior—and you'd be right. Consider this your broken-record reminder that the best way to succeed at self-control is to plan ahead so that you need as little as possible.

Fatigue Fallout: When There's Nothing in the Tank

We've already encountered this one through Roy Baumeister and his exhausted radish eaters, and the dangers of HALT (when you're hungry, angry, lonely, tired). Being fatigued, mentally or physically, always makes it harder to make the right choice. When we're hungry, blood-sugar levels drop and the body enters a state of mild stress, releasing hormones like cortisol and adrenaline. These hormonal changes can lead to irritability, difficulty concentrating, and increased impulsivity. Extreme tiredness can likewise severely impair our focus, memory, and decision-making, eroding our ability to resist immediate gratification in favor of long-term benefits. Self-control is a function of our physical state and well-being—and when these are off, so is our willpower.

Tools to Overcome It

The first line of defense here is, again, preemptive: better self-care. But no one wants to be told in an important moment that they should have gone to bed earlier last night or that they "should have eaten something before we left."

One useful choice-point strategy is to talk ourselves into *just getting started*, by narrowing our attention to whatever the smallest first step is. In chapter 1 I described my daily struggle with exercising: I wake up and think biking sounds *way* too hard. But maybe I could just put on my shoes? Putting on shoes is easy. Toddlers do it. I focus my attention on only that: shoes. And more often than not, once the shoes are on, I start to forget how tired I am . . . and decide that the next step, getting on the bike, isn't so hard after all.

If refocusing doesn't work, it may be time to deal with the HALT situation. If you skipped dinner to finish a work presentation and now you're feeling scatterbrained, you just might feel more productive with a burrito in hand. Or if you canceled plans with friends because tonight you're definitely going to the gym, but you find yourself dawdling . . . maybe what you're feeling is not laziness but loneliness. Would your friend be interested in exercising too? And if not, could it be that you need a heart-to-heart conversation right now more than you need half an hour on the treadmill?

It might also just be a day to cut yourself some slack. Maybe your emotional elephant needs a break. The key, if you decide this is the case, is not to frame it as some grand failure of your goals. It's an "only human" moment—and as humans, we have plenty of those.

Shortsighted Stumble: When Our Only Perspective Is Now

Researchers call this challenge "delay discounting," which is a fancy way of saying we value immediate gratification over longer-term effects. It's the "what we want now versus what we want most" effect. I want to scroll Instagram *now*, but I want to succeed at my job *most*.

There is a classic episode of *The Simpsons* in which Marge is telling Homer that someday he is going to regret not spending more time with the kids. Homer replies, "That's a problem for future Homer. Boy I don't envy that guy" . . . before pouring vodka into a mayonnaise jar, shaking it up and slugging it down. (This disgusts even me, a former alcoholic who drank rotgut wine that never saw a grape.) The scene gets to the core of this pitfall: that we are not thinking of our future self, or the future at all.

We all deal with shortsightedness on a regular basis. I'm so invested in this show, despite that it's 2 a.m. and I have work in the morning. I know I said I'd take the stairs, but the elevator just opened . . .

Tools to Overcome It

In recovery we used a reframing technique called "playing the tape all the way through." I might suddenly have a craving to get high, in the wake of which all I'd be thinking about is how good it would feel. Playing the tape through means thinking about what happens after I get high. I might feel good for a few hours, but then I would want to get high again, and with even more intensity. And I'd remember I didn't have any money, which would mean that I would have to steal something to keep it going, and oh yeah I was already facing fifty years of prison time . . .

Most of us aren't on the mayonnaise-vodka/if-I-do-this-I'll-go-to-jail trajectory, but all of us can mentally fast-forward to the outcomes of our choices. And that can be a surprisingly powerful tool for choosing better. If you're tempted to hit snooze again instead of getting up for work, take a second to picture what comes next: the frantic scramble, the awkward slide past your boss's office, the slow burn of shame and anxiety that sticks with you all morning. Suddenly, pulling off the covers doesn't seem so bad.

The scientific term for this strategy is "episodic future thinking," or any instance of imagining in detail experiences that might yet happen to you. The goal, whatever you call it, is to develop the ability to see and feel the likely consequences of your present choice. It's answering the "what do I want *now* versus what do I want *most*?" question with a Technicolor simulation.

Emotional Escapism: When We Check Out from Feelings

The lousier we feel, the more likely we are to seek fast fixes for our distress. This is rooted in our evolutionary history, where responding quickly to pain was often crucial for survival. (Is that a saber-toothed tiger bite? Plague? Frostbite?) In modern contexts the fast fixes to our emotional wounds might take the form of comfort eating, impulse buying, substance use, or social media doomscrolling. They provide temporary relief, a brief dopamine boost in a sea of complex feeling.

Emotional discomfort can also lead to cognitive distortions that justify self-control lapses. Thoughts like "I deserve this treat after such a hard day" or "Just this once won't hurt" become more persuasive when we're feeling vulnerable. Listening to these voices isn't inherently wrong—it might be time to give ourselves a break. But it's also true that giving in can make the situation worse, as the original feelings remain unresolved: Now it's joined by the quiet sting of letting ourselves down. This can create a downward spiral in which the negative consequences of the coping actions lead to more emotional discomfort, triggering further lapses in self-control.

Tools to Overcome It

In the immortal words of children's television host Mister Rogers: "Everyone has lots of ways of feeling. And all of those feelings are fine. It is what we do with our feelings that matters."

Emotional escapism is not about thinking too little, like acting on autopilot or ignoring future Homer. It's about thinking, or feeling, too much. In this state we want to practice something I like to call *emotional containment*. The roots of our distress are beyond the scope of this section; our goal right now is not to fix what's truly wrong, or even to feel better. It is to contain our feelings skillfully enough, for the moment, that we can do what we set out to do. (We should circle back to the roots of our distress later.)

To stop our feelings from spilling over, the first tool is attentional. Can I move my attention away from distress and toward what I intended to do? The recovery line "Sometimes you can't think your way into right action; you have to act your way into right thinking" applies here. So does another famous slogan: *Just do it*. Try to focus on nothing at all for the time it takes to get started, trusting whatever behavioral intention you set ahead of time. You might find yourself on the good kind of autopilot, able to separate action from your inner maelstrom.

Another tool is also attentional, and it has to do with lowering our emotional temperature. I like to think of this as self-directed calming. (It is also commonly known as self-soothing.)

Take five deep breaths. Put on a trusty playlist. Get a hug, if one is available. Try smiling even if you don't feel like it: Studies show that going through the motions of positive facial expressions can elicit the same hormones that come when we smile spontaneously. Again, the goal is not to address the underlying turmoil right now—you're not going to convince yourself to be over your breakup with a few deep breaths. But you might remind yourself that you didn't want to text him or her, or that you did want to put on real pants and go for a walk. And that will be one step in the right direction.

Self-Doubt Stalemate: A Can't-Do Attitude

Another challenge has to do with whether or not we believe we can change. When we lack confidence in ourselves, it's incredibly difficult to muster the motivation needed to stay on track. If we don't think we'll succeed, we are more likely to give up at the first sign of difficulty or to not even try at all. This pessimistic mindset becomes a self-fulfilling prophecy, as our lack of effort leads to the very failure we feared.

Writing this book has brought me levels of self-doubt I haven't faced in a long time. With each new page my brain asks me, "Who are you to offer wisdom to anyone?" or "Is there a more boring sentence outside of an accounting textbook?" It's painful and it makes procrastination tempting, whether with solitaire or with another rabbit hole of research—anything to avoid getting words on paper. Knowing that this avoidance can become a vicious cycle I find myself thinking of an old Henry Ford cliché: "Whether you think you can, or you think you can't—you're right."

Tools to Overcome It

As a coach I often heard clients say, "I'm just the kind of person who . . ." and they would finish that sentence in any number of self-dooming ways. *I'm the kind of person who has no willpower, can't finish what they started, can't stick with anything*, etc., etc. These beliefs were so ingrained that reframing them became a pillar of our work. Changing behavior is a skill, not something we either can or cannot do—but many of us need a lot of convincing to believe this.

As always, the first and simplest strategy is to just get started. *Just write*, I tell myself. Whether I'm a good or bad writer shouldn't be my concern right now. If the blank page keeps staring back at me, I might need to move to a reframing approach.

At this point, many a self-help guru would start talking about the power of "positive thinking." But I have to admit that going into full cheerleader mode (I can do it! I believe in myself!) is more likely to make me roll my eyes than turn my frown upside down. I have found it easier, and just as effective, to aim for neutral. Instead of saying "This book is practically writing itself! You *are* Hemingway!" which no amount of cognitive effort could get me to believe, I might ask myself: "Do you know you *can't* write this book?" The answer, even my most pessimistic self has to admit, is no, I don't know that. And in fact, the chapters I've already finished would suggest otherwise. I still don't know whether I can do it, but I also no longer believe I can't, which is a place to start.

Another strategy to address self-doubt is to focus on progress and growth over time. By setting incremental goals and celebrating small wins along the way, we build momentum. That word—*celebrate*—is more than window dressing. It's strategy. Every time we notice and honor a small win, we turn up the dial on motivation. Our brains learn to associate progress with feeling good, and suddenly the next step forward isn't something we have to force. It's something we actually want to do. And yes, this goes back to the planning stage—but there's no time like the present to start a better cycle.

Insignificance Trap: When It's a Drop in the Bucket

A final self-control challenge is similar to self-doubt, but instead of doubting our ability to accomplish the task at hand, we doubt that it matters at all. This happens when we fail to connect our actions to our values and long-term goals. What could one day of [insert habit] matter, we think? I need change today. When we fall into this trap, even the simplest acts of self-discipline can feel pointless. Our response might be to do nothing, or it might be to overcorrect—twenty push-ups? What about TWO HUNDRED?—which is a recipe for fatigue fallout later. (The rest of the week: zero push-ups and a lot of pain-killers.)

However grand our goals, if we can't see how our day-to-day

choices contribute to them, we're likely to falter. Why put in the effort to study for an exam when it feels like just one small test in a long academic career? Why bother saving a small amount of money when it seems insignificant compared to our overall financial goals?

Like so many of these pitfalls, the insignificance trap creates a bad cycle. If we dismiss the importance of our actions, we'll see fewer results and progress toward our goals. This reinforces the belief that our actions don't matter, digging us in deeper.

The way out of the trap is the premise of this book: to trust that *Little by Little, a Little Becomes a Lot*. It's to set aside our fear and skepticism in favor of accepting that the right choice, taken again and again, turns into something that matters.

I made a series of poor choices about money through the first forty-five years of my life. In saving for retirement, the key, as everyone knows, is to start early . . . which I didn't. I've since wised up, but when I look at the amounts that I will be able to save over the next fifteen years they seem too small. Not ENOUGH. Why bother? Of course, this is the thinking that got me here in the first place. And the reality is that $100,000 saved is not as good as a million—but it is much better than $10,000, and $10,000 is better than $0.

Something is better than nothing. This reframe is a good first response to the insignificance trap, because even a cynic has to admit it's *technically* true. Going further, we might be able to recognize that there is a reward right now for living according to our values. Even if a given choice doesn't have cosmic significance, it impacts how we feel about ourselves. Picking up litter while we jog might be a small act in the grand scheme of environmental conservation—but if it's something we've decided to do, in line with values we care about, following through will mean bringing ourselves that much closer to the person we want to be while we're here on this planet. And those are great stakes indeed.

MOVING BEYOND SELF-CONTROL

If all you wanted to know was how to introduce a new behavior or two into your life, you can close this book right now. I don't mind. (Unless you close it, pause meaningfully, then slowly slide it under a wobbly table leg. That might sting a little.)

What I mean is that we've gotten somewhere in these first four chapters. We introduced the theory of change that underlies every page, and that has animated every bit of progress in my own life: *Little by little, a little becomes a lot.* To identify the kinds of change likely to lead us in the direction of a more fulfilling, less conflicted life, we named our values and linked them to everyday actions. We then moved into the planning stage, looking at which contexts support follow-through, and which ones sabotage it. Finally, we entered the choice point: the moment in which to summon our internal resources and take a big little step.

But this book isn't only about how to cultivate new habits of **behavior**. It's also about how to cultivate new habits of **thought**. These are practices not tied to any single behavioral goal, but rather are useful across all of them. These habits are routes to feeling more in touch, more of the time, with our wiser, truer selves. They are ways of building sustenance, support, and well-being in the long middle of change—the quiet, ongoing "becoming" by which a little becomes a lot.

Parts II and III will dive into patterns of thought deeply worth cultivating and arenas in which to do so. Some chapters will explore how to process essential, but often unpredictable, elements of our everyday experience—such as how to deal with failure and how to accept support from others (and recognize when they need it). Others will focus on strengthening load-bearing aspects of our internal lives—such as self-compassion, perspective, and acceptance. We'll encounter each new wise habit with a combination of scientific grounding and timeless sources of insight.

If the journey of a thousand miles begins with a single step, we're easily a few exits down the highway. Or to go back to the old man on the sea, we've said goodbye to land. A fair wind is blowing and we have places to be.

> **ONE LITTLE THING** YOU CAN DO RIGHT NOW
>
> The next time "just this once" shows up, mentally hit fast-forward and watch a quick movie of how you'll feel **fifteen minutes after** giving in. Ask, "Still worth it?" If yes, enjoy consciously. If no, pivot to any constructive microtask (one push-up, one kind text).
>
> When you're ready to go a little deeper, flip to the appendix for extra exercises—or download the companion worksheets anytime at oneyoufeed.net/resources.

Part II

BECOMING

FIVE

Be a Friend to Yourself

> The curious paradox is that when I accept
> myself just as I am, then I change.
>
> —CARL R. ROGERS, *ON BECOMING A PERSON*

"Oh hit it, Alice!"
"You *idiot*."
"Hit the ball, you pansy!"

MY FATHER OFTEN TOOK ME TO PLAY GOLF WITH HIM GROWING UP, AND THIS was always the soundtrack. I both loved and hated those afternoons. They were a mix of fatherly love—him choosing to spend time with me—and four hours of tension as I waited for him to get angry over my next mistake.

But the above insults aren't ones I remember him directing at me. They were what he said to himself. If he left a putt short, sent a shot into the woods, or didn't put enough force behind a chip, he'd be ready with a fresh way to tear himself down. He could get angry when I didn't perform up to his high standards, but he used at least as much energy being his own worst critic.

We learn to talk to ourselves not only by talking with others, but by watching others talk to themselves. My father was, deeply and lastingly, an angry man. He was many other things too, but his temper was a defining characteristic for those who knew him well.

Which is to say: I come by a harsh internal voice honestly. A voice that, long after those afternoons on the golf course, sounded uncannily like Thom Zimmer.

Far from holding me accountable, I eventually learned, that voice was holding me back—at golf and everything else. From the vantage point of a thankful present, I can say that besides no longer using mind-altering substances to burn my life to the ground, no single change has made a bigger difference in building a life worth living than this: learning to treat myself with kindness.

...

Who do you spend the most time around? Your best friend? Your husband or wife? Your coworkers?

The answer is none of the above. The person you spend the most time with, by far, is YOU.

Part I of this book was a guide to kicking off positive change in our lives—a step-by-step initiation into the *little by little* school of pursuing wiser, healthier, value-driven habits. Now is when I have to remind you of one of the least exciting but most essential parts of this process: that it takes a while. Any road to change has a middle, after the spark of setting out and before capital-R Results. It is on that road that the magic of repetition will do its work—and also where we can falter in our commitments. Rather, where we almost certainly *will* falter, and will need to be able to see our way to getting back on track.

It's in this long middle that the wisdom of the following chapters sits. In part II, we'll be focusing less on habits of behavior than on habits of *thought*—on retraining the mental and emotional patterns that keep us from our wiser, truer selves day in and day out.

Another way to describe the coming chapters is that they're about the relationship we have with ourselves. Psychologists call it "self-talk" or the "inner monologue," but for most of us it's just . . . thinking. What might be more of a surprise is just how much our inner narrator is saying, and how fast; some estimates say that we talk to ourselves at a rate of four thousand words per minute. Our self-talk starts when we wake up in the morning and continues until we fall asleep (if it doesn't keep us from falling asleep). Like clockwork, the mind works away with or without us paying conscious attention, doing what evolution designed it to do: categorize, predict, explain, compare, worry, judge.

Also like a clock, our inner voice(s) love getting into a rhythm. I've already talked about being on autopilot—how we can act unconsciously in either useful or unuseful ways. Our inner monologue too is often automatic, our thoughts looping in deeply repetitive patterns. While the exact proportion of repetitive thoughts are hard to measure, studies show anywhere from 40 to 90 percent of our thoughts are the same day after day.

If this default mode (another term for our most common, cycling thoughts) is not inherently harmful, it's at least pretty boring. If I had a friend who was as tunnel-vision predictable as my inner narrator usually is, I'd never return another phone call from him. "Morning!" he says, every day. "Here's a list of your aches and pains. Here's who you're feeling bad about not emailing. Here's who hasn't emailed you back. We're out of milk. Here's your aches and pains again. Are you gonna go biking? Could make your back worse. Could be the reason it hurts in the first place. Have we talked about who hasn't emailed you back? Can we play solitaire? Wait, don't play solitaire. Here's your aches and pains again. You're trying to focus on writing? Seems like it's not going super well. Anyway I have more to say about your back pain . . ."

Seriously, if he was a friend I'd hide under the table when he knocked on the door.

But I know I can't do that. I'm stuck with me, and in accepting moments I'm grateful for it. The fact is that the conversations we have with ourselves are arguably the most important conversations we have. And luckily, our "habit-ridden consciousness," as Zen master Hakuin calls our default thoughts, is not the only form our self-talk can take.

In chapter 4 we introduced several of what I consider the most important tools for working with our thoughts and emotions more skillfully. As we go forward, you'll see that attention (what we focus on) and framing (the story we tell about it) show up again and again as tools for noticing our self-talk and creating the distance we need to change it.

We'll also build an arsenal of exercises—anchored in something I call "still points"—to disrupt unhelpful habits of thought and introduce wiser ones.

But before we get to the cognitive gym equipment, it's worth spending time with the simple truth that our inner life, the ongoing conversation we have with ourselves, actually is a *relationship*. As anyone with a long-term partner, roommate, colleague, friend—anyone who's ever had a family . . . heck, anyone who's stood in line long enough at the DMV knows—sharing your life with someone takes profound work and care. And the first step to improving any relationship, but especially the one with the person you're stuck with twenty-four seven, is to lead with kindness.

EVERYONE'S A CRITIC

Imagine this: Your most recent relationship has ended and you call a friend to tell them about the breakup. They say, "*Yep, I knew it was* coming. *You're old, ugly, and needy, not to mention fat. And boring, if I'm being honest.*"

Odds are that you are going to be looking for a new friend, or at least deeply questioning how you choose friends. But now imagine saying something similar to yourself. More believable? Maybe familiar?

Among the subjects our minds tend to go on about, our own (perceived) inadequacies are a classic. If my self-talk were a concert, the list of my failings would be "Free Bird" or "Hey Jude": the songs that get played every night, without fail. What we (hopefully) wouldn't tolerate from a friend is in constant rotation inside our own heads.

These days, thanks to years of work (and many tools you'll find in these pages), my inner critic doesn't have nearly the same power he used to. One of the biggest upgrades we can give our lives, it turns out, is to expect from ourselves the same baseline of treatment we expect from everyone else who knows and cares about us. We can demand a mind that is kind to itself. In the words of psychiatrist and philosopher Theodore Rubin, "Relative psychic peace can only exist in a compassionate emotional climate." You live in your head—why not make it nice in there?

Fine, sure, you might be saying. *Be nicer to myself. Is that it?* Not quite. As neatly appealing as "treat yourself with kindness" is, self-compassion is all too often both misunderstood (about what it's *not* as well as what it is) and underrated (in its practical implications on our well-being). And as with any wise habit, self-compassion is only valuable when we live it. We can underline, highlight, and star Rubin's words, but this doesn't do any good if we never end up telling the voice that says "I hate myself" that its contributions aren't welcome.

In the rest of this chapter, we'll cover what self-compassion really is, why it's such a powerful advantage on the road to change, and how we can take on our inner critics and cultivate our inner allies for a kinder, wiser life.

TRUTHS, FEARS, AND FACTS: THE UPSIDE TO BEING ON YOUR SIDE

Compassion is a two-sided coin, by definition. On one side is concern for the suffering of others; on the other, a desire to do something about it. The word is sometimes used interchangeably with sympathy, aka pity, or empathy, often defined as feeling someone else's pain. But these speak to only side one of the coin. Compassion means feeling for someone in pain *and* wanting to alleviate its cause. It is both kindness and action: kindness in action.

When I talk about *self*-compassion, the same idea applies. We'll get deeper into how it works, but at its core, self-compassion is **a balance between self-acceptance and self-improvement**. **Acceptance** is the sympathy/empathy side of things. We fall short. We mess up. We are not some flawless ideal—and that's not a problem; it's the shared experience of being alive. Recognizing this is not only useful but is also a better way to live. **Improvement** is the action-oriented side of things. Having self-compassion isn't telling ourselves we're perfect so nothing needs to change. It's saying that we're worthy as we are *and* that we're capable of growth. It's never lying to ourselves, but it's always rooting for ourselves. In the words of Shunryu Suzuki, "Each of you is perfect the way you are . . . and you can use a little improvement."

• • •

Now, if you had pitched the above to my dad, I'm pretty certain he would have thought it was a lovely idea but that it was likely to make you soft, indulgent, and probably selfish. And he would not be alone in feeling this way. Many people, myself included, have felt that being hard on ourselves, never "accepting" anything less than perfection, is the only way to hold ourselves accountable.

Long after I had memorized my dad's golf course insults, I found myself grappling with the language of 12-step programs—character defects, moral inventories. These were meant to be tools for self-improvement, and in many ways they were. But the way they were often used in meetings reinforced a familiar lesson: The best way to keep myself in check was to be suspicious of my own motives, to assume that deep down I was still broken.

Years later I was still suspicious of much of the language and the practices around self-compassion. Put a hand on my heart and refer to myself as "Sweetheart"? *Cringe.* Look in the mirror and "affirm" that I'm beautiful and good? Was this *Snow White*?

Finally, I began to wise up. The latest research on self-compassion—a booming field in psychology—convincingly shows that myself, my dad, and many of us were wrong about being hard on ourselves. Far from a sign of weakness, self-compassion makes us stronger, more resilient, more motivated, and kinder.

My dad, a veteran, would have been surprised to learn that self-compassion reduces the severity of PTSD in Iraq and Afghanistan war veterans. It is linked with better mental health in general, having been shown to reduce depression and anxiety. It makes people more resilient across challenging life situations, including divorce, domestic violence, and even natural disasters.

Being kind to ourselves doesn't make us selfish—it actually makes us better for others. People who have self-compassionate partners consistently rate those partners as better in categories such as emotional connection, supporting their partners' autonomy, and being less prone to being detached, controlling, and verbally or physically aggressive. It makes us more likely to forgive, better able to care for those who need it, and even more likely to help a stranger out. Turns out, being a better friend to ourselves helps us be better to everyone else too.

Maybe the biggest fear skeptics have—the biggest one I had—is that self-compassion equates to being overly lenient with oneself, which then leads to self-indulgence. But that's not what self-compassion is. Indulgence is about chasing short-term comfort even when we know it'll cost us later. It's the voice of desire we talked about in chapter 4, the one that shows up during emotional escapism to whisper "*I deserve this*" or "*Just this once won't hurt.*" True self-compassion isn't the devil on our shoulder, because self-compassion arises from a place of care for our well-being. It also arises from a place of alignment with our values—the things we won't wake up tomorrow and regret wanting in the first place.

When we actually value ourselves and our goals for change, we are more likely to succeed at them. In an analysis of multiple studies, researchers in Australia found that self-compassion was consistently effective in helping people eat better, reduce smoking, exercise more, and get more sleep.

How, exactly, does going easier on ourselves help us change? Let's imagine two students. The first, Bobby, is asked by his teacher what is 2 + 7 and Bobby answers 8. His teacher responds: "You moron, how many times do we have to go over this? If you can't figure this out you aren't going to amount to anything. You'll be lucky to get through the third grade, let alone college."

Now let's imagine another student, Sally, who is lucky because she has a different teacher. The question is the same—what is 2 + 7—and Sally doesn't know her addition any better than Bobby, so she also answers 8. Sally's teacher doesn't call her an idiot. She gently tells her that the answer is 9, and then goes on to explain why. She finishes with encouragement: "I'm sure if you try again, you can get it. And if you're still confused, stop by for a second after class and I'll explain more."

Which student, Bobby or Sally, do you think is going to have a better chance of learning math?

Say it with me: Sally. The reason behind this intuitive answer is that learning doesn't happen in states of stress. I'm going to oversimplify a very complex thing—our brain—but when we are in states of heightened emotion, we take energy away from the prefrontal cortex, which is where most learning happens. And when we are unkind to ourselves, we keep ourselves in higher states of emotional arousal.

Here is a big, open secret to change: We need room to learn from our mistakes. Many people will argue that being hard on themselves got them through med school or spurred them on to succeed in their career. And yes, self-criticism is a type of fuel. But my experience and that of many of my coaching clients has shown me that it burns dirty and eventually gunks up the engine. In a very real way, judgment collapses our consciousness, and we become unable to look at situations in our life in a way that we can learn from. Paul Gilbert, who created compassion-focused therapy (CFT), theorizes that when we criticize ourselves, we are turning on the body's threat-defense system—and if we keep doing it over and over, we create burnout, paralysis, and the kind of demoralization that comes from chasing your own impossibly high standards.

On an even deeper level, when you've tried and failed enough times, hope itself can start to feel dangerous. The idea of trying again at this point doesn't feel hopeful, it feels reckless. Why set yourself up to be disappointed by yourself again? Why risk finding out that you can't be the person you hoped you were? This is what psychologist Ross Ellenhorn calls the paradox of disappointment. The way that repeated failures can make us afraid of the very thing that we need in order to change, which is hope. This often ends up showing up as a voice in our head that says, "Don't even bother," as a way of trying to spare you the pain of trying again and falling short.

Self-kindness, on the other hand? It dials down the threat and opens us up. It puts us in a mindset where we can actually reflect and grow.

I could go on with finding after finding. The bottom line is that self-compassion offers two profound benefits: It makes our own heads a kinder place to live, and it can help us reach our goals for change.

So what does it really look like to be kind inside?

BEFRIENDING OURSELVES

The key to self-compassion is easy enough to say in one sentence: **Treat yourself like you would a friend or a child.** That's it. To go back to the thought experiment from earlier, just as you wouldn't tolerate a friend greeting the news of your breakup with all the reasons you're never going to find love, you probably wouldn't respond to their breakup that way either. So a useful way to start cultivating kindness from yourself is to imagine you actually *are* interacting with someone else.

Think about why you're friends with your best friends, or why you love the child(ren) in your life. Is it because they have the potential to be good . . . when they're not messing everything up? Is it because of external measures of success or desirability, like their job? Their appearance? How many A's they got on their last report card? Does how much you support them change with any of these metrics?

Probably not. You care about them because they are who they are, period. You root for them through ups and downs equally.

In his book *Compassion and Self-Hate*, Theodore Rubin articulates a script for applying this same attitude to ourselves. It starts with the idea that "I am because I am":

> I am because I am! *means I exist because I exist* and need no justification whatsoever for my existence. *The fact of my being is enough. I require no terms, conditions, or permits from myself or*

anyone else. . . . My life, my existence, and my being are not predicated on standards, values, achievements, or accomplishments . . . I do not exist because of them. . . . While they may give me satisfaction, they are a function of me. I am not a function of them.

How many of us have fallen into the trap of pinning our self-worth on our latest successes or failures? *What have you done for me lately?* our inner critic asks, like some bottom-line-obsessed manager. Instead, Rubin suggests, our worthiness lies in the fact that we are who we are, period.

With self-acceptance in motion, we can move to self-improvement. I'm betting you love your friends enough not to want to enable behavior or attitudes that you know will do them harm. And I'm guessing you trust your instincts when it comes to spotting those patterns—and knowing what you'd say if they asked for advice on how to stop being their own worst enemy (or even if they didn't ask).

Just as it's often easier for us to accept our loved ones' flaws than our own, as humans we tend to be better at delivering wise advice to others than to ourselves. This phenomenon even has a name in psychology: Solomon's paradox.

Coined by University of Michigan professors Igor Grossmann and Ethan Kross, Solomon's paradox refers to the biblical king renowned for his wise advice on his subjects' dilemmas . . . despite having an absolute mess of a personal life. Next time you feel like a hypocrite, consider the man who, while opining "Better to live on a corner of the roof than share a house with a quarrelsome wife," collected some seven hundred wives and concubines. (He also wrote "the borrower is slave to the lender," while driving the nation of Israel into debt with vanity building projects. Among other things.)

In the same way that Solomon put his best foot forward with everyone but himself, Kross and Grossmann found that it is easier to handle other people's problems with care than our own. In a 2015 study, they asked a group of people in long-term relationships to imagine discovering their partner had been unfaithful, and asked another group to imagine the same thing happening to a close friend. They then measured how each group approached the crisis.

"People were much wiser when they imagined the problem was happening to someone else," writes Kross in his book *Chatter*. "They felt it was more important to find compromise with the person who had cheated, and they were also more open to hearing that person's perspective." Those imagining the situation from their own perspective were apt to respond from a place of emotional volatility, even though the whole thing was hypothetical.

"We don't see ourselves with the same distance and insight with which we see others," Kross concludes. This is where the act of imagining that we're someone else comes in. It is our way out of Solomon's paradox, or at least a way to mitigate its effects.

One key to success is to do this imagining in as great detail as possible, literally down to the words we would say if we really were having a conversation with a friend instead of spinning our own mental wheels. Language matters, even internally. When my therapist in the early 1990s introduced the idea of engaging my "inner child," I cringed as hard as I ever have. But once the same ideas were explained as "developmental stages that I might have missed," or as the simple but revelatory truth that what happens to us as children affects how we are as adults, I was able to give "Little Eric" a genuinely healing mental hug. (I still don't love when people nickname him, but I think that's because my childhood self wouldn't have loved being called "Little Eric" either.)

By playing out how we would talk to a friend, we can find language that doesn't turn us off. There is a Russian saying: "You can't kiss your own ear." But when it comes to self-criticism, you're the only person who can—you just need to find the right angle.

A BETTER WAY TO ENGAGE WITH YOUR INNER CRITIC

To this end, I'm going to offer you a three-step guide for engaging with your inner critic in any situation. Just like you would with a friend in pain, you're first going to **greet** your critic by name and make space and time for a heart-to-heart. Next, you'll **listen** to what they're saying, from a healthy distance. Underneath their monologue of complaints, what are the real fears and desires going on? What's holding them (you) back, keeping them (you) stuck? Finally you're going to **respond wisely**, interrupting the cycle of self-loathing with a response that combines love, loyalty, and your best guidance for moving forward.

Greeting Your Critic

Naming your inner critic is a simple way to take away some of their power. When that list of your supposed failings starts playing in your mind, picture this newly ID'd character as the one talking. If the image is kind of ridiculous, all the better.

My inner critic these days is less angry Thom Zimmer than Eeyore from the Winnie-the-Pooh books. Known for his chronic pessimism and air of gloom, he's a gray stuffed donkey with a pink bow on his detachable tail. In a scene from *Pooh's Grand Adventure: The Search for Christopher Robin*, Eeyore says as he puts the finishing touches on a house he has been building: "Not much of a house. Just right for not much of a donkey."

By hearing my most morose thoughts in Eeyore's voice, I suddenly see them as simply that: a cartoonishly glum voice. Not the truth, not reality. As a bonus, I very often make myself laugh.

Ginny named her critic the Evil Queen from Snow White. Not the Queen in all her mirror-obsessed splendor; specifically the Old

Hag she becomes to tempt Snow White. Imagining her anxieties in the voice of a gnarled, wart-nosed crone brandishing a suspiciously shiny apple makes Ginny laugh too. Her critic thinks she's so intimidating when she's really just . . . so extra.

Identifying your critic as a separate entity is key in getting the distance necessary to engage with it in a healthy way. We need to be willing to turn toward our pain, to look at it and say, "Yes, I see you there." But we also need to avoid falling into its gravitational pull, becoming so consumed that we lose all perspective.

Dr. Kristin Neff, a professor of psychology at the University of Texas and leading researcher of self-compassion, refers to this safely distanced awareness as mindfulness. It's a type of consciousness that doesn't shy away from discomfort, but also doesn't blow it out of proportion. Without it, she argues, self-compassion becomes a Herculean task. How can we be a friend to ourselves if we're in denial about our suffering? On the other hand, if we're so entangled in our pain that we can't see beyond it, how can we step back and offer ourselves the care we need?

Mindfulness, which we can prompt by saying "Hey, Eeyore" (or whoever), allows us to recognize our thoughts and feelings for what they are—thoughts and feelings. Not irrefutable facts, not permanent states of being, but the day's grumbles from an animated donkey.

Listening (with Distance)

Once we've identified our inner party pooper, our interactions with them still tend to go one of two less-than-compassionate ways: We either argue or we agree.

I'm standing in front of a mirror, rehearsing a presentation. It's a TEDx Talk in front of more than a thousand people. My reflection stares back at me, a mix of hope and fear in his eyes. Right on cue, that familiar voice pipes up in my head. "Your presentation sucks, and so do you."

My response is a dejected sigh, followed by a mumbled "Yeah. You're right. Who am I kidding to try this? It's terrible."

It's funny to see it written out like that. This toxic oracle suddenly gets treated as if he has profound, exclusive insight into the situation. I don't like what he has to say . . . which must mean he's dishing the hard facts?

You could replace "my presentation" with any challenge you're facing right now. Maybe it's a job interview, a first date, or your attempt to kick a bad habit. The critic's script changes, but the essence remains the same:

CRITIC: You're not good enough.
US: Makes sense, no further questions.

If we ever want to get on that stage, go on that date, or create a better habit cycle, we can't blindly agree with the critic. Maybe we should argue with it?

"Hey, now, that's not true," I told my inner heckler that day, pacing the greenroom. "I'm intelligent and articulate. My speech is clear and effective. It's going to be great."

So far so good, according to plenty of cognitive behavioral therapy I've encountered. I'd used "positive self-talk," and given a "rational response" to the biased distortions of my critic. Undeterred, he came back swinging:

CRITIC: How do you know that? Are you sure? Okay, maybe you're not a total disaster, but let's be real—everyone else here is great. You need to be better than you are for anyone to even notice you.

With a thought loop like this, it's like trying to reason with a toddler having a tantrum. You can present all the logical arguments you want, but that toddler is still going to scream and throw their toys.

So what's the alternative?

Remember: The best way to be a friend to ourselves is to treat our inner critic like someone else we care about. If you're sitting down with a loved one in distress, your first instinct probably isn't going to be to shut them up, nor is it going to be to tell them they're not making any sense. Your first move is going to be to *listen to what's wrong*.

The same thing applies with our self-talk. The goal should not be to immediately silence the critic or to win arguments against it. The goal is to change our relationship with it entirely. We need to recognize it for what it is: a part of us that feels threatened. To find the fears behind the flailing, we need to listen with genuine curiosity.

"What is the propaganda campaign of your critic?" asked Dr. Aziz Gazipura, author of the wonderful book *On My Own Side*, in a conversation on my podcast. "Where is it steering you toward? It's telling you, 'You can't do that.' 'You're not attractive enough.' 'You messed that up? What's wrong with you?' And usually, it's steering you toward something." By getting curious about what that something is, Gazipura says, we can start to notice patterns. Maybe your critic is trying to keep you safe by lowering your expectations before anyone else can disappoint you. Or maybe, by convincing you that everything is your fault, it's preserving the fantasy that if you just stopped messing up, you'd be free from all emotional complications.

Whatever your critic's emphasis, argues Gazipura, its "function is, primarily, to keep you safe from harm, safe from pain, safe from emotion . . . the critic is just trying to stop it all." This often means discouraging you from taking action entirely, because why risk something you'll just mess up?

In case you haven't spotted the flaw in this logic, your critic is trying to shut down the whole experience of . . . having a life. Not ideal.

But by understanding where it's coming from, we can put ourselves in a better position to work with the underlying negative emotions.

With my TEDx speech, I could have chosen to acknowledge my critic's presence without either buying into its story or shouting it down with affirmations. I could have said, "I hear you're worried about the presentation. Thanks for trying to protect me, but I've got this." That might have averted at least a bit of angsty pacing. Turning down the volume of your critic is ultimately not about positive thinking or rational responses: It's about empathy.

Respond Wisely

Once you understand the hurt and rationale beneath your critic's nagging voice, it's time to make a game plan for feeling, and doing, better. This could mean prompting a behavioral habit ("Hey, I know you're feeling depressed, and I love you regardless—*and* I promise exercising is going to make you feel better than sleeping until noon would"). Or it could be purely in the realm of thought, letting some mental daylight into a spiral of negativity. It's here, in the role of self-adviser, that all your previous introspective work—identifying your values, making plans about what you want to do—will act as your compass.

The inner critic is usually, though not always, inhibitory: It's trying to stop you from doing something. When my inner critic whispers that I'm not good enough to write this book, the action that naturally flows from that belief is to not write at all. A wise response is to take the action that aligns with what you believe in and know is good for you, regardless of what the critic is saying. So for me, that means: Keep writing.

Wise responding may at times consist of correcting distorted thinking: "I'm not failing at everything—I'm struggling with this one thing right now." At other times it means acknowledging the fear behind the criticism: "I hear that you're worried I'll get hurt by putting myself out there, but I'm strong enough to handle whatever comes my way."

The beauty of responding wisely is that it doesn't silence your inner critic—it changes your relationship with it. Over time, that voice becomes less of a demon and more of a nervous companion that you've learned to reassure. It might never fully disappear, but it no longer has the power to thwart you from living the life you want to live.

COMPARISON

To illustrate our self-compassion playbook in action, I want to focus on one of the most common breeding grounds for unkindness toward ourselves: comparison.

There's a song called "High Lonesome" with the simple refrain: "I always kinda sorta wished I was someone else." It's about being young and self-destructive, about late nights in bars and dreams of being a cowboy and Elvis at the same time, but the key is that one line.

All of us have our moments where we kinda sorta wish we were someone else. In my case, from as far back as I can recall, I lived in the shadow of my own body. Shorter, skinnier. While we most often hear about women having body-image problems, men carry these burdens too, and mine were heavy despite my slender frame.

When I was a kid, swimming pools were terrifying. I'd stand at the edge of the water, calculating the social cost of taking off my shirt, certain that everyone would see what I already knew: I wasn't enough. The dismal math of adolescence had led me to believe no girl could ever be interested in someone built like me. Any invitation to swim was an invitation to feeling shame. I was intelligent, I was funny, I was kind—but I was small. And smallness, in boys, is not celebrated. There was this comic advertisement that tortured me from the pages of magazines: Charles Atlas's "The Insult That Made a Man Out of Mac." A skinny kid at the beach gets sand kicked in his face by some muscle-bound monster, who then goes on to steal his girlfriend. The solution? Get bigger. Get stronger. Order this exercise program and—ta-da!—he returns to beat the bully and win back his girl. That wasn't just an ad to me. It was my autobiography, minus the triumphant third act. I did not need to be told explicitly; the message saturated my environment.

If I was able to greet my inner critic back then, I would have seen that he looked and sounded a lot like the muscle-bound lunk in that ad. He (or she?) probably also would have reminded me of my mom, whose innocuous comments about other kids—"My, he's such a good-looking, strong boy"—cut me because I knew I wasn't the kind of son that prompted those observations. Or maybe my inner critic's final form was the Greek chorus of teenage girls I once overheard discussing me at the Worthington Square Mall as I passed by: "He's too skinny." Three words that confirmed all I feared.

When you're living on the wrong end of comparison, it's not some abstract concept. It becomes the funhouse mirror you can't escape, distorting everything about how you see yourself. It would take a long time for me to realize the simple truth that trying to be more like someone else is a losing game.

・・・

Let's move on to listening to our critic. What does comparison do for us?

Sometimes, our urge to compare isn't negative at all. We make "lateral" comparisons to people in similar situations, which can be genuinely informative (am I making as much as my peers for the same work?), and sometimes we make "downward" comparisons, boosting our self-esteem with "you should see the other guy!" glee. But for many of us, it's the siren song of "upward" comparison that calls the loudest. *He or she is better, funnier, richer, smarter than me.* And before we know it, we're spiraling—convinced we're falling short of everyone whose opinion we care about.

In a landmark book on disordered eating, psychiatrist Christopher Fairburn explains how comparisons get out of hand. We tend to focus too much on the parts of ourselves we don't like, and also to blow our "flaws" out of proportion . . . which only makes us feel worse. Think of that friend who's always been self-conscious about a trait you just *know* no one else even notices. You might very well be doing the same thing about a trait of your own.

We also often make quick, surface-level judgments about others without really knowing much about them. To this day I am no stranger to watching athletes on TV in a jealous fugue state, even though I know, logically, that their feats are far beyond anything I could ever have achieved. (And even if I *did* have a body capable of looking like a professional running back or power forward, I'm pretty sure I wouldn't want the life it takes to maintain it.) We're all drawn to comparing ourselves to unrealistic standards. Rather than looking at the wide variety of body types that actually exist in the world, LeBron or Elvis or a Kardashian become our benchmarks. This trend gets further amplified on social media, where we aren't just facing celebrities but seemingly ordinary people who are sharing "candid" access to their seemingly perfect lives.

The psychological costs of comparison are legion. Body dissatisfaction, depression, eating disorders, insomnia, narcissism, perfectionism, anxiety, even post-traumatic stress disorder and self-harm—all have been linked in studies to social comparison.

So: Let's say we've already named the voice inside and, with mindful distance, let it say its piece. We can't simply turn off our desire to compare (as a social species we are wired to do it), but we also know that allowing self-defeating comparisons threatens our well-being. How do we respond wisely?

We can learn to compare better. Our starting point should always be: "Is this useful?" Some comparisons are, and not just lateral ones. Comparing ourselves "upward" sometimes excites us to try harder or to aspire to something we hadn't considered a possibility. The more mindful of our inner states we become, the better we'll be at sussing out when comparisons cross the line from inspiring to demoralizing. Even comparing downward doesn't have to be as petty as it sounds: It can help our self-esteem to see how far we've come, or to cultivate gratitude for, and awareness of, any privileges that helped us get there.

If the comparison we're doing isn't useful, there are other tools to try.

We can broaden the scope of inquiry. "Social comparison, at its heart, is sort of a lack of information," explains psychologist Ellen Hendriksen, author of *How to Be Enough*. When we fixate on one characteristic, say differences in height, "we're just comparing point to point," she says, ignoring all the other context that differentiates us from our peers and somehow deciding that "am I good enough?" can be answered in the same way theme parks judge whether children can ride this ride. Instead, Hendriksen suggests, we should "flood the zone with information," considering so many comparison points at once that no single one has the power to define us. As she puts it, it becomes like comparing apples to tennis balls. The comparisons stop making sense.

What do your height rivals have going on in the hair department? Sense of humor? The more neutral the additional characteristics (i.e., the less sensitive you feel about them) the better. We can also become less selective in our comparisons: Instead of comparing yourself with people who rank higher in a given category, try comparing yourself to the first ten people you see.

On top of this "flooding the zone" or redirecting attention, we can also try a reframing that is as simple as it is profound: recognizing our common humanity. Dr. Kristin Neff sees this as a pillar of self-compassion on par with mindfulness and kindness itself. "Each person's experience is totally unique and different, and yet the fact that we do suffer . . . unites us as human beings," she explained on the podcast. Remembering how much we have in common can turn the sting of comparison into the solace of solidarity. "When we think, not only are we struggling, we feel all alone and isolated in that struggle," and this compounds our suffering," she explains. Recognizing our common humanity means "correcting that illusion we fall into of being alone."

"I am a human being; therefore nothing human is alien to me," wrote the Roman playwright Terence more than two thousand years ago (in Latin). However much divides us, we share the cosmic coincidence of being flawed, struggling, miraculously existing human beings, doing this life thing all at once. None of us is alien to anyone else in those trenches.

Or as you might respond wisely to a beloved friend or child: I'm here for you, and with you. You're not alone.

KINDNESS WITH MOMENTUM

Right now, you're standing at a pivot point. As these words reach you, you have the power to make a life-changing decision: to stop the cycle of self-criticism. This is your chance to say "enough" to turning against yourself, to end the habit of picking yourself apart and dismissing your own feelings. You can choose to stop the self-abuse and the relentless pressure you put on yourself. That doesn't mean the voices will vanish overnight, or that your inner critic will go silent. It simply means you're committing to a different path—a path where you no longer turn against yourself.

I wish I could say that Thom Zimmer found his bliss and quieted his inner critic. It wasn't in the cards. But someone who did is Sherry Borsheim, a former student of mine in the Wise Habits program, whose story shows just how transformative being kinder to ourselves, little by little, can be.

"Like so many women, my priority was always meeting other people's needs before my own," Sherry writes. "My guiding questions were, How can I be a better wife, mother, daughter, friend? What do they need? I didn't know how to ask myself what I needed. I'm not sure I knew that I was even allowed to."

Her husband liked cars, so she liked cars. She sometimes imagined spending summer evenings sitting around a bonfire, engaged in deep conversation—but her husband preferred TV, so that was that. She adopted her children's interests as her own. She had been taught that being a "good" wife and a "good" mother meant banishing her own needs entirely.

Then, with the spark of our Wise Habits, she got curious about self-compassion. "I was so good at offering compassion to others," she reflects. She began experimenting with being a friend to herself.

"What do I enjoy doing? What do I want to experience?" Sherry thought to herself, and she made asking these two questions a consistent practice. When critical inner messages cropped up in response—telling her it was selfish to focus on what she enjoyed—she replaced them with love and acceptance.

The world opened up to her. She discovered and pursued new interests: scrapbooking, kirtan, sacred women's circles, and community meetups. Something that became undeniable in this process was a truth she had known for a long time, on some level: that her marriage was not working. Despite the fact that her husband was "a kind and hardworking man," she was deeply unsatisfied as a partner. After years of counseling, being a friend to herself gave her the courage to finally leave the relationship.

As heartbreaking as divorce was to go through, Sherry confirmed just how right the decision had been for her. She was able to see that the most important question to ask herself was not "How do I make my husband love me?" but "How do I love myself?" In her words, honoring her own wants and needs not only created a kinder environment in which to live, but also helped her more authentically inhabit the roles she had once lost herself in. "I began to learn that putting myself first was not selfish or narcissistic, as I'd always believed," she writes, "but essential in allowing me to be the mother, friend, and family member I'd always hoped to be." This was a person deeply enriched by, but no longer *defined* by, her relationships with others.

"While the needs of those I care about will always, always be important to me, my own needs matter now as well," she writes. Through taking the time and care to be a good friend to herself, she has discovered new and enduring strengths and gifts. "I feel strong and capable in a way I never have before."

We can all use self-compassion to get in better touch with our wiser, truer selves. This is your opportunity to be done with the whole pattern of negative self-talk and harmful beliefs; you have the strength to make the choice to treat yourself with the kindness and respect you deserve. It's time to get on your own side, starting right here, right now.

ONE LITTLE THING YOU CAN DO RIGHT NOW

Give your inner heckler a name. Maybe it's an Eeyore, like mine, or just "the critic." Sometimes just this simple act reduces its power. Next time it shows up, greet it like an old acquaintance: "Oh, hey there again." You won't be fighting it or feeding it, just acknowledging that it's in the room.

When you're ready to go a little deeper, flip to the appendix for extra exercises—or download the companion worksheets anytime at oneyoufeed.net/resources.

TINY DISRUPTIONS: STILL POINTS

> At the still point, there the dance is...
>
> —T. S. ELIOT, "BURNT NORTON"

As powerful a tool as self-compassion is, it only works if we can access it when we need it most. Self-criticism and negative comparisons aren't like occasional thunderstorms, visible in the distance with plenty of time to get to shelter. They're more like a steady on-and-off drumbeat of rain, one which most of us don't have a reliable way to interrupt in real time.

These relentless thought patterns aren't just repetitive—they're often working against us. We spiral into worry, replay our mistakes, and beat ourselves up, all while barely noticing what's happening. Even when we do catch ourselves mid-spiral, we don't have a realistic way to shift gears (or come in out of the rain) in the moment.

We need something that helps us interrupt automatic patterns and do so frequently enough that the clouds start to part—the thought patterns start to shift.

My method for doing exactly that is called *still points*.

A still point is a moment of reflection or practice we intentionally build into our day. Because so much of what drives us happens below the surface, we can't brute-force internal change any more than we can will ourselves into a new habit overnight. What we can do is create small interruptions—tiny shifts that help our thoughts settle into better grooves over time.

That's what still points are. You can think of them as the fundamental building blocks of a new way of thinking: tiny disruptions that pave the way toward new horizons.

The formula is simple: **When-Then**. The "When" is a prompt. The "Then" is your chosen response. Think of it like the if-then plans we talked about for setbacks—but these are for everyday life.

Example: When I check the time, then I'll ask myself: *What am I thinking and feeling right now?*

The disconnect between the prompt (checking the time) and the response (checking in with my thoughts and feelings) is intentional. This is a feature, not a bug of still points. You can think of them as a container that you can drop any helpful response into.

The ideal **When** is something that occurs often enough to disrupt your mental status quo, while the ideal **Then** is something simple enough to do without resistance. For the **When** above, if I had chosen "when I get into bed at night . . ." that would give me only one time of day when I'd be checking in with my thoughts and feelings—a time I tend to use for reflection already. "When I check my watch" happens several times a day, including at times when my brain won't be expecting a prompt to check in with my mental and emotional state.

And if I'd made the **Then** "I will write two long paragraphs on what I'm thinking and feeling," my reaction the first time I checked my watch would probably have been along the lines of "ain't nobody got time for that." A simple mental check-in, though? That's something I'll actually do.

There are two core barriers to lasting change: We're too busy to add something new, and we forget to try in the first place. Still points solve both. Each exercise will look laughably basic on its own, but each can transform, with repetition, from insignificant to life-changing.

Here is a still point that I used for years. **When** I walked from my car to the office, I would **Then** do a practice called "Grounding in Our Senses." It simply meant noticing five things I could see, five I could hear, and five I could feel in my body. The goal? To practice presence.

Doing this once made no difference, but doing it twice every day—once on the way in and on the way out—started to change my capacity for presence. I found myself more able to take a step back from the stress of the day to notice the sway of the red oaks. The wrens in spring. The crocuses and tulips and marigolds. The bounce of my soles, the beat of my pulse. The grand natural cycles that couldn't help but make my emails and meetings feel trivial—which had the side benefit of making me feel a little more ready to handle the day's business.

All of that, and I never actually had to carve time out to access this still point. It was found time, a pocket of autopilot action and thought I co-opted for something a little more useful.

Let's start designing your own still points.

The When (Prompts)

In chapter 3 we introduced six types of intentional prompts:

1. Time-based
2. Location-based
3. Preceding event
4. Other people
5. Random

We can use any of these to set up our **When** moment. Again, the ideal is to choose a prompt that comes up often enough to matter. I can't tell you how frequently that will be for you, but it's probably not once a week. As with every little-by-little change in this book, try starting small, set up a consistent practice, then increase.

The Then (Response)

Broadly speaking, the **Then** falls into one of two categories: a reflection or a practice. A **reflection** brings to mind something important—something we want to remember or spend more time with. One of the habits of thought I'm currently trying to cultivate is to enjoy the good things in my life more. So a useful reflection for me is to simply pause and think of what good things are happening right now.

A **practice** is more like what I described earlier, when I used the walk from my car to be more present. Other practices might include deep breathing, writing out a list of three things you are grateful for, or reading a small inspirational passage.

Here is a list of **Then**s, both practices and reflections, for cultivating self-compassion:

1. **THE SELF-TALK CHECK:** Pause and ask yourself: Would I say this to a friend?

2. **THE COMPASSIONATE BREATH:** Take three deep breaths and remind yourself: I am human, and mistakes are part of growth.

3. **THE DAILY KINDNESS INTENTION:** Take a moment to think of one way you can be kind to yourself today.

4. **THE PROGRESS REMINDER:** Remind yourself: Progress is not linear, and growth comes from learning, not perfection.

5. **THE CELEBRATION PAUSE:** Acknowledge your effort and celebrate it, no matter how small.

If you're wondering where the **When**s for self-compassion are, the answer is that they are yours to choose. Each of these **Then**s can be paired with any of the types of prompts above; the right one is whichever fits into your life with the best chance of low-resistance, consistent practice (little by little). I suggest trying the Random prompt to start with, because it will allow you to start building repetition while you consider what other prompts might fit more naturally into your day-to-day.

In the following chapters I will continue to suggest **Then**s for each new wise habit, but the **When**s will always be up to you.

WHAT ABOUT MEDITATION?

I'm sometimes asked if still points are simply meditation by another name. To which the answer is: good question, but no.

Meditation can be a practice we use inside a still point, but in general it's something done for a longer period of time and outside the confines of our moment-to-moment life. We set aside five, fifteen, or thirty minutes to sit down and meditate. Meditation is an excellent tool for training many of the things that we will be discussing in the upcoming chapters of the book—but still points are designed to happen inside your busy day—not apart from it.

A guest of my podcast, Carmen Rita Wong, told me a story that perfectly describes how using still points can work. We were discussing a little habit that she has carried over from her days of being raised Catholic. Every time she gets in the car, before she starts driving, she does the sign of the cross that Catholics do. It's an ingrained habit, but instead of it being an old tic that she just keeps doing, she decided to turn it into something meaningful. Now every time that she does it, she reflects briefly on her mother (who has passed) in a loving way.

PROACTIVE VERSUS RESPONSIVE

There are two types of still points: proactive and responsive. Proactive still points are built into your daily routine. They train your mind in advance, making it easier to respond wisely later. Responsive still points happen in real time. They help you pause and choose differently *in the middle* of emotional intensity.

Proactive Still Points

Proactive still points are planned interruptions we integrate into our daily routines. They're designed to train our minds in new ways of thinking, preparing us for future emotional situations. This is our go-to for prompt types 1–5.

Key features:
- The **When** is a regular, nonemotional prompt (like checking the time)
- Practiced multiple times throughout the day (typically 4–5 times)
- Builds mental habits of wise thinking
- Prepares us to respond more effectively in future emotional situations

Example: "**When** I check my watch, **Then** I will take a moment to close my eyes and repeat, 'May I be safe. May I be peaceful. May I be kind to myself.'

Responsive Still Points

Responsive still points are triggered not by anything external to us, but by our emotions. They're designed to help us manage our reactions in moments of strong emotion. I call emotional states the Holy Grail of prompts because they involve being in touch with your own internal weather enough to recognize when it changes and then deciding to act in a beneficial way.

Emotion-based prompts often result in the behaviors we least want, as volatile or vulnerable feelings lower our self-control. I start feeling anxious (**When**) so I pick up my phone and begin checking email (**Then**); I feel sad (**When**) so I seek chocolate (**Then**); I feel frustrated (**When**) so I lash out (**Then**). The great news is that learning to recognize them and put in another response can allow us to upend some of the most entrenched reactions we have. This is what responsive still points can help with.

Key features:
- The **When** is an emotional prompt
- Used in the moment, as emotions arise
- Helps us pause and reframe our thoughts during emotional situations
- Encourages wise thinking and measured responses

Example: "**When** I feel angry, **Then** I will take three deep breaths and acknowledge that this is a moment of suffering. I will remind myself that suffering is a part of life, and I will ask that I treat myself with gentleness in this moment."

There's a symbiotic relationship between proactive and responsive still points. Responsive still points help us in the heat of the moment; proactive ones prepare us for those moments before they arrive. When we regularly practice proactive still points, we train our minds to default to more useful patterns of thought. Then, when emotional triggers hit—those intense, in-the-thick-of-it moments—we're more likely to meet them with the same wiser mindset we've been rehearsing.

Throughout the rest of the book you'll find plenty of examples in each category, as well as suggested new applications of still points, in line with each intersection of thought and behavior we'll be focusing on. I hope that for you, like me, still points will become rest stops on a long journey— providing a moment to pause, refocus, and realign oneself with the desired destination, ensuring that we don't get lost in the daily grind. The great thing is that like rest stops, the best ones don't feel like detours at all.

SIX

We Don't See the World as It Is, We See It as We Are

We are what we can imagine.

—ROBERT HASS

WHEN I WAS TWENTY-EIGHT AND A FEW YEARS INTO RECOVERY FROM HEROIN addiction, I had started piecing together something that looked like a "normal" life.

I had no college degree. No experience outside of restaurants. And yet somehow I'd landed a job at one of the world's first internet companies. I worked relentlessly—way out of my depth—and got promoted into a role for which I had no formal qualifications. My wife was pregnant with our first child, and I was our primary support. Every day I felt both insanely lucky and aware of the sky-high stakes.

One morning when I was about to leave for work, I got a call at home from HR. My company had been bought by AOL and they were making cuts. I was out.

A deep pit opened in my stomach.

In the days that followed what I felt most was fear. I recited to myself, over and over, what I considered a series of indisputable facts: I have a baby on the way and no way to provide for my family. It was a fluke to have gotten this job. No one else is going to hire me. Getting laid off means I have no marketable skills. Which means we'll go broke, which means I'll be back to working in restaurants, which means I'm near the party scene, which means relapse, which means I'll lose it all.

My thoughts cycled like a hamster on speed, more and more darkly. I was certain: My "normal" life was gone. Not slipping away, but gone.

・・・

This chapter is all about perspective.

The story above is the beginning of my own version of a famous Taoist parable about a farmer in ancient China. A lot happens to this guy: His only horse runs away. (Bad luck! say his neighbors.) But the horse returns a few days later with six wild horses. (Good luck! say his neighbors.) The six wild horses get rowdy and break his son's leg. (Bad luck!) But a few days later the military comes calling to recruit young men for war, and his son is spared thanks to his injury. (Good luck!)

At every turn, the neighbors are eager to label what's happened as either "good" or "bad," even as the wise farmer withholds judgment, replying to his neighbors only, "Maybe, maybe not." The moral is that "good" and "bad" are false categories to begin with—that we assign them based on narrow impressions of a situation, and they can transform if and when we gain a new perspective.

I've never been able to reach the total equanimity of Taoism (more on that in the next chapter). But I want to focus here on a central, eternal truth of the farmer's story and my own: that the meaning of any situation—the meaning of *life*—is, in very real ways, what we make of it.

So this is the bad—or good?—news: For us humans, there's simply no such thing as an objective view of reality. This has vexed and fascinated the people who think about thinking forever. Marcus Aurelius, the Roman emperor and philosopher, declared: "Everything we hear is an opinion, not a fact. Everything we see is a perspective, not the truth." Friedrich Nietzsche, in developing a school of thought called "perspectivism," threw up his hands with "Facts is precisely what there is not, only interpretations." And in one of my favorite phrases of all time, Anaïs Nin wrote simply (attributing the sentiment to the Talmud), "We do not see things as they are, we see them as we are."

Just to steer clear of the cultural battleground of facts versus opinions: Where I'm going with this is not to say that there is no truth, nor that all perspectives are equally valid. This is not relativism. What I am saying is that even when we think we're seeing all the facts, we're always seeing them through the colored lens of our own perspective. There is no view from nowhere—no omniscient, perfectly removed perch from which we can see all angles at once. And when we forget that, when we assume that the way we're seeing the world in a given moment is just *the way it is*, rather than *the way it looks to us*, we can cause ourselves a lot of needless suffering.

We know by now that we can't climb out of our own minds, however much we'd like to take a break from that chatty inner monologue. But what we can do is become more aware of how our minds are interpreting our experience. We might only be able to see from one angle at a time, but by expanding our awareness that there's a bigger, more multifaceted picture to see, we can lessen the power— and the error—of some of our most flawed, biased conclusions.

Like, for example, deciding that the news of your layoff might as well be the grim reaper handing you a one-way ticket downstairs, instead of what it will look like with more distance and less panic: the end of one job, and the start of something new.

• • •

Here's what actually happened after I decided my "normal" life was over.

I took some of my severance package and invested it in training in my field, which gave me both more qualifications and more courage for my next round of job applications. I ended up getting a job far better than the one from which I had been laid off, and another, better job after that, and a whole career in the software industry. Along the way my son arrived, and I was there to raise him, bringing me more pride than any paycheck.

The story keeps going, of course, and it wasn't all up from there. A few years later I started a solar energy company, and poured my heart and soul into it for five years. It was my (new) baby: I gave it everything I had. And it failed.

I was heartbroken, and I was once again afraid. Here I'd had this stable career and I'd risked it all—my hard-won normal life—on some entrepreneurial dream. Who was I to gamble like that? A failed business meant I was a failure after all. I wasn't qualified after all. I'd go broke, and relapse (again), and . . .

That was not what actually happened. Somewhere in that self-critical spiral I checked myself and took the opportunity of a closed door to see an open window. I took the entrepreneurial lessons I'd learned, took the spare time I suddenly had to get in touch with my values, and I started *The One You Feed*, which turned into the most fulfilling, surprising chapter of my professional life yet. And here we are, and I am way, way happier doing this than I ever would have been running a solar energy company.

In this chapter, we'll explore some of the most common distortions in perspective and look at ways to shift, expand, and refine the lenses we see through. We've already talked about *attention* and *framing* as key tools for making our habitual thought patterns more conscious and more useful; both are, at their core, tools of perspective, and you'll see them play a central role in the practical exercises ahead.

Whether you're using this book as a step-by-step guide to changing habits, or a more timeless resource for cultivating a relationship with your wiser, truer self, few skills are more useful than becoming aware of how you assign meaning to everyday experience. To hold the truth of the moment more lightly is, ultimately, to see more clearly that the moment is just passing through.

SEEING MAKES IT SO

When I say **there is no view from nowhere**, let me explain what I really mean. Do you remember the Dress? For a few days in 2015 it held the internet hostage. Some people saw the infamous photo of a striped dress as blue and black, while others saw it as white and gold. Everyone had to weigh in. The original *BuzzFeed* post received over thirty-seven million views, and over ten million tweets appeared in the first week, most of which were nuanced discussions of the role of color perception and the neuroscience of vision. Just kidding: Most of the conversation was people yelling that *of course* the dress was the color that they thought it was and everyone else was as blind as a tree sloth. Kim Kardashian (white and gold) disagreed with then-husband Kanye West (blue and black); Lady Gaga described the dress as, actually, "periwinkle and sand;" Taylor Swift tweeted that she was "confused and scared" about the whole thing. Politicians, government agencies, and major brands chose a side, and even the scientists who posted couldn't agree on why we all saw it differently.

The dress in reality was black and blue, but over two thirds of people thought it was white and gold. (Same.)

What this mega-viral moment shows, besides that humans are ready to argue about anything, is that we see things differently on even the most literal level. The five senses, traditionally thought of as the most unfiltered form of perception, deliver a separate cognitive verdict to each of us.

What that verdict might *mean* gets only more debatable from there.

In a classic Buddhist story, a man is walking along a path in the dark. It's hard to see, and he looks down and sees what appears to be a snake lying across the path. He is terrified. As he stands there, paralyzed with fear, clouds move away from the moon, allowing more light to shine on the path. With more light he realizes that what he thought was a snake is actually just a piece of rope lying on the ground. And just like that, the fear disappears.

To update the parable, imagine you are at a meeting at work and you share your thoughts on a topic. Afterward you look over at your boss and you think that she looks a little irritated. Was your idea bad? you wonder. After the meeting your boss doesn't stop as she normally does and ask you how your weekend went. You spend the next couple of hours fretting: Did you sound inarticulate? Arrogant? How do you fix her sinking opinion of you?

And then at the coffee maker a coworker mentions that your boss's son wasn't feeling well this morning, and she got a text during the meeting and had to rush off to pick him up. As though moonlight has revealed a snake to be a rope, your worry fades away.

Both of these examples combine what we might call pure perception (noticing a sinuous object in the road, or your boss's frowning face) with other kinds of context that influence meaning-making. A man walking along a deserted path at night is on the lookout for anything that might threaten him—which makes him more likely to see a fearful snake before he sees a harmless rope. At work, even if you have a good relationship with your boss, you're more likely to worry about her expression in a meeting than if it were a coworker—especially one who doesn't control your performance review—glaring at their phone.

The thing is, of course, that none of us perceive anything without context—or said differently, none of us perceive objectively. We constantly mistake snakes for ropes, and interpret our boss's glance through our own filters. Your mind is a projector, screening a movie onto the world around you that is a blend of your memories, expectations, and interpretations. Rather than seeing raw reality, you see a story whose plot, characters, and even genre are shaped by a vast array of factors including your past experiences, cultural background, education, beliefs and values, emotional state, expectations, and personality traits. Someone else watching the same screen could see a completely different movie.

There is no view from nowhere. For the rest of this chapter, I'll refer to the inexhaustible bag of conditioning we all carry around as simply *perspective*—and to the many ways it keeps us from seeing objective reality as *cognitive biases*.

In a neat irony, perhaps the single most common cognitive bias is naive realism, by which we tend to think that everyone else is biased but we see things as they are. This mental quirk is our brain's way of giving us the confidence to act—everyone around us might be stumbling around in a fog of subjectivity, it says, but we know exactly what's going on. Never mind how statistically unlikely this would be: We alone have been gifted reality-seeing glasses, while the rest of humanity is squinting through a kaleidoscope.

Okay, so we might not consciously claim to have Godlike omniscience. But our autopilot assumption is that what we see is *the truth*, and everyone who thinks otherwise must be mistaken. If you have doubts about our ability to double down on this kind of bias, remember that Galileo risked being burned at the stake for suggesting that the Sun didn't, in fact, revolve around the Earth—almost a hundred years after Copernicus had first mathematically proven this.

To begin working with our many biases, from the cosmic to the everyday, we have to say goodbye to naive realism. On closer examination of your reality-seeing glasses, you'll see that instead of crystal-clear lenses, what you're actually looking through are tinted shades. Trying to see different perspectives will be like pulling those sunglasses down just a bit. You'll be able to see that the world itself isn't (say) yellow, even though most of your field of view is still tinted.

It would be nice if we could just take the glasses off completely, but that isn't possible. What we can do is find the edges of the frames and remember that other views exist. We accept that the glasses will always be there, but we can gain awareness of, and wisdom from, the infinite vistas beyond them.

We've already seen the benefits of shifting the lens in previous chapters. The key to self-compassion was an exercise in getting outside our own perspective by imagining a dialogue with a beloved friend or child, instead of with our myopic inner critic. In chapter 4, pitfalls of self-control such as the "shortsighted stumble" and the "insignificance trap" were failures of perspective, to be overcome by giving ourselves useful distance from the struggle of the moment. And way back in chapter 2, we saw how the journey toward identifying our authentic values starts with becoming aware of "mimetic desires," by which a lifetime of messaging influences what we've decided is worth caring about.

Think of this chapter, then, as a skeleton key to a universal theme: a set of doors that open not just onto fixes for specific situations, but onto the deeper thing that needs fixing. That take us from a new vantage point or two to the larger goal of seeing life itself a little more clearly.

So how do we do it? How do we make the world come into focus?

RAISING AWARENESS

We can always begin working with perspective by asking two simple questions:

What am I making this mean?
What else could it mean?

These questions are useful in any situation, as we'll explore later with still point exercises. But they become most urgent in times of emotional distress. The fear that comes from imagining your boss is upset with you, or the despair that you've just been laid off from your last job ever, or the anger that hits when you realize that your sister invited everyone but you to Sunday dinner—these responses send our meaning-making engines into overdrive, while shrinking and distorting our capacity for perspective.

Using the heightened emotion itself as a prompt, our goal should be to challenge our interpretation of what's happening, and why. The simplest and most effective way to do this is by asking ourselves questions, starting with the two above.

Let's say you've just moved, and your new neighbor doesn't wave back when you greet him. You see only two possible explanations for this: either he's a jerk, or you don't really fit into the new neighborhood. Both of these interpretations are going to create anxiety, if not a slow-burning vendetta toward your new nemesis.

Before you call the movers back, ask yourself the first question: **What am I making this mean?**

This question makes us aware that we're actively creating meaning. It's a process that usually happens automatically and subconsciously, with our preconceptions serving up an outline into which our perceptions fit. By interrupting with a call to consciousness, we catch our mind's meaning-making machine in the act. Sometimes the question alone is enough to make us reconsider our conclusions.

To thoroughly answer *what am I making this mean?*, try to separate the *facts* of the situation from any other kinds of context. In our example, the only fact is . . . that you didn't see your neighbor wave at you. Everything else cycling through your mind—your insecurity about being below the average income of the neighborhood, or how the neighbor kind of looks like a mean old gym teacher you had in middle school, or how exhausted you're feeling after a long day of unboxing—wouldn't be admissible in court. As a rule of thumb for identifying the facts, keep it to what a video camera or a sound recorder would pick up. If it's something those impartial observers couldn't detect, you can be pretty sure you're into the realm of the subjective.

If you still find yourself wedded to first impressions, go on to the following question: . . . **and what else could it mean?**

The "could" here is key. The goal of this follow-up question isn't necessarily to change the meaning you've assigned to a situation. It's to help you recognize that other interpretations are possible.

It could be that your new neighbor waved before you saw him. Or he could be socially anxious and have a hard time meeting new people. Or maybe he didn't see you wave. He could be legally blind. It could be that you've moved in next to Mr. Scrooge, and he's going to hate you until a Christmas miracle says otherwise. We have no way of knowing which, if any of these, is true. But by prompting yourself to come up with alternative explanations, you create space around your biased (they're always biased) first thoughts. You let in the light of new possibilities and reintroduce choice into meaning making. Assuming we know why someone acted a certain way is an all-too-common cause of emotional turmoil; just by acknowledging your uncertainty, you lessen the power of the worst-case scenario.

The next step in refining your perspective is to gather more information. Keep an open mind for as long as possible, narrowing things down only when you've learned enough to do so.

Unfortunately, life often requires acting on one meaning over another without having all the facts (and we never have *all* the facts). Given this, I often find it helpful to follow the first two questions with a third: **What meaning is most useful?**

Psychologist George Kelly, creator of the school of thought known as personal construct theory, came up with the term "constructive alternativism." In his words, "Reality is subject to many alternative constructions, some of which may prove more fruitful than others."

Think of two people stuck in traffic. One sees it as wasted time, a frustrating delay. The other sees it as a rare pause—an unexpected moment to catch their breath, listen to music, or call a friend. In both cases, the situation is the same: Cars aren't moving. But the meaning each person assigns to it leads to very different experiences.

For our purposes, the central truth of Kelly's thought is that some interpretations are more helpful for living wisely than others are. If I am creating the meaning, and if I've identified several equally possible meanings in a situation, why not choose the interpretation(s) that empower me and reduce suffering?

To return one last time to Mr. No-Wave, if you ask yourself which meaning of his behavior is most useful, the clear answer is to give him the benefit of the doubt. He might be either Scrooge or Boo Radley, but assuming bad intent means writing him off, while deciding that he might just be shy preserves the possibility of friendship in the future.

I've used a relatively innocuous example here—you don't have strong feelings about your neighbor yet, so it's probably not hard to keep an open mind. But we fall into the same habit of assuming we know someone's motivation with people we're much closer to—and when the emotional stakes are much higher. Every time we do this, we lock ourselves into an unnecessarily narrow view of our relationships. By stopping to ask *What am I making this mean? What else could it mean?*, and *What meaning is most useful?*, we give ourselves the opportunity to make another choice instead.

Let me give you another example of how we construct meaning in the least useful ways. If you remember the section on comparison, I talked about my fears of being too short (I'm not exactly short, I'm an inch short of the average—said like a guy who still carries some of this comparison) or skinny. I wish I could say I left it in my childhood, but I didn't.

In the aftermath of my first marriage, when my wife left me for a taller man, this comparison came rushing back like a tidal wave. I compared myself to him in every way imaginable. I compared myself to all other men. When I began to look for a new partner, I was convinced that not being six feet tall meant I would never find love again.

I could cite you the research that shows taller men do better in everything from salary negotiations to dating. I could show you the online dating profiles where women said directly: "Under 6 ft tall? Don't message me." (Okay, I couldn't actually show you those, they're in the digital ether; the point is that they were data points I collected to reinforce my story.) I know from this remove how ridiculous that all sounds, and yet it was incredibly real and painful to me at the time.

This is a perfect example of the sort of meaning-making that we do all the time. And even worse, how we often argue for our own limitations when it comes to the meaning that we're making.

When I asked myself "What am I making this mean?" the answer was clear: I was making my height mean I was fundamentally unlovable. And when I followed up with "What else could it mean?" I had some room to consider alternatives. Maybe it meant nothing at all about my worth. Maybe our breakup had zero to do with height? Maybe those dating profiles represented a tiny fraction of the dating pool rather than every woman. This shift in perspective didn't happen overnight, but asking these questions opened the door to possibilities beyond the prison I'd built for myself.

MORE BIASES

To experience distortions of perspective is, as discussed, to experience the human condition—we can't take those sunglasses off. But some patterns of bias are so common and pernicious that it's worth calling them out by name.

Psychologists have been identifying cognitive biases for decades, from the "I knew it all along" hindsight bias to the "oops, too late to stop now" sunk cost fallacy. This body of work, which owes a great deal to Daniel Kahneman and Amos Tversky's Nobel-winning research in the 1970s, is a well-labeled zoo of the hundreds of ways our minds tend to be less than rational, ranging from trivial quirks to serious errors in judgment. The bias in our above example, by which we assume that we understand someone else's motivations, has an official title—it's called the observer's illusion of transparency.

We could easily fill three books with nothing but cognitive biases, while adding our own to the list. For example, the Dishwasher Loading Superiority Complex: the conviction that you are the only person in your household who knows how to properly load a dishwasher. But what I want to offer here is a quick triage tool: a cheat sheet of top offenders. When you question your perspective in the moment, your answer may more often than not involve one of these three biases:

Confirmation Bias

If you've heard of one cognitive bias it's probably this one. It turns us into information cherry pickers, sifting through vast groves of data to pluck only the juicy bits that align with our preexisting thoughts and beliefs. Our brains feel safe and validated when the world reflects what we suspected was out there, so even if what's around us is 90 percent apples, confirmation bias tells us we can hunt down what we came for and call the whole place a cherry orchard.

This bias rivals naive realism in its root-level power to prevent us from seeing with objectivity. Like an overzealous spam filter for reality, it discourages us from even noticing things that might confuse or contradict what we've decided to pay attention to. Which is to say, it discourages us from truly experiencing anything new.

As we ask ourselves "What am I making this mean?" and its follow-up, "What else could it mean?", it is the latter question that gets to the heart of the confirmation bias. To overcome it is to seek out ideas genuinely outside our default beliefs.

Fundamental Attribution Error

With this Shakespearean flaw of a bias, we give ourselves the benefit of the doubt while assuming the worst of others. When we disappoint ourselves, we "attribute" the lapse to external factors like luck and environment. With others, bad behavior can only indicate problems of character.

If I saw a man kick a vending machine, I'd assume he is an angry person, but if I do it, it's because that's the third time this week it's taken my money without delivering the Peanut M&M's. If I cut someone off in traffic it's because I didn't see them, but if someone else does it they are a jerk. If I'm late it is because my meeting ran long, but when my friend Bela is late it's because he is a disorganized mess. (Wait, I actually believe this. Bela is always late and I'm only occasionally late. This is probably another bias at work.)

The range of our attribution empathy can vary. It can extend to whole political parties: When a candidate on the other side runs a hateful attack ad, it's because they are shameless, but when my candidate does it, it's because they have to keep up with yours. On the other hand, it sometimes seems to apply most to those closest to us. If I get upset because my partner is talking to someone at a party, it's because I know that other person has a reputation for getting into illicit affairs. But if my partner gets upset with me for doing the same thing, it is because she is a jealous person.

This blind spot in our empathy is all the more indicative of the power of emotion to further distort our objectivity, and all the more argument for seeking new perspective.

The Availability Heuristic

The final bias on our short tour is a shortcut our brains use to make quick judgments based on information that comes readily to mind. While this can be useful in some situations, it's not a recipe for wisdom, especially in our relationships.

Take conflict with a spouse. When things get tense, the availability heuristic kicks in. Recent negative experiences crowd into our minds. The argument we had yesterday? It's front and center, replacing weeks or months of positive interactions. The support, kindness, and shared laughter from just a few days ago? They fade into the background, harder to recall.

The worst danger lies in how this bias compounds over time. As we focus on recent negative experiences, they become our go-to reference points for whomever we're in conflict with. This creates a feedback loop: Negative thoughts lead to negative interactions, which in turn create more negative memories, reinforcing our biased perspective. And to make matters worse, this often pairs with confirmation bias—our tendency to seek out evidence that supports what we already believe, even if what we believe is skewed.

Recognizing this bias is, as always, the first step in combating it. By consciously reminding ourselves of experiences that don't conform to the recent past, we can prevent the availability heuristic from unfairly skewing our perception of the present.

SHIFTING THE LENS

Once we've diagnosed a failure of perspective, we can seek to correct it. As we ask *what else* a situation might mean, below are some perennially useful ways to think outside our own boxes.

The Three P's

Dr. Martin Seligman introduced the concept of the Three P's in his work on depression and optimism, arguing that people who see setbacks in these following terms are more likely to experience depression and pessimism, whereas those less bound by these patterns are more resilient and optimistic.

The three P's are:

1. Permanent: Believing that negative events will last forever.

2. Personal: Seeing yourself as the unique target, or cause, of negative events.

3. Pervasive: Believing that a negative event will affect all areas of your life.

Next time you feel the walls closing in or falling down around you, ask yourself: Is this situation *permanent*? Is it *personal*? Is it *pervasive*?

PERMANENT. I've mentioned my struggles in the past with depression. One of the stories it told me, over and over, was that I would always feel as bad as I did in that moment. When I let it convince me of this, I felt even worse. But it was never true: My depression changed all the time. My mood would lift or shift.

Grief has been the same experience. I lost my beloved dog, Beansie, almost exactly a year ago as I write this. In the first days the grief was overwhelming, but over time it changed. I still miss her and get waves of sadness, but nothing like I did before.

Nothing in life stays the same. This is one of the key insights of philosophy and religion, but it's also about the most self-evident truth there is. Everything changes: That's the deal with matter and energy and life itself. You don't need to be an optimist to accept it. By reminding ourselves of this, we can start to create the mental and emotional space to hold on and believe things will get better.

PERSONAL. There is a reason phrases like "nothing personal" (although once you hear this phrase, watch out, because you'd rather not hear what is coming or was just said) and "it's not personal, it's business" are clichés—because our default is to take *everything* personally. This can manifest in various ways; maybe our tendency is to assume a bad situation is all our fault, or maybe it's to become righteously indignant because everyone is out to get us.

Not taking things so personally means, for one, questioning whether a situation is really as much "about you" as you've assumed. A huge part of coming to terms with being laid off from my first tech job was realizing how much it genuinely wasn't about me. I wasn't at fault, nor was I some specially targeted victim. A lot of people lost their jobs that day.

The other, related truth of "not personal" is that whatever has befallen us, we are not alone. Somewhere, someone has felt the pain we are feeling. Probably millions of someones. In a return to the building blocks of self-compassion, it can help simply to remember that we're part of the family of humans who have all known loss, pain, and fear. We fit right in.

PERVASIVE. We tend to generalize. We focus obsessively on the parts of our lives that are not going well, which makes sense from an evolutionary perspective (it's a natural means of self-protection and survival), but not from a happiness one. We extrapolate the bad things into every corner of our existence, casting a shadow over areas of our life that are, in reality, untouched by what's gone wrong.

There is almost always something that isn't as good as we want it to be. Maybe work is going well and your friendships are solid, but your romantic relationship is struggling. Or maybe our partnership is good but things are tough at work. If we wait until all parts of our lives are good to enjoy them, we will be waiting forever.

This is where compartmentalization can be helpful. We want to be able to acknowledge that yes, there's a part of life that's painful or not how we'd like it to be, but also to stay present to the parts that *are* okay, or even good.

We also tend to overgeneralize from a single failure. One bad date means no more good dates for us, ever again; one bad interview means a tanking career. It's as if we're taking a single puzzle piece and insisting it represents the entire picture of who we are. In all these cases, if we can step back to see the truth of our myopia, we'll suffer less.

Five Hours, Five Days, Five Months

One of my most-used perspective questions is a way of asking about permanence slightly differently:

Will this bother me in five hours, five days, or five months?

Asking this question is like exchanging the microscope I have trained on my own petty grievances for a cosmic telescope.

It turns out that the answer to most things that bother me is that they will not matter in five hours, let alone five days or months. That customer service call where I was on hold for an eon to a soundtrack of elevator jazz and whale sounds? I won't care by bedtime. My car isn't starting? In five days it will be fixed and I'll move on.

Now, sometimes the answer to this question is yes, it will matter. And that's great to know. Because those are the things that we want to devote our energy and attention to. Those are the mountains worth climbing, the dragons worth slaying. The trivial things that distract us from them are just that: trivial.

This question has saved me SO MANY hours of frustration and irritation.

Problems to Puzzles

A. J. Jacobs is a bestselling author and self-described "human guinea pig," known for hilariously extreme experiments in self-improvement, such as the year during which he tried to follow every rule in the Bible literally (see *The Year of Living Biblically*). I interviewed him on the podcast about his latest odyssey-turned-book, *The Puzzler: One Man's Quest to Solve the Most Baffling Puzzles Ever, from Crosswords to Jigsaws to the Meaning of Life*, without knowing exactly how his deep dive into the world of puzzles would fit the spirit of our show. I needn't have worried. In addition to a deeply funny and insightful conversation, A. J. had a key insight into perspective waiting for me.

He first referenced a quote from Quincy Jones, the legendary musician and producer who once said of his career: "I don't have problems, I have puzzles."

That reframing captivated A. J. "The word 'problem' is very intimidating and very negative," he explained. "It implies that maybe there is no solution. Whereas a puzzle is very inviting. It's like, 'I'm gonna roll up my sleeves, and I'm going to solve this puzzle." He has applied the shift beyond the actual puzzles he was solving. "I try to say, 'I'm having a conflict with my wife. All right, this is a puzzle. Let's see if I can make this marriage work better. That's the puzzle. If I'm struggling to figure out what my book is, it's not a problem. It's a puzzle. Let's solve this puzzle.'"

As A. J. describes, this shift in perspective is a way of seeing the world that is more oriented toward possibilities than limitations. It's a great way to cultivate a kinder learning environment for ourselves, in which we lead with curiosity rather than fear of failure—which, we know from the last chapter, is the best way to ensure we learn from our mistakes. A key theme of this book has been that making change isn't a matter of strength of character or feats of willpower; it's about having the right strategy. By reframing obstacles as puzzles rather than problems, we make the execution of that strategy something worth celebrating, rather than one more box ticked or hurdle cleared. We maybe even make room for fun.

Certainty to Doubt

"The fundamental cause of the trouble," Bertrand Russell once wrote, "is that in the modern world the stupid are cocksure while the intelligent are full of doubt." This may sound like a pretty cocksure thing to say, until you consider that Russell was writing in 1933 against the rise of the Nazis. The growing appeal of a group of confident fanatics was, as objectively as can be, the world's biggest problem at the time.

But I don't think the answer for our time is to let go of doubt. To use our intelligence wisely is to be able to question even our deepest-held beliefs and views. In a way this whole chapter is a warning against being cocksure, because to be so means to be content with viewing the world only through the film of our own biases.

In today's "modern world" we still tend to venerate certainty and insult its opposite. We call politicians who change their minds "flip-floppers," and look upon divorce as failure rather than as two people learning enough to make a new choice. We demand black-and-white conclusions where scientific evidence paints in shades of gray. But what if we celebrated doubt instead—as something honest, rigorous, even courageous? As an alternative to clinging to answers that, in the end, might turn out to be wrong?

The Three Essentials of Zen practice are *great faith*, *great doubt*, *great determination*. At first glance this appears confusing. How do you have great faith and great doubt? Another Zen phrase begins to clarify things: "Great doubt, great awakening. Small doubt, small awakening. No doubt, no awakening." The doubt of Zen Buddhism is an exhortation to keep questioning, to keep looking, looking ever more deeply. To throw off the shackles of our limited points of view and to see more and more of the world. To be freed from the deadening effects of certainty.

Once we think we know something we stop looking. We stop seeing. The world becomes one big confirmation bias. Welcoming uncertainty, by contrast, gives life the chance to keep surprising us. In describing the play he chose to call simply *Doubt*, the playwright John Patrick Shanley earns the last word on the subject: "Doubt requires more courage than conviction does, and more energy; because conviction is a resting place, and doubt is infinite. It is a passionate exercise."

WHEN IN DOUBT, ZOOM OUT

To begin this section with "last but not least" would be an understatement. I've saved for this chapter's finale the single most important, useful tool for gaining new perspective: *When in doubt, zoom out.*

This is, in one sense, the synthesis of almost every prompt we've explored so far. To ask if something is *permanent*, *personal*, or *pervasive* is to zoom out from a view with too little context. To ask *what else* something might mean, or to replace certainty with doubt, or to outsmart the availability heuristic with the deeper past—all are ways of stepping back from the claustrophobia of the moment. Back in chapter 4 we saw another zooming-out trick with "play the tape all the way through," by which we imagine the full scope of one action's consequences.

To truly zoom out, however, is to go from the practical to the poetic.

One of my favorite pieces of art of all time is the cartoon strip Calvin and Hobbes. I first started reading it when I was in the halfway house and looking for something to cheer me up, and was struck not only by its hilariousness but also its deep philosophical tendencies. The whole strip is, in a way, a commentary on perspective, given that when only our two main characters appear, Hobbes is a talking tiger, but whenever an adult is present, we see only a little boy and his stuffed animal. (Which version is real? There is no view from nowhere.)

In one strip, little Calvin is taking a test. The question asks about the significance of the Erie Canal, and Calvin, in all his six-year-old wisdom, writes: "In the cosmic sense, probably nil." Then he looks out at us, the readers, and declares, "We 'Big Picture' people rarely become historians."

There are one hundred to four hundred billion stars in the Milky Way and more than one hundred billion galaxies in the Universe— maybe as many as five hundred billion. If you multiply stars by

galaxies, at the low end you get ten billion billion stars, or ten sextillion stars in the universe—a one followed by twenty-two zeros. So there are likely five to ten times more stars than there are grains of sand on all the world's beaches. In this view we are infinitesimally small. A speck. Less than a speck. A speck of a speck of a speck.

Calvin is absolutely right that in the cosmic sense, the Erie Canal isn't the biggest deal—to say nothing of our own daily strife. The smaller our perspective, the more we tend to suffer; zooming out allows us to reveal mountains as molehills. And the bigger the picture we can keep in mind, the better.

I interviewed a man named David Christian, who is one of the foremost proponents of a view of the world called Big History. He says, "Big History views the past at all possible scales and from many different scholarly perspectives, with the belief that a sort of triangulation will yield a richer and deeper understanding of history." His discipline brings together the fields of cosmology, geology, biology, and history, weaving together their insights into a more holistic worldview. It is the ultimate form of zooming out: It stretches our temporal horizon from mere centuries to billions of years, while refocusing the spatial center of action from Earth to the entire universe, reframing our understanding of our place within it.

Calvin was not quite as right, it turns out, that there's no place for thinkers like him in history.

Big History is an excellent insight into perspective shifting, training us to view ourselves and our world through an ever-expanding lens. If our goal is to widen our view, it's a perfect example and thought exercise.

It's also worth remembering that gaining a new sense of scale is not always about going bigger, technically, at all. What if instead of grains of sand on the world's beaches or stars in the sky, we think about atoms? If you were to make a pile of 10 *sextillion* atoms . . . it would be about four times smaller than a dust mite. Which means that a grain of sand has more atoms than there are stars in the universe. A single atom is so small that if you took all the atoms in a grapefruit and made each of them the size of a blueberry, that grapefruit would be the size of the earth.

Through this lens we human beings are enormous.

My own day-to-day struggles seem no less insignificant next to the wonder of quantum physics than next to the Milky Way, but it does give me a different kind of pause. Centuries ago, William Blake wrote about the longing to zoom in, and out, at the same time:

> To see a World in a Grain of Sand
> And a Heaven in a Wild Flower
> Hold Infinity in the palm of your hand
> And Eternity in an hour.

At my most zoomed-out, I think I know what he means.

So which are we? Big or small? Infinitesimal or infinite? Is the Dress blue or gold?

Yes.

ONE LITTLE THING YOU CAN DO RIGHT NOW

Whatever's on your mind right now, ask yourself: "Will this bother me in five hours, five days, or five months?" Be honest. If the answer is no to all three, you've just given yourself permission to let it go. If it's yes to one or more, you know where to focus your actual energy. Either way, you've gained perspective.

When you're ready to go a little deeper, flip to the appendix for extra exercises—or download the companion worksheets anytime at oneyoufeed.net/resources.

SEVEN

The Middle Way

> Love says: "I am everything."
> Wisdom says: "I am nothing."
> Between the two my life flows.
>
> —NISARGADATTA MAHARAJ

IN THE VILLAGE OF BAKRAUR (FORMERLY SENANIGRAMA), IN NORTHEASTERN India, across a river from where the Buddha is said to have attained enlightenment, is a place dedicated to another person without whom modern Buddhism would not exist. The Sujata Stupa, a colossal half pyramid of brick, has stood in some form since the second century BCE, attracting a steady flow of pilgrims across the millennia.

Sujata, the namesake of this ancient, enduring place, was not wealthy or powerful. She was a young milkmaid. And what she did, the act of literally monumental importance that became a turning point in the creation of a world religion, was also deceptively humble: She gave a snack to a hungry man.

The story goes like this. The Buddha himself started out as

a prince who did all the fun things spoiled princes do—a lot of wine, women, and song. When he realized that his life felt empty of meaning, he did a more surprising thing for a spoiled prince, and took a hard left turn into isolation and asceticism. He took this lifestyle just as seriously as he'd taken messing around, practicing extreme fasting, meditation, and sleep deprivation in hopes of finding meaning without the distraction of earthly pleasures. It was said that you could see his spine through his stomach at one point. After seven years of nothing but contemplation, he felt no closer to the big answers he craved. Then, exactly as you'd expect from a man living off a grain of rice daily: He collapsed.

Enter Sujata, who was walking by with a bowl of *kheer* (rice pudding) she planned to offer at a nearby temple when she saw the Buddha lying in the dirt under a banyan tree. She stopped and offered the food to him instead—and this time, after years of self-denial, he took it. Sujata helped him to eat and bathed him in the river before they both went on their separate ways.

That chance encounter was, for the Buddha, a turning point. It marked the end of his asceticism and the beginning of his following a way of life focused on seeking balance in all things. Soon after, he "woke up," finding the enlightenment he had sought all along. He began teaching his many followers that the path to truth was neither in a life focused on comfort and sensory pleasures, nor in the kind of deprivation he had practiced as a forest ascetic. Both of these paths were "painful, unworthy, and unprofitable," he said. The road to follow was, instead, a "middle way."

Sujata's role in the Buddha's embrace of the middle way has, over the centuries, been reduced to more or less the same function as the apple falling on Newton's head (to cite another famous "guy surprised by food under a tree" scene). But it's worth spending another moment with her before we dive into what this rich philosophy of wise living—a philosophy steeped in compassion, patience, tolerance, and gratitude—really means. Because Sujata was not only the maker of an unexpectedly important afternoon snack; she also embodied middle-way principles the Buddha would later articulate.

In the details of the story as it has been passed down, she was someone living according to her values, taking time out of her day to pay tribute at a local temple—but also not so caught up in the perfect execution of her goals (in this case offering a spiritual sacrifice) that she missed a better use of her time and energy (in this case helping out a person in distress). She was also, unlike the Buddha at the time, living in the real world, accountable to practical concerns like food and cleanliness. She didn't have her whole life to wander around the forest thinking, or to follow the Buddha wherever he went next. She had a day job, thanks to which she had the rice and milk to give away in the first place. What she did have to spare, in time, material resources, and empathy, she used wisely. And her big little actions made all the difference.

All this context is, I think, essential to the gift Sujata gave to the Buddha that day. She showed him another way to be even as she helped him take his first steps toward it. What matters is never only the gift of wisdom (or rice pudding and a bath), but also the giver. What matters is not only the idea of a better way to live, but proof that it can work in real life.

• • •

This chapter is all about the middle way. Even if you don't consider yourself an aspiring Zen master, don't skip ahead. Buddhist practice embodies this lesson for living wisely, and gives us the perfect name for it, but the middle way echoes throughout traditions of thought and spirituality, not to mention the science of behavioral change.

Let's get the basics out of the way. The middle way, as the Buddha and many others have articulated, is about balance and moderation. It's about eschewing extremes that don't serve us in favor of steady and sustainable commitments, pleasures, and challenges. You can probably already see the relationship to a little-by-little mindset: The middle way is about finding the gear in all things that lets us keep going without burning us out.

As with self-compassion, the middle way is both a process, useful for changing habits of thought and behavior, and an end in itself—a better way to live, more often than not. In the language of perspective, it's an always useful lens to try, especially when we're navigating emotional extremes or aiming to act with less bias in the moment.

Also like self-compassion, the middle way is easy to misunderstand or dismiss. It sounds good in theory but can be harder to put into practice.

In this chapter we'll dig into exactly what the middle way is and isn't, trace the ways we've seen it crop up already, explore where it's especially useful, and learn new tools for reframing any situation from a middle-way perspective.

Let's get to the middle of things.

MODERATION, NOT MEDIOCRITY

A confession: I don't love the term "moderation." To me it has a strong association with moderation in the sense of drinking, which is not exactly personally applicable. Beyond my hard-won sobriety, there is also the me who was drawn to pushing my mind and body to their limits in the first place, who for a long time rejected moderation as the province of the boring and uninspired. Extremes of any kind—wild new experiences, adrenaline rushes, do-or-die romantic drama—were where I thought *real* living happened.

When I think of the seduction of this mindset, I think of myself at twenty years old, when I picked up my life to relocate across the country to San Francisco. I wanted to be the protagonist in *On the*

Road: "Nothing behind me, everything ahead of me." I was anxious about my drinking and drug use and thought a change of scenery would help, plus I had a friend in San Francisco and it felt like the place to be—the Beats, after all, had set up a home base in the fabled City Lights bookstore. I was going to leave my old life behind by sheer grandness of gesture: no half measures, no baggage, just fearlessly stepping into the unknown. My second night in San Francisco I came out of a blackout lying on a park bench, which tells you most of what you need to know about that experiment.

I'm hardly alone in having overlooked the middle way for the highway, so to speak. "Everything in moderation" might be a cliché of virtuous living, but in many ways, we Americans especially celebrate anything but. We champion eternal striving, max efficiency, never settling for less. We venerate those who push themselves to the limit, who work the hardest, who dream the biggest and live the largest. We love excess in pretty much any form: One of the most popular events on our nation's birthday is a contest to see who can eat the most hot dogs. To talk about aiming for the middle of anything, whether of sensory experience or emotion or productivity, isn't exactly sexy.

Here is what the middle way isn't. It isn't mediocrity, and it isn't settling for less. It isn't the sapping of ambition and experience I feared when I clung to extreme behaviors that, let me tell you, were not worth it. These days I have learned to set aside most of my biased associations with moderation, while at the same time realizing that to live on the edge is, far more often than not, to miss life at its fullest.

To refine what the middle way *is*, I like to begin with the Swedish concept of *lagom*. Appropriately, the term doesn't quite translate into English, but hovers somewhere in the realm of "just right." Imagine Goldilocks if she was a Swedish lifestyle guru. In our world of constant optimization and more-is-more, *lagom* stands as a quiet rebellion. It's not about having it all, but about having enough. And yet it's also not about dimming your light or saying goodbye to your dreams. Rather it's about finding that elusive sweet spot between too much and too little. It's the art of savoring your coffee without turning into a caffeine-addled workaholic, or enjoying a piece of cake without spiraling into guilt-induced fitness mania. It is the Swedish cousin of the middle way, dressed in minimalist Ikea furniture and sipping lingonberry juice.

• • •

I first encountered the middle way through Buddhism, but there are countless entry points in its history among philosophers and religious thinkers.

Aristotle introduced some clever branding with the Golden Mean, by which he meant the idea that any virtue lies at the midpoint between two vices, one of excess and one of deficiency. Courage, for Aristotle, was the mean between cowardice and recklessness; assertiveness, the mean between aggressiveness and passivity. Generosity would be the balance between "here's my other kidney" and "I charge friends for using my toilet paper," self-respect the midpoint between commissioning a fifty-foot sculpture of yourself and apologizing for your presence in the world . . . you get the idea.

This legacy of thought shows that there's nothing *middling* about the middle way. It's about using an awareness of the poles of "too far" and "not far enough," in any given realm of action, to guide us to something better than either extreme: a meeting point of complex harmony, informed by both sides but avoiding their pitfalls.

In ancient China, the concept of yin and yang took shape . . . and I guarantee you're now picturing a circle divided into two swirling sections, one black and the other white, with a smaller circle of the opposite color nestled within each half. Before the yin-yang was a hippie decal to put alongside flowers and peace signs, it was an expression of Taoist cosmology: Within a circle that represents the universe, a union of opposing forces—a primal masculine energy, or yin, and feminine energy, yang—is not only balanced but interconnected. The black dot in the heart of the white section, and the white dot in the black, shows that light emerges from darkness and vice versa.

One of my all-time favorite books, the *Tao Te Ching* of Lao Tzu expands on this principle of interconnectedness, teaching that there is no light without darkness, no up without down. All contrasting elements are manifestations of a shared underlying essence, and they exist only in relation to one another, transforming back and forth in endless cycles. Day turns into night, and night into day. Life leads to death, and death paves the way for new life. According to Lao Tzu, we should align with this natural flow of things whenever we can, which is to say, we should live by the principle of balance, of yin-yang give-and-take.

Chapter 9 of the *Tao* observes that continuous filling of a bowl will lead it to overflow, and constant sharpening of a knife will make it dull. I like this because it speaks to how unsustainable it is to live at the limits of experience, without making experience itself the enemy.

Another figure of ancient China, Confucius, developed the concept of Zhongyong, often translated as the Doctrine of the Mean. It emphasizes balance and discernment in all our actions and thoughts. Confucius viewed it as a supreme virtue—and a hard one to find: "The virtue embodied in the doctrine of the Mean is of the highest order. But it has long been rare among people."

Islamic philosophy speaks of *wasatiyyah*, encouraging moderation in all aspects of life. The Hindu text Bhagavad Gita introduces *yukta-vairagya*, a measured approach to detachment. And in the classical and medieval Christian understanding of virtues, moderation (or temperance) was considered one of the four cardinal virtues, along with prudence, justice, and fortitude.

At this point we start getting to some of the baggage that made younger me allergic to the very word "moderation": the puritanical tradition by which excess got a little, well, excessive, with deep shame as the cost of violating social norms. Under such strictures moderation can seem more like a prison than a golden mean, much less the center of nature's dynamic, eternal flow.

The truth is that while moderation describes many useful approaches to following the middle way (as we'll see), the two terms aren't synonymous. F. Scott Fitzgerald once wrote, "The test of a first-rate intelligence is the ability to hold two opposed ideas in mind at the same time, and still retain the ability to function." When I think of the middle way, I think of the productive tension at the heart of that idea. It is about choosing the way through any situation that closes the fewest doors to us: a needle-threading, truth-balancing path rich in nuance and possibility.

The middle way is an approach to life that energizes rather than wears us down. It widens rather than narrows our perspectives. And like any "way," it helps us to move forward.

On that note, let's explore how the middle way is also a path to lasting change.

CENTERING CHANGE

Picture an actual *way* for this part. A road or a trail. It stretches into the distance, straight and well maintained as far as you can see. You're in the center, facing the direction you want to go. The middle way toward a given goal isn't always this obvious, but we can get better at seeing it on the metaphorical horizon.

Middle-way principles have been at work throughout this book. Self-compassion is a thoroughly middle-way idea, for instance, taking us between the extremes of self-indulgence and self-criticism. On one end we have an overactive "treat yo'self" mentality, where you justify every whim and mistake with a shrug and an "I deserve it because I'm breathing." On the other end we have the internal critic that treats every minor slipup like a cardinal sin, keeping up a monologue of "You idiot" and "Why can't you do anything right?" Self-compassion sits between this rock and a soft place, saying, "Hey, you're human. Mistakes happen. Let's learn from this and move on."

Or remember the "fuck-it"s from chapter 1? How often have you found yourself on a new diet and then, having given in to diner pancakes for breakfast, gone on to consume an entire sleeve of Oreos, a pint of Ben and Jerry's, and McDonald's for dinner? (Just me?) "F*&! it, I've already messed up" is the anthem of days like this: Since we didn't act perfectly from the jump, we go to the other extreme and don't try at all. A middle way would be to accept that, yes, we didn't stick to the plan at breakfast, but it doesn't have to affect what we do the rest of the day.

These kinds of pitfalls on the road to change can be grouped under one of the most common cognitive biases: "all or nothing" thinking. This is the antithesis of the middle way. I've said it before and I'll say it again: *A little bit of something is better than a lot of nothing.* You're never going to be perfect, but that doesn't mean you're a failure. However slowly you're hiking or driving that metaphorical trail, every foot you've covered puts you that much further than you were yesterday.

It's helpful to recognize our personal tendencies when it comes to stepping off the path. I've had clients who were so hard on themselves that they needed to practice being way more understanding, and others who avoid responsibility by any means possible. Telling the first to be more accountable to themselves would be like adding gasoline to a bonfire. Meanwhile, advising the responsibility dodger to "take it easy" would essentially be giving them a PhD in procrastination. I gave the two groups what sounded like polar opposite advice, ultimately guiding everyone toward the same balanced midpoint.

Think about what tends to stop you from acting as your best self. Do you lean toward the momentum killer of depression, or the detour of anger? Does the downhill of fuck-it/self-indulgence call your name? Or are you more often tempted to make things harder than they need to be?

For any tendency that gets in your way, whether in forming new habits or simply in finding purpose and joy in the everyday, there is a middle-way corrective. I could fill another book with specifics, but fortunately, there are some all-purpose tools useful for gauging when we're drifting off course, and for guiding us back.

WORDS OF WISDOM

Q: What do you call a psychic who enjoys exercising moderation?
A: A happy medium.

Were you not expecting a pun? I have a reason for whipping out one here, promise: because paying close attention to language is a prime way of flagging when we're veering off the middle way.

As I sit here and write this my back hurts. I've had the good fortune to be traveling for a bit and have been walking . . . a lot. So I woke up, as is often the case, with a sore lower back and shoulders. And what my brain says to me is "My back is killing me." If I am in a less than fully aware state, this is what I wander around saying to myself. If I stop and actually check in with the signals my back is sending, however, the reality is much more like "my lower back is kind of tight right now." Which of those two messages do you think is more useful for my state of mind?

Extreme language produces extreme emotions. Even if something like "it's killing me" is obviously hyperbole, to use that script internally is to reinforce that what's happening is fairly dire. To disrupt this, I use the basic perspective exercise from the last chapter, asking myself, *What am I making this mean?* and then *What else could it mean?* Then, following George Kelly's personal construct theory, I ask myself a third question: *What meaning is most useful to me right now?*

This is where middle-way thinking comes in. This morning I realized that the best way to move forward with my day was to scale back how I was describing the pain to myself. (Internally, the whole conversation went more like "*eyeroll emoji*—I feel your pain, Eric, but a tight lumbar is unlikely to be your cause of death.")

Take another situation all too common for some of us. Your two-year-old has another tantrum and you say, "I can't stand it!" It's a throwaway line, but it's also emotional code for *This is relentless. I'm completely overwhelmed. And if this is what parenting is, I might not be cut out for it.* Now imagine saying to yourself something more like: "Raising a toddler is an exercise in absurdist theater, where one finds oneself negotiating with a tiny tyrant over the existential importance of wearing pants. It will pass." Not an easy thing to remember in the moment, I know. But parents—tell me that's not the truth.

I can't believe they did that!! Think about that statement. You mean you genuinely, as an intelligent human being, have an inability to believe that someone's done something that you didn't want them to do? Now let's come back to the truth. You can believe it; you just would have chosen for that person to act differently. Try rephrasing to "I wish they hadn't done that." If you're auditioning for *The Real Housewives* you may want to stick with the original, but assuming you want a calmer existence, the reframe is the right way to go.

Again: **Extreme language produces extreme emotions.** Whether we're talking to ourselves or anyone else, more measured language creates space for a more balanced, middle-way perspective. Even our most basic linguistic tics can reveal deeply ingrained tendencies—so prepare to get dramatic with the grammatic. (Sorry.)

Adjectives, Adverbs, and Pronouns

I never thought I'd be treating the lessons of third-grade English like a red-string conspiracy board, but here we are. Adjectives (which modify nouns), pronouns (which replace nouns), and adverbs (which modify verbs and adjectives) can, if we're not careful, become little bombs of extremity in our descriptions of reality.

An example of an **adjective** to watch out for is *horrible*. This one is a favorite of my mom's (sorry, Mom), although it's pronounced more "haaaarrible" when she says it. Describing things that are unpleasant or tedious as "haaaarrible" can tip our negative feelings over into despair or hopelessness. Similarly dangerous words include *disastrous*, *unbearable*, *awful*, and *disgusting*. Less common, but among my favorites to say (no one said drama-queen words weren't fun): *flabbergasted*, *flummoxed*, *catastrophic*, *astronomic*, and *preposterous*.

Among **adverbs**, suspects worth questioning are *always* and *never*. Want to turn a discussion into a fight? Just accuse the other person of *always* or *never* doing something. It works like a charm. Why? Because when looking at our own behavior we know that it's a patchwork, not an on-off switch. I have not forgotten to do the dishes *every* day, which is what the statement "You never do the dishes" would cause me to rebut. Or I don't *always* get grumpy after work. Adverbs like these provoke defensiveness and shut down the productive, nuanced conversations that should happen about not only the dishes but why the dishes have been causing resentment in the first place.

These wonder twins of adverbs don't just mess up our communication with others, they skew our internal monologues. I've seen this with countless coaching clients: "I never finish anything I start" . . . which, of course, is not true, but certainly keeps us feeling like failures. Or "I always mess up" . . . which is the reverse of the above but contains the same seeds of an anxiety spiral. We can add *constantly*, *completely*, *absolutely*, *utterly*, and *totally* to our mix.

Pronouns (she, he, they) seem innocent enough at first glance, until you add *everyone* and *no one* to the mix. "No one loves me" is a classic of the genre. "Everyone thinks I'm stupid," you say after a presentation to five people goes a little less well than you had hoped.

When you notice yourself using any of these red-flag words, experiment with substitutions that reflect the nuance of reality. We could replace my mom's old standby, *horrible*, with something like "That doctor visit was unpleasant." We could say "I'm having a hard time right now" instead of "Everything is terrible" (two red-flag words for the price of one in that sentence). Describing a family visit that didn't go well, try replacing "He astronomically miscalculated the impact of teaching his parrot swear words" with "Grandma did not like the colorful avian commentary." And if your first thought is "You never listen to what I say," try instead "Sometimes I think you don't give me your full attention."

Note that our goal here is not to gloss over things that are difficult or make us unhappy. It is to remind ourselves that reality is rarely black and white, and that there are a lot of benefits to seeing in full color.

And

Another powerful nudge toward middle-way thinking is one magic word: **and**.

Simply start replacing *or* or *but* with *and* to see how quickly this tweak can disrupt all-or-nothing thinking. Instead of "I'm a decent person *or* a stack of flaws in a trench coat," consider "I'm a decent person *and* a stack of flaws in a trench coat." That still sounds like a

Jekyll and Hyde situation, so better yet: "I have qualities I'm proud of *and* I sometimes make mistakes." Instead of "This week is going great" or "It's completely ruined," reframe it as "I had some successes this week *and* faced a few challenges."

In making the switch to *and*, we're acknowledging a big truth: Life is a mixed bag. A well-known phrase in Eastern philosophy speaks of "the ten thousand joys and the ten thousand sorrows." In Taoism and Buddhism, "ten thousand" stands in for everything, the full range of human experience. The idea is that all those ups and downs are often happening *at the same time*.

But we tend to lean toward the negative. We zoom in on what's wrong and lose sight of everything that isn't. One bad moment, a fight with your partner, for instance, can take over your whole mental landscape. Suddenly, you don't notice the beautiful day, the kind thing a coworker said, or the delicious lunch you just had. Your focus narrows to the one bad thing, and everything else fades.

As we explored in the last chapter: When in doubt, *zoom out*. Using *and* helps us do just that. It invites our joys and sorrows to share the stage.

My car is in the shop *and* my friend is nice enough to come pick me up for lunch. My job is a struggle *and* my family is healthy. I have a headache this morning *and* the way this dog and this little girl are staring at each other in line at the coffee shop is adorable. We don't have to get rid of the bad things on our horizons—in fact we often can't. But seeing both sides gives us a way to live more fully in the middle of it all.

The Third Thing

This idea is based not in words but numbers. Faced with two options, how can we create a third one instead?

Zen tradition offers a great example of a third thing. Master Gosho, a Zen monk who lived in the twelfth century, posed a koan: "When you meet someone who's truly enlightened, you can't greet them with words or silence. So how do you greet them?"

At first glance it seems like a dead end. No words, no silence—what's left?

Eventually, Zen students figure out that there are actually lots of ways to greet someone: a smile, a tune, or handing over some flowers. Once you realize how you've boxed yourself in with either-or thinking, the solution seems so obvious that we are amazed we didn't see it right away. It's a perfect illustration of a third thing, or in this case multiple third things. Notice that each possible answer is not a compromise, but a synthesis: the kind of solution that doesn't immediately present itself when we're caught in binary thinking.

A third thing often emerges out of paradox, which is an apparent contradiction in which two things seem to exclude each other, but actually need not do so. "Square circle" is a contradiction, whereas "saintly sinner" is a paradox, as is "holy fool." When we accept that seemingly irreconcilable things can be true at the same time, we start getting creative. It's something great thinkers have always experimented with. F. Scott Fitzgerald's praise for "the ability to hold two opposed ideas in mind at the same time" echoes John Keats's celebration of Shakespeare, whom he described as having enormous "negative capability." By this Keats meant the capacity to hold countless ideas lightly, as though seeing the truth in each thought as well as the truth in the negative space around it.

You don't need to be a Zen master or Shakespeare to find the elusive third thing. You just need curiosity and patience. I spent ten years in a marriage that wasn't healthy for either me or my partner. It slowly ate away at all aspects of my life. The dilemma was a familiar one—we both wanted to "stay for the kids." Our sons were thriving in the stable home we had created for them, and I was the last person to take stability for granted. But no matter how much we tried to repair the marriage it just wasn't working.

I was so stuck on the two choices of stay or go. Over and over, a thousand times: Stay or go? Like a Clash song stuck on repeat. Neither of those options felt like an answer.

I was reading about decision-making, and one crucial idea I learned was that the key to good decisions is to get as many ideas as possible on the table. I only had two: Stay or go. But I began to wonder if there were other options I hadn't explored, like in Gosho's koan. Was it possible to stay *and* go?

Through a lot of discussion, my ex and I found our way to a third option. We would stay in the house together and co-parent the boys, but we would end our marriage. At first we didn't tell the boys anything, and it was rocky, but the little bit of space we had opened up between us helped. As time went on it became clear that telling the boys was the right thing. So we sat them down and told them that we loved them and wanted to keep the family together until they went off to college, but that our relationship as a couple was done. What had seemed like a contradiction—how can a family "stay together" when the headline is a split?—actually wasn't. The relationships that bound us to our sons, and even to each other as parents, existed independently from the relationship that wasn't working. As participants in those other relationships we wanted to stay under one roof, so we did.

No, it wasn't all calorie-free chocolate and self-folding laundry from there, but things were so much better. We managed to get the boys off to college and then went our separate ways.

This would not work for everyone, but it was the middle way that worked for me in this case. As with the many potential answers to Gosho's koan, the beauty of the third thing is that when you decide that one and two aren't the only options, a universe of possibility opens up.

THE MIDDLE WAY OF LIFE

Thus far I've been treating the middle way mostly as a handy addition to our cognitive toolbox. It is a new lens on emotionally fraught moments, a way to minimize the all-or-nothing thinking that gets in the way of change, and a set of prompts to encourage balance and nuance. It is also even more capacious than this. It will be up to you how you integrate its wisdom in your day-to-day, but below are a few areas I navigate with my feet planted on the middle way.

Between Optimism and Pessimism

An optimist and a pessimist walk into a bar. The optimist says, "This is great! The glass is half full!" The pessimist grumbles, "Yeah, and it's probably backwash." The realist bartender rolls his eyes and wonders why these weirdos can't just enjoy their drinks like normal people. You might be able to guess who I am in this scenario.

I've written elsewhere about my allergy to "positive thinking," the self-help cousin to blind optimism. "Manifesting" and "good vibes only" may work for some people, but I've never been convinced that telling myself I can write like Hemingway or bike like a Tour de France champion is going to make those things any truer.

And yet, I know I need to counteract my susceptibility to the other extreme: the negativity bias. I come by this bias honestly, as we all do. Our evolutionary ancestors who were more attuned to threats had a better chance of survival, which led to this trait being passed down through generations. Being on red alert about the possibility of a saber-toothed tiger attack is, unfortunately, far more useful than obsessing about a typo in an important email or the one flaw in a delicious meal.

As the self-doubt stalemate demonstrated in chapter 4, my solution for everyday pessimism is to aim for neutral—telling myself

I don't know that I *can't* write this book, for example, though it's anyone's guess how well it will turn out. I'm not saying I would hire my internal realist as an inspirational speaker, but he's a guy I believe, which makes all the difference. This is a deeply middle-way strategy.

I've also taken to a middle-way approach to thinking about, well, the rest of the world. One of the books that has most influenced me in the last decade is *Factfulness* by Hans Rosling. The book and Rosling's work in general is about fighting ignorance with data. It is common today to hear that this is a terrible time to be alive, and the fire hose of distressing news and hot takes available to us twenty-four seven is one big, never-ending recency bias, making it *feel* true that everything is burning down all the time. This view always felt limited to me, but I didn't have the framing to suggest otherwise until I read *Factfulness*.

Rosling shows that there are real ways in which the world is not getting worse—in fact, quite the opposite. Here are just a few statistical counterpoints:

- The share of the human population living in extreme poverty dropped from nearly 35 percent in 1987 to under 11 percent in 2013.

- Child mortality has decreased substantially. It has fallen by more than half since 1990.

- Maternal mortality declined by 43 percent between 1990 and 2015.

Of course, any amount of extreme poverty, child and maternal mortality, child labor, and illiteracy is too much. But to focus only on the world's ills is to make them seem inevitable and intractable rather than responsive to solutions.

"People often call me an optimist, because I show them the

enormous progress they didn't know about," Rosling once said. "That makes me angry. I'm not an optimist. That makes me sound naive. I'm a very serious 'possibilist' . . . I see all this progress, and it fills me with conviction and hope that further progress is possible." Rosling associated optimism with a sort of fingers-crossed faith, whereas his outlook was about "having a clear and reasonable idea about how things are. It is having a worldview that is constructive and useful. A solution that works for me is to persuade myself to keep two thoughts in my head at the same time." (I wonder if Rosling was an F. Scott Fitzgerald fan?)

We are back to something foundational here. We are looking for a "worldview" that helps us move forward, holding apparently contradictory ideas in our heads and reconciling them into a third thing. Not optimism, not pessimism, but "possibilism." *Welcome, reality*, we possibilists say. *We're ready for you.*

Between Ordinary and Extra

In our culture of relentless self-improvement and achievement, we've collectively bought into a seductive idea: that each of us is destined for greatness. This notion, championed by everyone from celebrities to business moguls, has become so pervasive that it's practically heretical to suggest otherwise. We all need to, as Steve Jobs said, "make a dent in the universe." But if we consider the implications of this belief, it says that a life is only worthwhile when it stands out from those around it. What does that say about the vast majority of human existence? It's a perspective that, taken to its logical conclusion, devalues most of humanity and most every experience. Somehow being average has become a new way of saying "failure."

I felt this pressure for so much of my life. I had some sense that I was destined to do something "great." It was not motivating, however. It was a weight I carried. As a teenager I had a paper route and I would spend the whole time on the route developing these fantasy tales in which I always did something amazing and saved thousands of people and of course got the girl at the end. Later I'd watch a college football game and feel vaguely sick that I was sitting at home while the quarterback was getting so much attention. This outlook was driven by my insecurity about my value as a person, and it continued to drive some of my worst tendencies. If I was going to be a drug addict, I was going to be the most extreme.

The idea that "everyone can be extraordinary" is often more comforting than true. Remember Big History? In the grand scheme of time and space, our individual actions are insignificant. We barely make a dent in our neighborhood, let alone the universe. Even figures like Steve Jobs, idolized as singular visionaries, likely accelerated changes that would have happened eventually, with or without them.

Embracing our ordinariness can be profoundly liberating. It lifts the constant pressure to be something other than what we are, to see wherever we are as less than where we could be. It stops us from thinking we need to raise two MacArthur Fellows children, look like a twenty-year-old Instagram influencer, and also solve the problem of water scarcity for all of Africa. Paradoxically, accepting our own mundanity can give us the freedom to pursue what truly matters to us, unburdened by grandiose expectations.

This isn't an argument for complacency or a rejection of self-improvement, it's a shift in emphasis. Instead of seeing our lives as a constant striving toward some make-believe version of success, we might see more chances for engagement, connection, and meaningful contribution. We will be able to discover peace in a solitary walk, the joy of mastering a new skill, the delight of a spontaneous conversation with a stranger. We can rediscover the profound contentment of watching the clouds side by side with someone dear to you.

Sujata, with whom we began this chapter, would have been no less worthy a human being if no one ever linked her story to the

Buddha's, much less built a giant brick monument to her. That's not to say I'm not glad we know about her, and indeed I wish she got her due more often. It's just to say that it's a losing bet to link your self-worth to how big a temple the world builds in your honor.

Between Choice and Chance

One of my favorite books is *East of Eden* by John Steinbeck. As I've been thinking about the middle way, I've been thinking a lot about a word at the novel's heart: *timshel*, which in biblical Hebrew means "thou mayest."

In the novel, which includes characters named after Cain and Abel, among other heavy-handed biblical tie-ins, a voice-of-reason character describes how English translations of the Bible use the phrase "Thou Shalt," to convey God's unambiguous orders for how humans are supposed to behave. He points out that the Hebrew translation of this phrase is different, however:

> *The Hebrew word, the word* timshel—*"Thou mayest"—gives a choice. It might be the most important word in the world. That says the way is open. That throws it right back on a man. For if "Thou mayest"—it is also true that "Thou mayest not." Don't you see?*

This becomes something like the moral thesis of the book: that we can choose whether or not to be good, and in this is the possibility of redemption. It's a beautiful articulation of a middle-way view of human agency.

Whether or not you believe in the Judeo-Christian cosmos (or ever had to memorize all those "thou shalts/thou shalt not"s of the Ten Commandments), there are plenty of ways to question whether what we do matters, and even if we have the free will to decide in the first place. Are we "programmed" by our genetics and environment?

Are we doomed by inherent weakness, as original sin would have it? Are our choices essentially made for us by big government, big capitalism, [insert institutional system here]?

Or, at the other extreme, is everything bad that's ever happened to us somehow our fault? Can we take credit for everything good in our lives?

You know where I'm going with this. None of us have the big answers; that's part of the deal with being a tiny speck in a wondrous universe. But I've found the middle way a sustaining, purposeful, and even comforting place to live on this topic. Between the extremes of determinism and libertarianism (between no free will versus total autonomy), I prefer the idea of co-creation. Yes, our biology (genetics, brain structure, hormones, etc.), our conditioning, and countless other factors affect the course of our lives and our behavioral tendencies and habits of thought. *And* our ability to make our own choices, to change and grow in new directions, is real. We co-create our experience.

Free will might seem like a lofty place to leave this chapter, but it's not just some abstract philosophical quandary. It cuts to the core of how we see ourselves and our place in the world. A realistic, "possibilist" idea of our ability to change is crucial for the journey. If we expect too much from ourselves we become disappointed and disillusioned. But if we believe, deep down, that due to our circumstances or our nature we can't change, then we'll keep finding ways to make it so.

The same character in *East of Eden* who gives us *timshel* is, I think, secretly a Zen master. Elsewhere in the novel he gives one of the best summaries of a middle-way approach to life I've ever come across. "Now that you don't have to be perfect," he says, "you can be good."

ONE LITTLE THING YOU CAN DO RIGHT NOW

Catch yourself using an extreme word today—always, never, horrible, disaster. Replace it with something more accurate: sometimes, often, unpleasant, challenging. Notice how this small shift changes how the situation feels. You're not minimizing real problems—you're seeing them without the emotional magnification.

When you're ready to go a little deeper, flip to the appendix for extra exercises—or download the companion worksheets anytime at oneyoufeed.net/resources.

EIGHT

We Find Ourselves in Others

Sticks in a bundle are unbreakable.

—KENYAN PROVERB

ON THE DAY BEFORE MOTHER'S DAY IN 1935, A DOWN-ON-HIS-LUCK STOCKbroker stood in the lobby of the Mayflower Hotel in Akron, Ohio. He had traveled from New York for a business deal that had just fallen through. The air was thick with the sounds of clinking ice and laughter from the hotel bar. He hadn't touched a drop in over five months, but the thought that flickered through his mind was dangerously familiar: *I need a drink.* As he glimpsed the happy crowd at the bar, he could almost feel the companionship and relief alcohol had once provided. In that moment it would have been so easy to give in, to slip back into old patterns and lose the life he had fought to regain. But something stopped him—a slender thread of hope that maybe, just maybe, there was a different way through this familiar crisis. His name was Bill Wilson, and he had no idea he was on the verge of transforming his personal desperation into a global lifeline for millions.

Instead of stepping into the lobby bar that night, Bill's eyes caught sight of a row of phone books. He reached for one, chose a church at random, and asked the clergyman on the other end if he knew of anyone struggling with drinking. The reverend made a connection to a man named Dr. Bob Smith—a once-respected surgeon who was now spiraling into the abyss that Bill knew all too well. The two agreed to meet.

It was supposed to be a fifteen-minute conversation. Dr. Bob was taking a lot on faith, after all, by agreeing to connect with an out-of-town stranger about his darkest shame. But as the two men sat down and began to talk, Dr. Bob quickly realized that this Bill Wilson "knew what he was talking about." Dr. Bob had read a lot about alcoholism and had heard the opinions of fellow professionals who had treated it, but Bill knew what it was like to *be* an alcoholic. "In other words, he talked my language," Bob later said. "He knew all the answers, and certainly not because he had picked them up in his reading."

What was supposed to be the briefest of encounters stretched into six hours, as the two men shared their stories, their fears, and most important, a sense that they were stronger in solidarity than either had been on his own. Their meeting would become the founding moment of Alcoholics Anonymous, an international organization whose model for battling addiction still rests on the simple, powerful realization Bill and Bob each had that night: that by helping each other, they might just save themselves.

⋯

I've mentioned the old phrase that if you want to go fast, go alone. But if you want to go far, go together.

If you had asked me when I started *The One You Feed* what I thought was the most important thing in personal growth, I would have said very confidently, "the ability to go inside yourself." If you had asked me what I thought the most important thing was in hitting our goals, I would have said "inner discipline." Now, five hundred-plus interviews and almost ten years later, I would answer both of those questions very differently. I've finally—gratefully—accepted that the most important factor in any personal journey, up to and including life itself, is the help and support of others.

Programs like AA are described as "self-help," but the term itself is misleading. They are better thought of as "mutual-aid" societies. Members help themselves *by* helping one another, as Bill Wilson began to do that night with Dr. Bob, and as Dr. Bob would do by becoming a mentor (or "sponsor") for other alcoholics, and so on through many generations of recovering addicts, eventually including yours truly. Yet when it comes to changing most habits of thought and behavior, communities like AA are more the exception than the rule. For every "two heads are better than one" cliché, there is another entry in the canon of pop psychology, hustle culture, or "new year new you" game-planning that paints a rosy picture of going it alone, telling us that the self we want is wholly in our power—and ours alone—to achieve. Such promises can empower us, but they also exaggerate their case.

Remember in chapter 4 we discussed how relying only on self-control was problematic? And in chapter 3 how we stressed the environmental factors involved in change? Whatever your environment is, other people (or the lack thereof) shape it more profoundly than any other single factor. And beyond the province of realizing goals and changing habits, science is increasingly clear that the quality of our relationships is the most important determinant of our well-being, both mental and physical. In 2023, the U.S. Surgeon General Vivek Murthy declared loneliness so harmful and widespread as to be a public health crisis, while unhealthy relationships can be, quite literally, toxic to us. On the brighter side, strong community ties and stable, supportive relationships are linked to longer lives, lower stress, greater resilience, and a deeper sense of meaning and purpose.

"No man is an island," wrote John Donne four hundred years ago. His words are both a frank description of reality, none of us is free of the influence of others, and a warning that echoes with as much resonance as it ever did. Think of yourself as an island, and you might just end up feeling like a castaway.

This book has, in many ways, been a journey inward. We started with the deceptively simple questions, *Who do I want to be?* and *What do I want to do?* We got in touch with our deepest values, practiced emotional awareness (the Holy Grail of prompts), and took a closer look at our ingrained habits of thought, from cognitive biases to pesky internal critics. Don't get me wrong—all this internal spelunking remains essential to cultivating wise habits and a joyful, fulfilling life. Of all the people it's worth working on your relationship for, *you* are still at the top of that list. That said, no amount of introspection can lessen the importance of what will always be, by definition, outside our own heads: the people we surround ourselves with.

Relationships come in approximately eight billion flavors, from fifty-year marriages to head-nodding terms with your local barista. There are the ones you already know are worth prioritizing—family, close friends, long-standing professional ties—and then there are the looser ties that often get overlooked or undervalued, but which, properly tended, add richly to our sense of belonging and support. I'll speak to some of this infinite variety in types of connection, while ultimately zooming out (when in doubt!) to what we can say about the role of other human beings in any definition of living well and wisely.

In the Buddhist tradition there is a recounting of a conversation between the Buddha and his cousin and main attendant, Ananda.

Ananda enthusiastically suggested that good companions were half the holy life. In a classic bit of overstatement for a guy who also proclaimed a need for the middle way, the Buddha replied: "'Don't say that, Ananda. Don't say that. Admirable friendship, admirable companionship, admirable camaraderie is actually the whole of the holy life."

Whether it is half, or the whole, or maybe two-thirds or three-quarters, the truth at the heart of the Buddha's statement is that the people around us are more than fellow travelers. In this chapter we'll cover the science and wisdom of exactly how and why our relationships are so valuable, how to recognize when they need attention, and how to find new sources of community, even (or especially) when we feel most alone.

In retrospect, I should have recognized from the beginning of *The One You Feed* that there is no such thing as a lone wolf. A wolf alone in the wild, any biologist will tell you, is a sick wolf. And the parable referenced in the title isn't "inside you there is one wolf," after all.

NO (HAPPY) MAN IS AN ISLAND

When it comes to the link between relationships and the good life, Robert Waldinger fits just about every definition of "expert." He is a professor of psychiatry at Harvard Medical School, a Zen teacher, and the director of the Harvard Study of Adult Development, the longest-running study of personal happiness ever conducted. The study has followed the lives of hundreds of individuals for over eighty-five years now, tracking their well-being through triumphs and struggles, marriages and divorces, careers and retirements. What began as a study of privileged undergraduates, paired with underprivileged boys from Boston, would grow to encompass their spouses, children, and descendants.

Reflecting on his decades of research in our interview, he had a concise takeaway: "If we had to take all eighty-four years of the study and boil it down to a single principle for living . . . it would be this: Good relationships keep us healthier and happier. Period."

At first, he and his team found this conclusion tough to believe. Their initial hypothesis pointed at blood pressure and cholesterol as key indicators of well-being in old age—traditional measures of what it means to feel physically fit. But as their research unfolded decade after decade, and as other studies broadened the field and replicated their results, one of the clearest messages was that the quality of our relationships holds sway over both our happiness and our health.

Waldinger compared relationships to stress regulators, explaining that a gesture as simple as a partner taking your hand in a tense moment "literally makes blood pressure go down." On the flip side, in the absence of warm, stable relationships—or worse, in the presence of toxic ones—the body's stress response remains on high alert, degrading multiple systems over time. (Think of redlining a car's engine, over and over.) Connecting with friends and family isn't just a feel-good ideal, it turns out, but a lifeline. Psychologist Nicholas Epley observed that a lack of strong relationships often contributes more to unhappiness and psychical stress than a lack of financial resources.

For many of us, the above may come as an inconvenient truth. Community used to be something we couldn't escape from—it was simply there, part of the default setting of being human on an evolutionary level. Losing your tribe(s) used to mean losing your survival. It wasn't a choice; it was everything. As animals, we've never really lost that instinct for close, layered social bonds, but we've also never had to re-create them from scratch.

Now, we have choices—too many, maybe. The opportunity cost of reaching out or opting in is high when there are so many appealing ways to spend our time alone, most of which don't demand anything from us. It's easy to say you want community because it feels like the right thing to do, but it's harder to convince yourself to go to a neighborhood dinner or take a work acquaintanceship to the next level when the lure of Netflix is strong and infinitely accessible. And let's be honest, the moment something new is asked of us—our time, our energy, our vulnerability—the appeal of whoever is doing the asking is in danger of fading. Sit in the back of a town board meeting? Maybe. Actually have to, say, spearhead a park cleanup day, or head up the carpool, or host the next PTA meeting? Another thing entirely.

In his landmark work, *Bowling Alone*, sociologist Robert Putnam documented the decline of many of America's longest-serving social hubs, from churches, to civic clubs (do *you* belong to the Elks Lodge?), to once-robust recreation outlets like bowling leagues. Putnam's book was published in 2000, before the internet gave us most of its thousand new ways to feel connected-but-not-really and the COVID pandemic gave us all permanent Zoom fatigue. Today more people live alone than ever, and many (especially men) report having few to no close friends.

Okay, so that's the bad news. We need other people whether we like it or not, and the modern conveniences that have eroded traditional sources of connection aren't filling the void. The good news is that there are more ways to build strong relationships, and more ways in which they can add meaningfully to our lives, than we tend to realize. Assembling a personal tribe takes time, effort, and reinforcement of the basic building blocks of connection. In other words, it takes a little-by-little approach. It also takes a middle-way approach to the idea of what constitutes a worthwhile relationship or community, which is to say, knowing which ties genuinely serve us, without letting some idea of "perfect" be the enemy of the good. It can be the most surprising bonds that end up feeling most valuable of all.

I've found it useful to think about four basic ways in which community and relationships enrich our lives:

- **IDENTIFICATION.** To see ourselves in others, and to be seen, is to feel—and be—less alone.

- **ENCOURAGEMENT.** A helping hand or partner in arms equals momentum, accountability, and solidarity.

- **DISCERNMENT.** We often can't see ourselves or our situations clearly from the inside.

- **EMERGENCE.** When things really are greater than the sum of their parts.

One relationship might serve more than one of these roles. The closer and longer-term a bond is, the more likely it will evolve across roles. But connections that stay in one lane are also well worth cultivating; growing with a relationship often means being realistic about what you're asking of it, and celebrating its value often goes hand in hand with accepting its limits. At the same time, if a relationship or community offers *none* of the above, or if it offers them in reverse—if time spent with a person or group tends to leave you feeling alienated, discouraged, or like you've lost perspective instead of gained it—you're in red-flag city.

The devil's in the details with all of this. So are a lot of angels, and so are the social works-in-progress that are all of us in between. In the next section we'll explore what makes various kinds of community so worth cultivating—and then we'll get into how to actually seek out and build those worthwhile relationships.

Let's dig into what works and what doesn't.

Identification

We've already encountered some of the power of identification. It's the recognition of common humanity that Dr. Kristin Neff calls essential to self-compassion, and the perspective-enhancing answer to "Is it personal?" (Probably not.) Identifying shared experience or sensibilities can do wonders to create trust and intimacy, at any scale from one-on-one to much larger groups. One of the most powerful social movements of recent years had as its rallying cry two simple words: "Me too."

Without diminishing these truths, there is also more to identification than realizing we're not alone.

I don't know what I expected when I first cracked open the AA Big Book, but it sure wasn't sobbing like a baby two pages in. I had never heard anyone describe addiction without turning it into some tragic romance or cautionary tale. There it was—the fear, the confusion, that sense of being torn in two that I had been living with. Someone else had felt it. Someone else had survived it.

And that was the start. As I progressed in the program, I found comfort in the idea that I wasn't some broken, one-off freak. Other addicts felt like I did, thought like I did, hurt like I did—and they got better. That epiphany was healing. The kind of healing that makes you feel less isolated, more connected to the world.

But just realizing I wasn't alone didn't keep me sober. I had to see how other people made it out of the mess. This second element of identification is where we watch how others cope with the challenges of life. As Gershen Kaufman wrote in his book *The Psychology of*

Shame: Theory and Treatment of Shame-Based Syndromes, "Knowing how another human being functions on the inside—handling the vicissitudes of life, coping with joys and frustrations, facing critical choices, meeting failure and defeat as well as challenge and success—enables the child or adolescent to feel prepared for life."

Bill Wilson captured this idea in his first meeting with Dr. Bob Smith. "You see, our talk was a completely mutual thing . . . I knew that I needed this alcoholic as much as he needed me." One of the outcomes of that meeting was the idea of each member of AA having—and eventually being—a sponsor, which is best thought of as a guide for life in recovery. The program suggests choosing someone with character traits or life choices that you want to emulate.

I learned what this meant, as with so many things, the hard way.

My first attempt at picking a sponsor was based on his name, Thor. Who doesn't want a hammer-wielding god associated with lightning, thunder, and storms as their guide? My second sponsor I chose, I'm equally embarrassed to say, because he drove a Mercedes. It seems that years of being a penniless heroin addict caused me to really want money. With all due respect to these men, it turned out I had little in common with them on any level but the most superficial—and this didn't make for a helpful road map to the next chapter of my life.

Eventually, I figured out that the real criteria for choosing a sponsor were things like kindness, thoughtfulness, and experience with staying sober while raising a child. In other words, I learned that the right approach was to choose a guide consistent with my values. Watching my guides live was key: not just hearing what they said, but seeing what they did—in meetings, at home, in the chaos of everyday life. How did they deal with stress? How did they show up when life was less than perfect?

I hope it's not a stretch to apply this to your own life. Who have your own guides been? Your mentors, the people you've looked up to, either as you target specific goals or as you contemplate future chapters of your life? Have you had any "Thor" or "guy with Mercedes" detours, walking a mile in shoes that don't quite fit? Is there any chance you're on one of those detours now?

• • •

Stay with me for one more beat in the AA trenches. It's not just your sponsor you learn from—it's the whole group. And in this context, the people you identify with readily are no less valuable than those who, at first, might seem miles from sharing common ground with you.

When I first got sober at twenty-four years old, I was still living with my dad out in the Columbus suburbs. At local recovery meetings I was surrounded by people much older than me—most in their late thirties or well into their lives. I often felt like an outsider looking in, like I was going to this party for adults who hadn't invited me. Things changed when I moved into a halfway house and found an AA group with a younger crowd, closer to Ohio University: I recall walking into the meeting room and feeling like I'd been hearing music in the wrong key, then suddenly found a melody I recognized. I was thrilled and, frankly, terrified—I was extremely self-conscious, and was barely ninety days sober. But I saw a glimpse of what real belonging could look like.

Slowly, I began to fit in. I made friends, and this group gave me something I wasn't getting from the older crowd: Yet, over time, I also found myself missing the richness and variety that the larger, more diverse meetings offered. One line in the AA literature says, "We are people who normally would not mix." And there was a profound truth in that. I saw myself reflected back in people who, on the surface, could not be more different from me but were united by the shared understanding of what it's like to suffer under addiction.

We need both the intimacy of the small, close-knit circle and the diversity of the bigger group. It's a paradox of community in general. We need places where we feel confident in being understood, so that we can take new steps to open up and learn what it feels like to belong. And we also need the places that challenge us to exit our comfort zones, to bridge distances with those we may not have realized we could relate to at all.

This gets at the final piece of using identification wisely, which is to recognize its limits. Identification does not mean imitation, nor does it mean closing the doors to difference. As important as it can be to say "Me too!" or "I want to be like you!" it's equally important to be able to say "I am who *I* am, and you are who *you* are." Each of us can be only our own self, working toward the best version of ourselves. However much you identify with someone, whether they're your father, your friend, your boss, your sponsor, or your own child—to reduce that feeling to "we're the same" is to create a prison for everyone involved, most of all yourself.

Okay, that got a little intense. Bottom line: To make "we're the same" a condition for community is to leave yourself with no one new to meet and nowhere new to grow. But by looking widely for common ground, we can figure out how to be ourselves, a little better each day.

Encouragement

My arms are trembling, my hands slick with sweat. I feel completely exhausted. "I'm done," I say, expecting to be lowered back down. "Just rest a minute and try again," my climbing instructor responds calmly. Frustrated, I take a breath and give it another shot. "I can't—I'm really done," I insist, hoping he'll finally let me down.

"Hang on," he says again. "Rest. Then try it again. Maybe a different way." On my fifth attempt—certain this time that I have nothing left—I somehow find a way to haul myself up with one final surge of effort. Exhausted but victorious, I glance down at my instructor, who only moments ago I was cursing for refusing to lower me. Now, it hits me: He wasn't ignoring my limits. He was challenging me to push past them. Without him, I would have given up halfway.

The fact that encouragement helps us to reach our goals might seem like a point from Captain Obvious. But just how helpful it can be is remarkable. One of the most insightful studies on how the people around us boost our success is Rena Wing and Robert Jeffery's 1999 research on social support in weight loss programs, which showed that participants who entered a weight loss program with friends had significantly better outcomes than those who signed up alone. Over a ten-month period, people who participated with a group of three others not only had greater weight loss, but they were also far more likely to maintain it after the program—66 percent of those who joined with friends maintained their weight loss, versus only 24 percent of those who joined alone. That's nearly triple the success rate.

What's particularly fascinating about this study is that the results weren't just about showing up with friends. Participants were also more engaged when social support strategies were built into the program, in the form of things like team-based activities and group competitions. Even when total strangers were put together into teams, working together in what I would call mandatory fun, the support that emerged was real.

It's a reminder that encouragement can come in many forms. Sometimes this means solidarity: knowing that your peer is going through what you're going through, being able to commiserate, share strategies, and check in emotionally. Other times support comes from a cheerleader who can bring new perspective. With my rock climbing, it wasn't that I didn't have the strength or the training to climb the rock. I got myself most of the way there on my own. But when I hit the wall, I needed my coach. He believed in my ability when I couldn't believe in myself. He held the rope steady so I could lean back, catch my breath, and shake out my aching muscles. And he held me there a little longer than I thought I could manage, just so I could find the courage to try again.

Still other times, the secret sauce of encouragement is accountability. People who participate in Facebook health communities are 15 percent more likely to achieve their health goals compared to those who don't engage in these online communities. The comments, likes, and shares are part of the boost to motivation, but it seems that the most powerful part is the act of sharing itself. People who regularly share their physical activity on social media are 20 percent more likely to maintain consistent exercise habits, and those who post before-and-after pictures were shown to have a 25 percent higher success rate in reaching their fitness goals. By publicly committing to their goals, these posters create a contract for change that is harder to break than the kind we make without witnesses.

Social media may not be your thing, and that's more than okay. Encouragement, like community in general, comes in a few billion flavors. The truth to accept is that there are moments in life, whether we're striving for a goal or just trying to survive, when our own strength isn't enough. We need someone to hold us steady, to insist we keep going, and to see the potential in us that we can't. Or at the very least, to see that we're trying.

The influence of encouragement can be a double-edged sword, as evidenced by another kernel of recovery wisdom: "If you stay in the barbershop long enough, you're bound to get a haircut." Which is to say, for better *and* for worse, you're susceptible to the energy of those around you. If you're feeling peer pressure to maintain a healthy lifestyle, great! But if your friend group is all about the joys of heroin, well . . . not so great.

The answer is not to weather challenging times alone. The answer is to be generous and wide-ranging in asking for and offering support, and to stay mindful of whether the encouragement we're receiving actually points us toward our goals. We stand on the shoulders of giants, and we didn't get up there without a good climbing instructor.

Discernment

Imagine standing in front of a foggy mirror, trying to make sense of your own reflection. No matter how hard you look, the details remain blurry. That's what it's like to try to see ourselves in the midst of difficult situations. Remember Solomon's paradox in chapter 5—named after the biblical king famous for his wisdom, who could give sound advice to others but struggled to make good decisions for himself? When we're too close to a situation, we're entangled in the nuances of our own fears and biases. What we need at moments like this is *discernment*.

Discernment comes from the Latin word *discernere*, meaning "to separate." It's about separating what's important or true from what's not—whether it's understanding what's truly driving a situation, sensing what might be the best path forward, or distinguishing between what's genuinely good and what just appears that way.

Should I stay in this job or get a new one? Is what my husband did really a bad thing or am I just too sensitive? I found weed in my son's pocket when I was doing the laundry, what's the best way to handle that? Community can provide the missing clarity in such complex personal situations—but only if we ask the right questions.

The key in seeking discernment is to distinguish it from encouragement. What we usually want when we're in an emotionally fraught place is unequivocal validation. We might say we want a "sounding board," but what we really want is to be told that we are right. We want to hear that our interpretation is correct, we should be upset, and honestly good for us for reacting exactly like we did.

It's become a common trope in pop psychology that this is all people need when talking through a challenge. They don't need someone to fix them, or to offer solutions—only someone to listen and understand. As with much of our sound-bite culture, there's a partial truth here. Real, generous listening, the kind done with curiosity and empathy, is a skill and a gift in any relationship. But to seek only head-nodding agreement is to miss out on the wisdom of a wider perspective.

For a closer look at this trade-off, let's visit Becky and Jess.

Becky sat slumped on her couch, phone pressed against her ear, the whole story of a long week of restless nights told by puffy eyes. On the other end, Jess's voice was low and concerned; for the third time that evening, Becky started in on the details of the fallout of her latest fight with her boyfriend, Greg. It wasn't the first time they'd reached this point. Whenever things got rocky in Becky's life—work stress or family drama, or, like now, the spiraling mess of her relationship—Jess was the person she went to. And Jess was good at being there. Maybe too good.

Every time Becky hesitated, trying to back away from her rant, Jess pulled her back in. "I can't believe he said that to you," Jess interjected heatedly. "You deserve so much better." And with that spark of validation, Becky would plunge back into every detail—Greg's dismissive tone, his failure to reply to her texts, how she'd felt ignored and invalidated.

As weeks went by, it was more of the same. They would dissect every interaction. It felt great at first—to have someone in her corner, confirming that her feelings were valid, that Greg's behavior wasn't okay. But as the nights stacked up, so did Becky's anxiety. Far from giving her much-needed perspective or clarity on the issues, the conversations almost seemed to feed her worries, making them all the larger and more hopeless.

When they hung up each night, there was a sense of satisfaction—through all that shared intimacy, their friendship had grown stronger. But beneath the sincerely warm feeling, Becky was more troubled than ever. She knew she was starting to fear even minor interactions with Greg, expecting something to go wrong. And the more and more Jess validated her fears, the deeper those fears became. They were caught in what psychologist Amanda Rose calls a *co-rumination cycle*—the corrosive dynamic in which talking about problems with a friend feels like a show of support but is really miring a person deeper in negative emotions.

When we share our pain, we often get a sense of relief, a temporary lightening of our load. And this has real upsides, not only lessening our pain but nurturing our connection to the person or people we've trusted to hear us out, as Jess and Becky felt with each other. But true recovery, Belgian psychologist Bernard Rimé argues, only happens when sharing leads to *cognitive reappraisal*—when we are helped to see the situation from a genuinely new angle.

Timing and context matter when it comes to getting to the stage of reappraisal. If we try to offer solutions too soon, then attempts at reframing will fail. Think of any time you've told a friend "Have you tried . . . ?" Or "Have you thought about . . . ?" only to instantly regret it, or when you've heard the same questions and responded with "AS IF I DIDN'T THINK OF THAT" or "EXCUSE ME, I AM ONLY ONE-THIRD THROUGH THIS RANT." (Just me?) All of us need to feel heard and validated before we can truly be open to other perspectives.

One of the best examples of striking this balance are the Circles of Trust created by spiritual guide and author Parker Palmer, based on a Quaker tradition known as listening circles. I've had the pleasure of interviewing Parker multiple times over the years, and I continue to find him a source of deep wisdom and inspiration.

"Left to our own devices," Palmer writes in his book *A Hidden Wholeness*, "we have an endless capacity for self-absorption and self-deception." By this he means Solomon's paradox in action: the fact that it is simply impossible, some of the time, to see ourselves clearly. His Circles of Trust are built on the principle of deep listening without judgment or advice. Here, people are invited to show up as they are, with all their doubts, fears, and hopes, and to speak their truths into a space held with reverence. He told me that "we need communities that practice 'no fixing, no saving, no advising, and no correcting.'" Instead, participants offer only open-ended questions to guide the speaker to more fully articulate their own perspective.

At first this may seem like emotional support with no cognitive reframing. But the format of open-ended questions nudges participants toward new thoughts and away from simple validation that whatever they already think (or *think* they think) is the whole truth. Palmer himself realized in a listening circle that a prestigious university job he had just been offered wasn't what he wanted at all—despite coming into the circle eagerly talking up how great the opportunity was. Each question from his peers prompted him to shed another layer of rote justification and get at the heart of how he really felt.

If discernment boils down to one thing, it is this: Ask more questions. When you're done being listened to, ask for advice, far and wide. Any one person or group will have their own biases about your situation, and that's okay; even the wisest of us see through our own reality-tinting glasses. Your coupled-up friends might encourage you to make it work with the relationship you're in, while your single friends might encourage you to rethink it. (Your parents just want grandkids.) Your local friends might encourage you not to take a job in another city. That's no argument for not seeking their perspectives—it's an argument for asking around even farther and wider.

Emergence

There is an idea that has long haunted me. It is the claim that you are the average of the five people you spend the most time around.

This line bothers me because it seems so true, and yet I hate the sentiment. It's almost always used by people from hustle culture; it is attributed to Jim Rohn but you hear it everywhere, used in the sense of making you more successful, more productive, more eyes-on-the-prize. To be fair, a lot of what I've said in this chapter would seem to support it. Hang out in the barbershop, and you're going to get a haircut—but hang out with people who dream big and work diligently, and receive the encouragement you need to reach your goals. Identify with the people you actually want to be like, not the guy with the cool name or car. Seek new perspectives from people with wisdom to give.

Yet I resist the line. My biggest objection is that it treats relationships as commodities—acquisitions to be added up and used for the purpose of making ourselves better. If we want relationships that feel like more than transactions, the kind that make up half or three-quarters or all of a fulfilling life, we shouldn't always be asking, *What am I getting from this?*

I also take issue with the simple math of the expression above. As long as we're looking quantitatively at how our relationships enrich us, I think the insinuation that the outcome is an average is all wrong. Personal-influence-divided-by-x; a result the size of a self, a pastiche put together from a few other selves—this vision of the time we spend with others misses out on one of the greatest benefits of being in community with others.

This brings me to emergence.

Scientists use "emergence" to describe effects that only appear when large groups are together. These could be large groups of atoms, which, when together, act in new ways to produce the complex systems we call chemistry; large groups of flora and fauna, which together produce the ballet of coexistence we call ecosystems. Or humans—who, back in the day, gave rise to civilization simply by deciding to stick around one another long enough to build something together. (I'm no historian, but at that level of generalization, I think I'm safe.)

For our purposes, emergence is the truth that not only are two heads better than one—in the right circumstance, they can do things one head simply never could. The magic of relationships in all configurations, from one-on-one to larger groups, is that they can produce results greater than the sum of their parts. Insights, creativity, ambition, wisdom.

The Beatles are a perfect example. As Ian Leslie put it in our conversation about his wonderful book *John and Paul*, "There was something about their combination that brought out this third thing—something neither of them could have done alone." John and Paul "completed each other's thoughts," and had an "almost instinctive ability to shape, challenge, and complete each other's ideas," he said. "It's like they were extensions of the same creative mind." Each brought something distinct, but it was the dynamic between them—friction and flow—that sparked the brilliance.

In a recent *Nature* article, scientists Itai Yanai and Martin Lercher shared their favorite approach for generating new ideas: "Talk to someone." They explain that when you talk, it's not just about exchanging insights—you're actually creating new thoughts in real time. Ideas that would never have germinated in your own head, or your conversation partner's, suddenly take shape in dialogue. They note that speaking forces our messy web of thoughts into something more structured and logical, turning chaos into a coherent stream of words. In an added boost, conversation partners gain motivation from the process.

The key insight here is not that you're just adding your thoughts to someone else's, ending up with twice the thoughts. You're generating new ideas by the very process of conversation: $1 + 1 = 3$. Yanai and Lercher suggest that two is the ideal number for these discussions: large enough to spark creativity but small enough to stay focused (and avoid any grandstanding).

"A single bracelet does not jingle." This Congolese proverb is, to me, about emergence. It's about the kind of beauty and creativity that can only exist in communion with others.

Speaking of beauty, I'm sitting this morning writing from the lovely Honfleur, a French town nestled among orchard trees and facing the Seine estuary, staying in what used to be a modest inn that helped launch an artistic revolution. Here, at La Ferme Saint-Siméon, with its rustic charm and simple accommodations, in the mid-nineteenth century a group of artists found more than just lodging. The inn's communal dining room became an informal salon, where painters like Claude Monet, Eugène Boudin, and Johan Jongkind gathered for camaraderie after long days of outdoor painting. Over hearty Norman fare and flowing cider, they exchanged ideas, techniques, and critiques, each conversation adding another brushstroke to the emerging picture of Impressionism.

It was here that the young Monet began to see the world through new eyes. The mentorship he received at La Ferme Saint-Siméon wasn't confined to formal lessons, but took place in shared moments of observation, in discussions about light and color, and in the collective pursuit of capturing the ephemeral on canvas.

By Monet's own account, his situation was one of an individual mentorship, with Boudin, nestled amid a larger group. Boudin had told Monet he was wasting his talents doing caricatures in Paris, and had been the one to invite him along on painting trips around Honfleur in the first place, encouraging him to paint the natural world. Monet afterward described the experience as an epiphany: "It was as if a veil suddenly lifted from my eyes."

But the lightning strike that was the Ferme Saint-Siméon scene was also collective. While each artist maintained a unique style, their group presence fostered a shared, emergent vision—one that sought to capture the transient effects of light, the movement of clouds, and the essence of place. As they painted side by side, experimenting and encouraging one another, the artists reached toward a radical rethinking of what art could be, paving the way for a new era of visual expression.

Okay, so not all of us are going to go on vacation with our friends and come back with a new artistic movement. But we can all experience the kind of interplay between small-circle intimacy and larger-group richness that Monet found at Saint-Siméon. Lord knows I accomplished things through AA I would never have been able to do on my own, and part of that was simply knowing I was a part of something bigger than myself. There was nothing average about the experience of realizing my life had been saved.

JOINING THE CLUB(S)

Up to this point in the chapter we've focused on the *what* of community: the rewards that make relationships of all kinds worth cultivating. But I'll admit I've been stingy on the *how*. Among the questions I get most often from students and clients: How do you make new friends as an adult? How do you find groups that feel stimulating rather than draining? How do you find a partner? How do you deepen the relationships you already have?

If I had the answers to all of the above I'd be, as they say, a rich man (and each of those things is a book on its own). Or maybe I'd be the Buddha. In any case, what I do have are some expert insights and a little more advice from a lifetime of trial and (a lot of) error.

Slow and Steady and Mutual

To speak another inconvenient truth, connection doesn't just happen—it's something that takes intention, effort, and often patience. Even in the best of circumstances, community requires work. In my early days in AA, I learned that I wasn't just there to take. I was there to contribute, even in small ways, like washing ashtrays (yes, people smoked indoors back then—hard to imagine now) or greeting newcomers. I was encouraged to walk around, shake hands, and welcome others. This was an enormous lesson: that I wasn't just there to receive, I was there to give, and that giving is (paradoxically) what makes a relationship more than a transaction.

Mutuality is the key. It's about understanding that relationships are reciprocal, that our participation matters. This is how we move from feeling like outsiders to feeling like we belong. We offer what we can, even if it's small, and we remain open to what others offer in return.

Still, these things take time. Research by Jeffrey Hall has shown that transitioning from an acquaintance to a casual friend takes approximately 94 hours, from a casual friend to a friend about 164 hours, and from a friend to a close or best friend an average of 219 hours.

It's no wonder that so many of our friendships as adults form in the workplace, where we naturally accumulate hours together. Sharing meaningful experiences can help to shorten this window (Have you ever gotten real deep, real fast with someone while traveling?), as can being willing to get vulnerable in conversation, which means giving the gift of trust. Even then, patience is necessary. The process of truly integrating into a community requires us to endure the initial discomfort of being on the outside.

This has been one of my biggest barriers to finding new communities in adulthood. Many times I've attended a meeting or event once or twice, not felt a deep connection with anyone, and decided it wasn't right for me. My introverted tendencies have made it easy to retreat. When I began volunteering with Food Rescue US, for a long time I stayed with it only because I cared about the mission.

My role was solitary—picking up perishable surplus food and delivering it to places that needed it. But one summer, we started receiving a semitruck of produce every Saturday morning, and it required a group effort to unload and distribute. Suddenly, I was surrounded by other volunteers, many of whom already knew each other. The first week, I barely spoke. The second week, there were a few smiles, a few greetings. Slowly, over the course of the summer, I began to come out of my shell. By the end, I was laughing and joking with others—feeling like I belonged. It took longer than I might have liked, but it was exactly as long as I needed.

Choosing Your Tribes

We often hold ourselves back from community because we want it to be perfect. We want to immediately feel a sense of belonging, to be welcomed with open arms, to find people who understand us without effort. But this expectation is what keeps us from finding what we're looking for. We need to be willing, instead, to look for opportunities that stretch us. Real communities are messy. They're imperfect. They require us to show up—not just physically, but emotionally—and to do so repeatedly. They require us to prioritize connection over comfort.

What is worth considering is where you'll have the time and space to integrate. A weekly hiking group, a consistent book club, a regular volunteer shift—these kinds of ongoing commitments give connection the time it needs to take root. It's not that shorter-term activities or workshops are a bad idea, but if our goal is to make meaningful connections, we need to either move quickly or accept that it might not happen. In those cases, I've found it helpful to identify just one person I seem to resonate with and make an effort to follow up. More than one can feel overwhelming, but one connection? That's manageable.

Ultimately, it's better to invest deeply in one community rather than remain on the surface with several. True connection means sticking around even when we feel awkward or out of place, trusting that those feelings will eventually fade. It means understanding that there will always be people we don't click with, always moments of doubt. If we continue to show up, we give ourselves the chance to find something real.

One bit of good news is that "social fitness," our ability to connect with others, is similar to any other kind of fitness—which is to say, it can improve. Building social fitness is like returning to physical exercise after a long break, in that it feels awkward, exhausting, and unnatural at first. When we restart a fitness routine, we often think, *I don't remember it being this hard.* The discomfort can make it tempting to give up, but over time, we catch our stride, and things get easier as our muscles grow stronger. Social fitness works the same way: The more we practice, the more natural it becomes. Just as our bodies adapt to physical workouts, our social muscles need consistent use to develop.

More good news comes from Robert Waldinger, the Harvard happiness expert. Community is not a one-size-fits-all prescription, Waldinger says. Some people thrive with a few close friends, whereas others need a broader network. It is not about the number of relationships in our lives; it's about recognizing and paying attention to how each of them shapes us, supports us, and makes us feel. While getting out of your comfort zone is healthy, your goal doesn't need to be becoming the world's biggest extrovert. We don't have to gather more connections just for the sake of it—only to foster the ones that help us feel seen, valued, and supported.

Where to Start

To (sort of) quote Dorothy from the end of *The Wizard of Oz*, start right here in your own backyard. When many of us think of building our social lives we think about finding new communities, but it's always worth looking first at the connections we have, even (or especially) the ones we've allowed to fray.

Whether by choice, chance, or obligation, all of us can claim membership in many communities already. Family and friends count, and so does your neighborhood, your workplace, your kids' school, the library, a local religious community, your coffee shop, the dog park, even your favorite subreddit or Facebook group. (Online communities can be real too—it just takes participation and reciprocity, same as any other!) Where do you go at least once a month? Where are you getting emails from (that aren't spam)? Who's in your text history? This is your community backyard. Where might you want to deepen our involvement? What relationships do you want to nurture?

As with everything in this book, it's about small, repeated actions. Maybe it's reaching out to someone we haven't spoken to in a while. Maybe it's offering to help with an event, or simply showing up more consistently. Whatever it is, it starts with choosing to invest our time and our energy. It starts with choosing to reach out, even when it's uncomfortable, even when it feels uncertain.

I often spend just half an hour going back through all my text messages and seeing who I haven't talked to for a while. I'm surprised by how many texts from people I care about got very little or often no (the horror!) response from me.

If you're looking for ways to expand your community backyard, maybe your workplace offers affinity groups or social committees you haven't explored yet. Websites like Meetup.com can connect you with groups passionate about environmental action, animal welfare, women's rights, or just about any shared interest you can imagine. Religious communities often have smaller interest groups within them too, if that resonates with you.

Another of Waldinger's findings over the years is that it is not just about having relationships, but about sustaining a relationship through the chaos called life. "When I was in my twenties, I thought, well, I have my friends, and they'll always be there," he told me. But as time went on, he watched as good relationships often withered from neglect. His solution? Intentional, consistent effort. "Now I make sure I go on walks with friends every week," he said, "or send small texts—just something to remind them I'm here." Small, deliberate acts (sound familiar?) can strengthen bonds in profound ways, even with people we may not happen to see all that often.

If you find yourself fearing that whatever text you're thinking of sending right now may be awkward or ill-received, Nicholas Epley has another useful takeaway: Our fear of rejection or discomfort is typically an error in perspective. In a study called "Hello, Stranger," Epley and his colleagues encouraged London train commuters to strike up a conversation with a total stranger, then surveyed them before and after their act of social bravery. What they found was a pretty familiar pattern: People thought talking to a stranger would be awkward. Then they did it—and actually felt better. Not just "not awkward," but uplifted.

Epley kept pulling the thread. What if it's not just small talk? What about saying thank you or doing something kind? Same thing. People wrote gratitude letters or gave tiny gifts and almost always guessed wrong about how it would land. They thought it'd feel weird or be met with blank stares. Turns out, people were moved. Genuinely moved. Even deeper stuff—asking real questions, getting personal—people tend to steer clear of because they assume it'll be uncomfortable. But Epley's research shows those kinds of conversations ended up being the most rewarding. Less awkward, more meaningful, and they leave both people feeling more connected. We are not great at predicting how social interactions will go. And most of the time, we're selling them short.

The main takeaway from Epley's work is that our expectations about social interactions are often incorrect. This is perhaps no surprise, in the abstract, now that we're aware of operating from within our own bubbles of bias; but it's still something that takes practice to overcome in the moment. By pushing past our fears of discomfort or rejection—whether it's by striking up a conversation with a stranger, reconnecting with someone we've fallen out of touch with, or performing an act of kindness—we have only our preconceptions to lose.

CHOSEN FAMILY

One of the most rewarding parts of teaching my Wise Habits program over the years has been the friendships that form between my students. Some of the program's small weekly discussion groups, in particular, really take on a life of their own.

Jane's Wise Habits group has been meeting weekly for nearly five years. (The program was eight weeks!) They are, she writes, "quite an eclectic group at first glance—there are six of us, we have a thirty-year age range, we are from six different states and two different time zones. We work in different professions, some of us have families and some do not and each of us had very different life paths." Yet, she says, "over time we have become a chosen family."

Reflecting on where they were five years ago as the first meeting approached, members said: "I felt like it was just one more thing to do that I didn't have time for," "I was terrified of being seen," "My expectations were low but I thought maybe I'd learn a thing or two," "I already had a weekly guys' night, I didn't need another weekly group, and besides, small groups never last and I didn't want to be disappointed."

But they all showed up anyway. And then they kept showing up. And with patience, empathy, and courage, they trusted one another enough to get vulnerable (about . . . oh, you know, the stuff in this book) and invited the same in return. Today, Jane writes, "We have cocreated a space of practice, accountability, compassion, non-judgment, acceptance, and deep connection."

They get in the weeds of real life, practicing both encouragement and discernment. "We have supported each other during big life challenges like divorce, job changes, the death of a parent, geographical moves, illnesses and caring for elderly parents, as well as the daily frustrations of life," Jane writes. "We offer suggestions and different perspectives if they are asked for." And the fact that they are so eclectic is a plus. "We each bring our own natural talents, abilities, and strengths to the group and we each do our part. There is no BS, our conversations are real and deep and ones that often we can't have anywhere else in our lives." At the same time, they feel these conversations help strengthen other relationships: "We are better family members, community members, neighbors, coworkers, and friends because of our work together.

"While most of our work together is done via Zoom, our virtual connection has led to multiple in-person meetups. The meetups are full of laughter, tears, the tightest hugs. . . . We leave each other feeling nourished." And then they show up to talk the next week, again and again.

• • •

I end with Jane's story not to give the reader FOMO, but because it's a perfect encapsulation of so many truths about healthy, sustaining relationships. Here were six complete strangers, not even in the same time zone, who took the leap to connect with one another, little by little. We can all do the same.

"It's never too late," says Robert Waldinger, in what I think is one of his most important findings of all. Across his decades-long study, he saw that many of the people who were followed "have these surprising events in their lives where they find relationships or they find love when they least expect it."

It's our job to keep an eye out, a door open, and a hand extended.

ONE LITTLE THING YOU CAN DO RIGHT NOW

Scroll through your phone and find someone you've been meaning to reach out to but haven't. Right now, send them something simple—"Thinking of you," "How are you doing?" or a photo that made you think of them. Don't overthink it. Your fear of an awkward or unwelcome exchange is almost always wrong, and connection happens in these small moments.

When you're ready to go a little deeper, flip to the appendix for extra exercises—or download the companion worksheets anytime at oneyoufeed.net/resources.

SETBACK. RESET. REPEAT.

In my early thirties, after my first marriage imploded, I had a serious bout of depression. There were days—despite being sober—when I could barely get out of bed. It was like I was looking at the world through a gray window, weighed down with a bone-deep sense that everything was wrong. Imagine going to the library and being unenthused by the entire concept of books, or opening Spotify and wondering how any song ever brought you joy.

All my daily rituals felt pointless and daunting. I was paralyzed in a sea of feeling (or was it numbness?) that made it impossible to keep up many of the practices that had given my life structure and meaning throughout the years of my marriage and sobriety. Exercise? Barely. Depression has a cruel paradox: It often lifts a bit when we move—but makes moving feel impossible. Eating right? Please. Cooking a meal required a level of executive functioning I was currently using to stare blankly at the same wall for forty-five minutes.

It was a long road back from that place.

Part of what makes depression so hard to deal with—what has made *my* depression so hard to deal with—is that there are too many doors to walk through, too many treatments, too many variables. If addiction was a locked room with a single key, depression was a house of mirrors. Every turn offered a different reflection of the problem, each one pointing to a different solution.

One of the most significant realizations I had during this time was less about depression itself, exactly, than about the feelings of shame I let build up around it. My inner monologue reminded me constantly that I was failing to keep up with everything *else* in my life. This was never going to motivate me to get better, I finally realized. Quite the opposite: It was compounding my sense of the futility of getting out of bed.

Depression might be what sidelines you in pursuit of your goals for growth and change, or it might be some huge unforeseen event, or it might be nothing big at all. What I can confidently predict is that you, too, will find yourself off track.

This section is about what to do next. However far you think you've strayed from your best-laid plans, a key part of any journey toward wiser habits is being able to reorient and keep going. One step at a time.

• • •

To reiterate the bad news: You're going to get off track. That's not some cynical prediction—it's just reality.

Whether you're trying to exercise more, be truly present with your family, write every day, or just practice a little self-compassion along the way, you're going to stumble.

You're going to miss some days, forget, resist, and sometimes outright rebel against the changes you're trying to make.

This is where most of us think the story ends. We blew it. We're not cut out to be the best version of ourselves. We don't have what it takes to live according to our values. We've failed. But that's just the voice of shame trying to narrate your life. The truth is, that moment isn't the end of the story. It's a pivot point.

If you take one thing away from this section, let it be this: Don't think of these moments in terms of failure at all. "Failure" suggests some final, conclusive state of being, and that's not what getting off track is. It's a setback, and setbacks are part of the process.

In recovery, we have some very imperfect—but strangely useful—language around setbacks. We talk about *slips* and *relapses*. A slip is a one-time stumble: an unplanned drink, a bad decision, a moment of forgetting. It's like hitting a bump but staying on the road. A relapse, on the other hand, is when we veer off completely—when the internal "why bother" takes over and we stop trying altogether. Here's the important part: A slip *can* lead to a relapse—but it doesn't have to. It's the story you tell yourself about the slip that determines what happens next.

Maybe you planned to work out five times this week. You make it once. That's a slip. But if your next thought is "I always screw this up" or "I just don't have discipline," you're flirting with relapse—not because of your behavior, but because of the meaning you've attached to it.

A *slip* is part of the path. A *reset* is how we stay on it. And what we need to reset in these moments isn't more judgment; it's a system for getting back on track. We've already seen tools that help us reset—self-compassion that reframes mistakes as learning, perspective that lets us zoom out, and support from people who bring both encouragement and discernment. Even though you and I are trying to take things one step at a time, it's always possible to take a false step. Careful progress doesn't mean you don't make mistakes; it does, however, mean it's easier to get back on track.

But in case you don't want to reread this whole book next time you're feeling discouraged, I give you the **RENEW** framework.

THE RENEW FRAMEWORK FOR GETTING BACK ON TRACK

R–Recognize It's Normal to Get Off Track

No one does this perfectly. No one. And the people who *seem* like they do? They've just learned how to return more quickly. Setbacks are not signs of failure. They're signs that you're trying to do something hard and meaningful. Take a deep breath. This isn't the first time, and it won't be the last. But you're still in it.

E–Embrace Your Why

Remind yourself why you started. We lose momentum when we lose meaning. Your goal, whatever it is, wasn't random—it mattered to you. Reconnect with that. What is this change in service of? Who are you trying to become? Go read the note you wrote to yourself. Look at the picture. Open the journal. Remember.

N—Neutralize the Emotional Drama

This one's huge. Emotional drama is all the stuff we *add* to the setback. It's the story that says: "You always do this." "You're never going to change." "Why even try?" It's shame dressed up as insight. And it's not helping. When you notice that voice spinning up, try this: Imagine it's not you talking to yourself. Use the self-compassion playbook and imagine you're in conversation with a coach, a teacher, a friend. Would you talk to them that way? Do you think they would trust you if you did?

Your brain loves to catastrophize. To make a stumble into a failure. The truth is much simpler: You were doing something, and then you weren't. Now you can do it again. That's it.

E—Extract the Lesson

There's always something to learn if you get curious. What threw you off? Was it a certain trigger, time of day, or emotional state? Did your plan ask too much of you? Were you just tired or lonely or distracted? This isn't about blame—it's about data. Get interested in what happened, and adjust the system.

W—Walk Forward with Action

Not a grand gesture. Just one small, concrete action. Something doable. Something now. Put your shoes on. Text a friend. Take a deep breath. Drink a glass of water. Write the first sentence. Do something so small it feels almost silly. Then do another one tomorrow.

This is how momentum is built—not through resolve, but through motion.

· · ·

I've said before that no one gets it right all the time. The people who succeed at change aren't the ones who never fall off—they're the ones who keep getting back on. *Reset* becomes the most powerful skill we can develop.

Patience and Fortitude—the lions that guard the New York Public Library—are the perfect mascots for this part of the process. You'll need both. Patience, to meet yourself where you are. Fortitude, to begin again. These aren't the flashy traits. They don't make highlight reels. But they're the ones that get you through.

THE STAKES OF CHANGE

Again, if you take one thing away from this section, I hope it's that getting off track doesn't mean "failing" yourself in any permanent way. It just means a setback en route. But while I don't believe in labeling these moments as "failures," I do believe the consequences of staying stuck matter. When we think about change—whether we manage to make it or whether, yet again, we don't—we tend to measure it by its most visible results. The pounds not lost. The pages not written. The cognitive fog that creeps in when we don't get enough sleep. These are real, tangible consequences, and they matter. But I've come to believe the deeper cost of failing to change is something quieter, something we don't always notice right away.

It's the slow erosion of self-trust. The quiet crumbling of faith in ourselves.

Each time we plan on doing something and then don't—when we tell ourselves this time it is going to be different, then realize, actually, it is not—we lose a little bit of our faith in ourselves as individuals capable of shaping our own lives. It isn't simply that we get stuck in the same rut; it is that we lose our vision of our potential to be something other than that. That kind of disappointment does not always arrive in a big crisis. More often, it creeps in slowly, day by day, until one day we look up and don't even bother to try. We just assume we won't follow through.

And that's where the real danger lies—not in failing to reach a particular goal, but in the quiet shift from *I want to change* to *What's the point of trying?*

I've often told my coaching clients that what I really teach isn't just habit change, or mindset shifts, or productivity hacks. At its core, what I help people do is learn how to make and keep promises to themselves. Because that's what self-trust is: a track record of keeping our word to ourselves. Every time we follow through, even in the smallest way, we reinforce the belief that we are the kind of person who can be counted on. And when we don't, we do the opposite.

The good news is, trust—whether in a friendship or in ourselves—is built the same way it's lost: little by little. We don't have to make sweeping declarations or change everything overnight. We just have to start keeping promises again. Especially the smallest ones. Even the ones that seem too insignificant to matter. Because as we begin to believe in ourselves again, we don't just change what we do—we change what we see as possible. And we turn failure into setback, and then into success.

• • •

There's something else I want to offer you here. Something visual. Something tangible.

I had a client who was working hard to stay sober. But every time she slipped, she felt like she had to start from zero again. In the recovery world, we mark days sober—thirty days, sixty, ninety, one year. And when you mess up, you go back to day one. That can be devastating.

So she created a new system. Every day she was sober, she put a marble in a jar. Just one marble. One day. Another marble. Another day.

And over time, the jar filled up. Some days she didn't earn a marble. But she didn't throw out the jar. She just started adding again. That jar became a visible record of her progress. A proof of effort. A beautiful, lopsided, nonlinear path to change.

We need more grading systems like that. Not 0 or 100. Not all or nothing. Just forward.

We need something more like the **80 Percent Rule**. Perfection isn't the target. Never was. I've been sober for over sixteen years—zero slips, no missed days—but that level of consistency is rare even in the world of addiction recovery. In every other area of my life? I miss all the time. I forget to check in with friends. I skip meditation. I eat cinnamon rolls in cafés on vacation. Okay, that was actually a good decision—the first time, anyway.

But here's what I've found: If I do something 80 percent of the time, I get almost all the benefit. That's what I aim for. Eighty percent. That's a passing grade in any real school. If you meditate 292 days out of 365, it will change your life. If you move your body most days, you'll get stronger. If you show up for your people most of the time, you'll have real relationships. You don't need perfection. You need consistency.

And when you miss a day? A week? A month?

You reset.

You don't throw out the jar. You don't start the story over. You add another marble.

• • •

Last thing: If you've been off track for a long time, lower the bar. No shame, just recalibration.

You don't go from zero to marathon. If you haven't run in months, don't lace up with your old best time in mind. Start with a walk. A lap. A stretch. Set the difficulty level to match your current motivation—not your ideal self from a year ago. That's how you rebuild. That's how you remember you can still do this.

Let yourself start again.
Let it be imperfect.
Let it be small.
And let it count.
Because it does.

Part III

BEING

NINE

Allowing Everything to Be Exactly as It Is

> The boundary to what we can accept is
> the boundary to our freedom.
>
> —TARA BRACH

ONCE UPON A TIME THERE WAS AN OLD BUDDHIST SAGE BY THE NAME OF Milarepa. He lived in a cave, as mythical old sages sometimes do, and one day he left to gather firewood. When he returned, he found that his cave had been taken over by demons. They were everywhere: shadows twisting in the firelight, scaled bodies uncoiling, veined wings beating around his head. "Be gone!" he shouted, panicking. He lunged toward the demons, snarling and sweeping his arms. They were unfazed. Again and again he charged, kicking and grasping—but the demons were always somehow just out of reach, his limbs meeting only air. Whenever he stopped, panting, they settled back in, each to its favorite cobwebby niche or warm spot by the fire. The more he chased them, the more at home they seemed to be.

Realizing that his efforts were the definition of futile, Milarepa took a new approach. If chasing his houseguests out wouldn't work, then maybe hearing the teachings of the Buddha would change their minds. (He probably meant this in the sense of enlightenment, but I like to imagine him also wondering about some kind of vampire/crucifix-type allergic reaction.) So Milarepa took his seat and began teaching about existence and nonexistence, compassion and kindness, the nature of impermanence. After a while he looked around: All the demons were still there. They stared at him with the bulging, unblinking eyes that had become all too familiar.

At this point Milarepa let out a deep breath. The only way forward was surrender, he decided. The demons would not be manipulated into leaving; maybe he had something to learn from them. He looked deeply into the eyes of each one and bowed, saying, "It looks like we're going to be here together. I open myself to whatever you have to teach me."

In that moment all the demons but one disappeared. This hulking and especially fierce specimen, with flaring nostrils and dripping fangs, was still squatting at the edge of the firelight. Crossing the cave to it, Milarepa fully accepted his own vulnerability. "Eat me if you wish," he told the demon, and placed his head gently in its mouth.

Except that there was no mouth. At that moment the largest demon bowed low and dissolved into space.

• • •

I have a simple question for you. What would today be like if you were to *allow everything to be exactly the way it is?*

"Sure, Eric," you might say. "Reality isn't really up to me." Fair enough. What I mean is: What would it be like if you greeted everything that happens today with a default attitude of acceptance, rather than with a vision for how things could be/should be/lord-you-wish-they-were different?

Wake up and look at yourself in the mirror: no "I'm starting the diet tomorrow," no "I wonder if those expensive moisturizers actually fix wrinkles?" Just *allowing everything to be exactly as it is.*

Sit in traffic; no "Siri, you're fired," no "I think the slow-up is around the next bend? Maybe they've cleared things? . . . Maybe now?" Just *allowing everything to be exactly as it is.*

Have a conversation with a loved one in which you feel a sense of distance: no "I feel like this used to be easier," no "I just wish they weren't so ___." Just *allowing everything to be exactly as it is.*

By now you might be getting a sense of how hard, even radical, acceptance can be as a practice in daily life.

In a book about change, the idea of letting things be might seem like a swerve. It's anything but, for a host of reasons we'll get into this chapter. For a life of joy and purpose, one in which we're able to appreciate where we are while also charting our next steps forward, acceptance is one of the most worthwhile habits we can cultivate. To start answering why, here are three simple lines that may already be familiar to you:

God, grant me the serenity to accept the things I cannot change,
the courage to change the things I can,
and the wisdom to know the difference.

This is the famous Serenity Prayer, recited at nearly every AA meeting the world over. I've lived with, and tried to live by, these words for decades. We have spent a lot of time on the middle of those lines, exploring what it means to make real, lasting change. We've also explored some of the ways of thinking and being that millennia of seekers have connected to that third line: wisdom.

But both change and wisdom are targets that are always out in front of us. We are never done changing; we are never done facing the challenges that life brings our way. And I, for one, don't want my life to feel like a constant self-improvement project.

Think of a beautiful building that's always covered in scaffolding and Under Construction signs. We don't want to be in a place where we always think that real life is around the next corner. If we just had this, or did that, then we would be happy. Or think of fiddling with the dials of a thermostat: We can get sucked into trying to adjust life to meet our every expectation and desire, preoccupied by the infinity of preferences and alternatives that keep us out of the moment and in our own heads. The renovations on that building will never be done, and "perfect" is not a temperature setting on that thermostat.

This is where acceptance comes in.

In the TTM (one more time: The Transtheoretical Model of Behavior Change), the last phase of change is known as maintenance. It's what comes after all the steps covered in part I of this book: precontemplation (*thinking about* thinking about change, which relates to the values work in chapter 2), contemplation (thinking about change, aka getting specific with your goals), preparation (minimizing the need for self-control with all the structural setup in chapter 3), and Action (the choice point strategies of chapter 4).

In the long middle of change, new behaviors or thought patterns transform from a one-time experiment, to a few days strung together, to a regular practice, and finally to a noticeable difference in how we see ourselves and the world around us. This is the quiet miracle of little-by-little change.

What we arrive at, according to behavioral science, isn't some grand finale. We get to the "maintenance phase." And as much as I respect this term, I don't think I'm alone in not loving it as a description for how I'm supposed to live the rest of my life. True, it gets across how both our habits of mind and behavior require showing up with ongoing care and commitment. But "maintenance" also sounds like I've become a machine, one eye twitch away from collapse if I don't keep adjusting the gears. And that doesn't quite do it justice either. I picture Milarepa in the anxious grasping-and-kicking phase of keeping his demons at bay. Somehow I don't think the Buddha attained enlightenment and then thought, "Ah, yes, time to enter my maintenance phase."

In this last section of the book, we will explore what it means to live with change without living *for* change. In the midst of our day-to-day, with all its challenges and opportunities, we need to learn to enjoy the things that are good in our lives. We deserve to savor both the journey and the view from the top of each mountain we climb. We also have to learn to recognize—and live with—the parts of our experience that were never meant to be approached with a change mindset in the first place. Or as the Serenity Prayer says, we need the wisdom to know the difference.

I think of the subjects of this and the next chapter—acceptance and presence—as a kind of final exam of wise habits. Practicing them draws on everything we've built so far, even as they come with their own distinct (and often steep) learning curves. They are deeply interlinked: To fully experience one you need the other. To be truly present anywhere, you have to agree on where you are.

We have focused on changing and becoming. Now we turn our attention to being.

• • •

Back in my heavy 12-step days you would hear this in meetings a lot: "Four forty-nine, man, look at page four forty-nine," or "You need to apply some four forty-nine to that." People even had bumper stickers that said "449." Now, 449 is not a cleaning solution like 409 or a lubricant like WD-40. It's a page in the AA Big Book.

What was on page 449? This statement:

"Acceptance is the answer to all my problems today."

Of everything that I cover in my Wise Habits course, year in and year out my students rate acceptance as the lesson they struggle most to practice in their own lives. (Self-compassion comes in second, but it's not close.) Rebellious young me agreed; hearing "acceptance is the answer to all my problems today" drove me crazy more often than it brought me serenity. Because of course, as I would point out to whatever well-meaning soul dared speak those words, acceptance isn't the answer to all our problems. Nothing is an answer to *all* our problems. But then again, as with any spiritual truism, there is wisdom at the core of page 449. Not all "problems" are things we can change today—or, sometimes, things we can change at all. They might not even be problems, strictly speaking.

Our biological hardwiring tells us that pain, discomfort, or loss of any kind are enemies to be fought. The fight-or-flight responses that helped us survive as animals on the savannah are still right there, ready to flood us with adrenaline. But as humans, we face the unique challenge and opportunity of rising above these automatic impulses. We can pause. We can reflect. We can recognize that sadness over the death of a loved one is a different kind of pain than a persistent backache, which is a different kind of pain than a sense of injustice, which is a different kind of pain than existential dread. (The downside to self-awareness as a species: lots of feelings.) We can learn to recognize when our instinctive resistance to any of these is doing more harm than good.

In the rest of this chapter we'll dig deeper into what acceptance really means, and doesn't, and how to discern when it's the wisest response to what life, the universe, and our own brains have to throw at us. We'll also explore a range of tools for getting to acceptance when every instinct is telling us to keep trying to hurl that last demon out of the cave.

If it were entirely mine to tell and not a time-honored Buddhist parable, I'd make one edit to Milarepa's story. Many of our personal demons, when faced head-on, reveal themselves to be shadows—fed on darkness and fundamentally immaterial. Anxieties, regrets, assumptions: We put effort into keeping these things at bay when, if we took the time to understand them, they might just dissolve in the light. But not all demons are like that. Some are the kind that stay. Some, we have to acknowledge, have the power to destroy us if we let them. Addiction is like that for me, and so is my tendency toward depression. When I faced down these parts of myself, they didn't disappear. I learned to live with them. The good news is that eventually they felt less like demons than like roommates with sharp teeth, who just need to be reminded every once in a while that they can't be waking me up at 3 a.m.

True acceptance requires courage. It requires a willingness to see things as they are. When we stop resisting the truth, we unlock the energy needed to move forward. And sometimes, we learn to appreciate that we're exactly where we need to be.

WHAT ACCEPTANCE MEANS — AND DOESN'T

My biggest issue with page 449, back in the day, was that it seemed to involve saying that you were okay with everything. I'd think, What if Nazis invaded today? Should "acceptance" be my answer to that? Should I accept the existence of domestic violence? Elder abuse? What's next—accepting that my neighbor runs his leaf blower at 7 a.m. on Sundays? Where does it end?!

This response contains the most common misconception about acceptance: that it means approval. Acceptance doesn't mean liking, condoning, or resigning yourself to a situation. It means allowing reality to be what it already is, so you can respond with clarity and wisdom.

In Buddhism we have the idea of "near enemies." These are states of being that almost look like the path of wisdom, but crucially still miss the mark. Love's near enemy can be attachment—the kind that clings out of fear, while calling itself devotion. Compassion's near enemy might be pity—feeling *for* someone in a way that quietly reinforces your own superiority.

With acceptance, approval is perhaps the nearest enemy, no less wrong for being easy to confuse with the right idea. Another near enemy is repression, aka stuffing your feelings down until they're in danger of exploding. ("No, really. I'm fine. Totally fine. I am fully accepting this while seething internally!")

I made the mistake of confusing acceptance with repression in my previous marriage. To briefly summarize a nuanced situation: My then-wife's communication style tended toward attack, while mine leaned toward retreat. To avoid conflict, I got into the habit of "accepting" things I didn't actually agree with—things that bothered me on a deep level, even if I didn't always admit it to myself. I came to realize, far too late, that keeping the peace while letting resentment build wasn't communication—it was its opposite. There is a place for delaying confrontation while you sort out how you really feel, but that's not where I was. I wasn't pausing for clarity. I was just folding.

On the way to making that realization, I met a few more near enemies of acceptance. Low-grade denial, it turns out, also isn't a path to wisdom. ("You know what? It's not even that big a deal. I'm cool. It's fine. It's fine!") And avoidance? Definitely not acceptance. ("I'm just going to let this whole thing . . . exist . . . somewhere over there . . . while I pretend it's not slowly eating me alive.") Neither is consciously settling for less, which is no more a route to a life well lived under the banner of acceptance than it was under the middle way.

Turns out, acceptance takes a bit more honesty and less self-delusion than all those. Who knew?

With some wrong answers out of the way, let's look closer at what acceptance actually is. Starting with a little math:

Suffering = Pain x Resistance

Meditation teacher and neuroscience consultant Shinzen Young came up with this equation and has my deep thanks for its simple, undeniable formula. "Pain" is the constant in the above. To be human, to be alive, is to experience pain—our bodies betray us, people we love hurt us, dogs must be put to sleep, we lose jobs, we grow old, and people around us die. "Resistance," by contrast, is the variable in the equation. It's our (negative) response to pain. Resistance is THIS CAN'T BE HAPPENING. WHY ME? I DEMAND TO SEE THE MANAGER OF THIS SPACE-TIME CONTINUUM. Put the two together—the pain we experience, plus our internal spiraling about it—and you have suffering.

An example might help. Let's take a problem common to many of us: a throbbing headache. We wake up one morning, and our head hurts again. We feel that familiar pressure start to build behind our eyes. There are pain signals traveling from our body to our brain. These are real. But quickly, we leap into the meaning-making game: "Great, and I have that big meeting in two hours." "I *just* started drinking more water—why is this happening?" "What if it turns into one of those headaches that lasts all weekend?" "Is it a brain tumor?" The physical sensations, along with all of this mental anguish, constitute our "suffering."

But if you noticed, most of that suffering is my reaction to my pain. Here is why the idea that Suffering = Pain x Resistance is so powerful. Let's imagine that our pain and suffering are all on a point scale of 1–10. And that our pain level (the actual sensation of pain) is at 4 points out of 10, and our resistance level is at 5 points, so 4 x 5 = 20 total units of suffering. But if I can lower my resistance level from a

5 to a 3, voilà, I now have twelve units of total suffering. And I didn't have to change the underlying situation at all. (Which is great news because we often cannot change the situation).

Resistance is the far enemy of acceptance. Another way to say this is to say that they are opposing forces. Resistance often comes with an unconscious belief: that by rejecting what is, we can somehow change it. But resistance is like holding a beach ball underwater; the harder we push, the more violently it springs back when our grip falters. Acceptance, on the other hand, begins by simply acknowledging what's true. Not fighting it, not pretending it's something else. From that place of clarity, we can choose our next move with perspective and intention. In this way, acceptance becomes a path to less suffering

As an old phrase puts it, "What you resist persists." The art of acceptance comes in training ourselves to meet our resistance with curiosity rather than force. What's really behind this clenching? What am I trying to avoid? What might happen if I stopped fighting and simply allowed myself to experience what's here?

• • •

One more equation: **Happiness = Reality – Expectations**.

While acceptance lessens our suffering it can also, in equal measure, increase our everyday joy. "This is the nature of life," said spiritual teacher Lodro Rinzler when I interviewed him for one of the first episodes of *The One You Feed*. "The more fixed expectations we carry, the more likely we are to be let down."

So many tourists feel let down by the reality of Paris that their disappointment has a name as a medical pathology: Paris Syndrome. I've been to Paris. You can't tell me anyone would be disappointed with the City of Love and Lights if they hadn't come in with impossible expectations. Meanwhile, in world happiness surveys (which, yes, are a thing), Denmark and Finland consistently come out on top, and psychologists speculate that this is, in part, because Finns and Danes tend to have lower expectations for how happy they'll be—which is to say, they don't demand to be happy all the time.

"There's a sort of binary distinction there between really wanting something to happen in a certain way, which is totally fine, and demanding that it absolutely must be that way," said author Oliver Burkeman on the podcast. "You don't necessarily have to give up all [your] desires . . . it is [your] demands, ultimately, that cause huge amounts of suffering." This is a way of softening a whole legacy of spiritual gurus who advise seeking enlightenment by emptying ourselves of earthly desires. "The Great Way is not difficult for those who have no preferences," wrote the Third Zen Patriarch. I'll take his word for it. Over here in real life most of us are going to continue to have preferences, and that's okay. It's when they become hard-line, no-alternatives demands of reality that we set ourselves up for a bad time in Paris.

Expectations are premeditated resentments. They're the back-seat drivers of our mental road trip, yelling, "Are we there yet?" when reality hasn't had time to figure out where it's going. Acceptance is how we transform demands into preferences, paving the way for greater emotional freedom—and maybe a little less internal yelling.

Acceptance may be the opposite of resistance, but it is not the opposite of *action*. Nor is it the opposite of change. It is, rather, a complement to both.

When I was twenty-four, strung out and homeless, merely accepting my situation wasn't enough. If I had simply accepted where I was without taking steps toward change, I might have stayed stuck—or worse, spiraled deeper. Change was necessary. But to initiate change, I first had to accept my reality. The first step in 12-step programs is to admit that we were powerless over our addiction. I had to face the truth about my addiction and the fact that my life simply was not working. Without that clarity, meaningful change wouldn't have been possible.

Acceptance, in this context, was the groundwork for change.

It's also important to say that not all resistance is bad. When we are confronted with injustices like the Holocaust, systemic discrimination, or climate change, resisting is what calls forth the best in us. The cry of "This is not okay" has been behind many of history's greatest changes.

Acceptance, in this light, is not a negation but a counterbalance.

Without it, resistance can curdle into denial, despair, or burnout. Climate nihilism, activist fatigue, and the quiet drift into numbness are all reminders that resistance without grounding can paralyze rather than empower. Acceptance says, "This is happening. Let's take a breath, step back, and check in with ourselves and others. Now, how do we respond?"

Ultimately, resistance and acceptance are both far enemies and constant collaborators. ("Far frenemies," if you will.) Working with both of them means embodying the middle-way principle of holding opposites in creative tension—the paradox kind of opposites, not the true contradiction kind. Resistance without acceptance can become rigid, while acceptance without resistance may lack the drive for progress. When the two are balanced they create resilience, as exemplified by Martin Luther King Jr., who accepted the long arc of the struggle while holding infinite hope. Acceptance is a way to face the world's imperfections while working to heal them.

THE WISDOM TO KNOW THE DIFFERENCE

To state the obvious, not all suffering—which is to say, not every situation in which we wish things were different—is alike. For every time our resistance is a weather vane pointing us toward meaningful action, there are other times when it is just a lightning rod for more suffering, when it comes in the form of denying/avoiding/repressing the truth of something for which change isn't the answer. In both cases the way forward starts with acceptance, but the endgame is different.

This is the confusion for which the Serenity Prayer seeks clarity. Or, in the words of the eleventh-century Jewish philosopher Solomon ibn Gabirol, "At the head of all understanding is distinguishing between what is and what cannot be, and the consoling of what is not in our power to change."

The starting point of acceptance is to do the simple, hard work of agreeing that whatever is happening to us is actually happening. *My back hurts. The communication in my marriage isn't working right now. My dog has passed. An injustice has occurred. The Seine has some trash floating in it.*

The next step is to answer a simple, hard question: **Can I do anything to change the source of this pain?** Not "Do I want to change it"; not "I wish I could." You already know the answers to those. (The only variation I'll allow is in honor of page 449: **Can I do anything to change it** today?) Depending on your answer, acceptance becomes either an important check-in point or your final destination in navigating a challenging moment.

Life rarely supplies obvious answers in the "wisdom to know the difference" department. It asks us to balance conflicting truths and invites us to wonder whether to blame the world around us or our own perspective. Am I unhappy at work because my boss is actually a jerk, or because I'm being triggered and there's something in *me* that needs attention? Is this business not working because it's not a good idea, or do I need to hang on a little longer? Is my phone glitching because it's truly outdated, or is the universe trying to teach me patience while I Google "how to fix slow phone"?

The Stoic philosopher Epictetus may not have wondered about the phone thing, but he did frame the ability to know what is and isn't within our control as the cornerstone of a life well lived. His teachings start with a radical and liberating truth: There is a vast portion of life over which we have no say. The weather, the opinions of others, a roll of the dice—to expend our energy wrestling with these elements of existence is to guarantee frustration, like trying to capture the ocean in a bucket.

In his work *The Enchiridion* (The Handbook), Epictetus urged his followers to anchor their attention and efforts where they will matter most. He includes a neat division between what is and isn't under our control:

In Our Control:

- **OUR JUDGMENTS:** How we interpret events or actions.

- **OUR DESIRES AND AVERSIONS:** What we choose to pursue or avoid.

- **OUR CHOICES AND ACTIONS:** The decisions we make and how we act upon them.

- **OUR ATTITUDE:** Whether we face a situation with courage or despair.

Not in Our Control:

- **OUR BODY:** Its health, physical condition, or eventual decline.

- **OUR REPUTATION:** What others think or say about us.

- **WEALTH:** Whether fortune or misfortune grants or takes it away.

- **THE ACTIONS OF OTHERS:** How they behave, what they choose to do, or how they respond to us.

As brilliant and timeless as Epictetus's central insight is—that it's worth focusing your time and energy where they will have the most impact—you may have some qualms with these lists. I do! I can agree that we can't control the fact of aging, for example, but I'd point out that we can make choices about our health today that give us a better chance of aging well. And yes, we can't control the stock market, but we can make choices about how to save and invest.

Fast-forwarding a couple of millennia, Stephen Covey built on Epictetus's work when he introduced the concept of the Circle of Concern versus the Circle of Influence in his popular classic *The 7 Habits of Highly Effective People*. Covey visualized the division between what we can and can't change as two overlaid circles: a large circle representing everything we care about (the Circle of Concern), and a circle within it representing what we can actually influence (the Circle of Influence).

The Circle of Concern encompasses everything that weighs on our minds—global crises, the opinions of others, or the weather on our commute. The Circle of Influence is much smaller. It contains everything our thoughts and actions can actually impact: our choices, our responses, and how we show up in the world.

Here's the key, according to Covey: The more time we spend in our Circle of Concern—but outside our Circle of Influence—the more we burn energy without results. But when we focus on our Circle of Influence, not only do we make an impact where we *can*—we often watch that circle expand.

Think of scrolling dire news headlines, getting more and more anxious, versus choosing an issue and organizing friends into a local activist group. That one step connected you with others who care, some of whom may have even broader reach than you started with.

Covey later added a third, innermost circle to his visualization: the Circle of Control. This category narrows the field of focus even further, containing only the things we have *direct and immediate control over*, such as our thoughts, actions, and choices in any given moment. While the Circle of Influence includes areas where we can affect change indirectly (like improving a relationship or contributing to a team effort), the Circle of Control emphasizes personal accountability. When we want to change the world, it prompts us to start with ourselves.

William Irvine, a modern philosopher who writes about Stoicism, takes a middle-way approach to the many situations where we have some degree of influence but not complete control. When I interviewed him, Irvine used the example of a tennis match:

> *Suppose you're scheduled to play against your archrival in a week. So what can you control? Well, you can control how hard you train. You can control the strategy you go into the match with. You can control what you eat the day before the match. So that's what you should focus your attention on. What you don't have control over is how the other person trains or the strategy they have. So you shouldn't be thinking so much about those.*

He went on to imagine the aftermath of the match: What if you focused on all the right things, and you lost anyway? Should you think of it as a failure? "Well, in one sense, obviously you lost the match, but in another sense, you did the best you could," he said. "And there's a saying for that. You did what you could, with what you had, where you were. And that's all you can ever do in life."

As you might have figured out about me, I dislike binary, simple answers. So I appreciate Covey's and Irvine's expansions of Epictetus—and the Serenity Prayer, for that matter—because they bring more nuance to the question of what we can and can't change. Ultimately, however, I think I'm even further on the spectrum of "it's complicated." Our actions, judgments, and choices, which all these thinkers put in the "we can control" bucket, come from a complex stew of motivations, not all of which are even conscious. "Control" itself is a slippery concept as soon as you stick "self-" in front of it. And what even counts as a "choice"? As discussed at the end of chapter 7, I have a middle-way view of the big picture human agency, in which we are the cocreators of our lives along with the many factors—biological, cultural, economic, and otherwise—that shape the tools with which we choose.

Is it a choice to drink, when you're deep in the patterns of an alcoholic? Is it your "fault"? Not exactly, I would argue, but at some point there is some choice to say "no more." It's your responsibility to make that choice, because no one else can. This is where I find a line in all this complexity: in the distinction between fault and responsibility. It's also not your fault if something completely outside your influence goes wrong—lightning strikes a tree and it falls on your house, say—but it is your responsibility to fix the situation (or to hire the right people to fix it).

This shifting of the lens from what we can "control" to what we are responsible for has often helped me to move away from the treadmills of guilt and shame and toward what is in my power to do next. In other words, it has helped me to move from resistance to acceptance.

• • •

If you really want a clear boundary between what we can and cannot change, or at least a clear sense of where seeking change has diminishing returns, look no further than the people around you. A friend of mine is extraordinarily frustrated with her husband: He has high blood pressure, high cholesterol, smokes, and is overweight, yet will take none of the doctor-recommended steps to address his health. His own father died in his early fifties from heart disease, yet even this reality hasn't moved him to take the actions that, to her, are so obviously of life-or-death importance. Time and again she has wondered: What can she do? How can she change someone who doesn't want to change?

My first answer to this is not what most people in a situation like my friend's want to hear, but it's the truth. As a well-handled kernel of wisdom has it, consider how hard it is to change yourself and you'll understand what little chance you have in trying to change others.

My second answer is to get as specific and realistic as possible about what is and isn't worth approaching from a change mindset, when it comes to advising others on how to be. In *Far from the Tree*, author Andrew Solomon examines the complexities parents face when their children differ from their own (or society's) expectations for what it means to thrive. He articulates this dilemma:

> *All parenting turns on a crucial question: to what extent parents should accept their children for who they are, and to what extent they should help them become their best selves?*

There is no one-size-fits-all answer here, of course; as Solomon said when I interviewed him, it is in many ways a parent's job to "change" their child. "You educate them, you teach them a sense of moral values, you try to teach them some manners, you try to give them all kinds of knowledge they didn't have." At the same time, "You have to accept your child for who he is or she is and make him or her feel good about who they are or what their identity might be." And between what should be changed and what should be celebrated, "there's a great deal that falls in a gray foggy middle."

Part of what Solomon found in researching *Far from the Tree* is that it's often far more rewarding to err on the side of acceptance. In studying individuals with challenging medical conditions, he found that people who know their condition to be irreversible are often happier than people who believe it can be changed. As he explained on the podcast: "If you know that there's nothing that you can do about having lost part of your leg . . . you figure out how to live a good life with that condition. If you have a condition which is easily fixable, you fix it. . . . But a lot of people have conditions which might be fixable or might not be fixable, [or] somewhat fixable but not fully fixable, where there's a lot of vagueness, and those people tend to live with a sense that their condition requires them to keep trying to fix it. And they keep trying and often the fix doesn't happen at all or it doesn't happen [to] a sufficient degree. And so those people end up terribly frustrated." The constant cycle of hope can become a wearying form of resistance, compounding personal suffering.

Returning to parenting, he used the example of autism as a condition in the "gray foggy middle" of acceptance and change, as it can present in countless ways with just as many potential paths forward for parents and children. Therapies that dramatically help some autistic individuals to live more independent, socially integrated lives don't work at all for others—while still others on the spectrum of neurodivergence, and their parents, would prefer not to think of their autism as something needing "treatment" at all. Regardless of the case, Solomon says that thinking about autism as something to be "fixed" does a disservice to any child, who deserves "to be accepted and even to be celebrated" for who they are in the present tense. "Sometimes that's very difficult for people who keep thinking that *there's something wrong with my child and I need to make it right*," he says. "And it comes more readily to people who think *my child is who my child is and I just have to deal with what I've been given*."

That may not sound like the most Hallmark-card version of parental devotion, but it's real, honest acceptance. And that foundation is sturdy enough to hold a lifetime of love and support.

My friend's husband has been walking a little more often these days. He enjoys taking the dog out and has begun lengthening their walks. But as much as my friend is heartened by this sign of progress, a part of her own learning curve has been to resist immediately pressing for more. She is focusing on accepting her husband for where he is right now, keeping hope alive but recognizing that only he can make the decision to change his relationship to his health further.

In my own life, I've had to remind myself how little power I have to change other people many times, and with no one more so than my own father. For years I fantasized about having a closer relationship with him. I longed to be able to share emotions with each other, to have long flowing conversations in which we'd talk about something besides the weather and his golf game. In my younger years I wished he'd take an interest in me as a musician, in me as who I *was* in any real way; later, when I had my own son, I added to this the longing to be able to talk about fatherhood itself.

For years I'd show up to play a round of golf with him and think, "Okay, *this* is the day I'm going to break through. We have four hours out here on the course, and I'm going to get him to open up." And then we'd start playing, and my grand plans would seem like what they were: an exercise in futility. But instead of truly accepting that, I'd let my disappointment in myself for not achieving the impossible, and my disappointment in him for not being a different person, cast a pall over the whole afternoon.

When I eventually realized that a storybook relationship with my father was not in the cards, it made it far easier for me to live in the relationship we did have. I stopped fretting that our phone calls didn't last a long time, and that he and I didn't have much in common. In making peace with not having the father I'd dreamed up, I even found myself better able to appreciate the one I had. I was able to see echoes of good qualities between us: a capacity for hard work, a certain consistency and steadiness.

And I was able to just enjoy a nice afternoon of golf.

HOW TO GET THERE

If you're currently yelling EASIER SAID THAN DONE at the page, I sympathize, and also, sorry to whoever's nearby.

Let's review: We know what acceptance is, we know why it's a wise way to approach a lot of things in daily life, and we know a bit about how to think through when it's a complement for change versus an end in itself. But how do we do the whole . . . accepting part?

In this section I'll offer a range of guiding tools, from the big picture to everyday, from conceptual to literally embodied. As with all wise habits, the best combination of practices and reflections is what works for you.

Start Small and Obvious

When I teach acceptance people immediately jump to the hardest things. You mean I should accept that I was abused as a child? I should sit with the fact that my mom has cancer? I should look in the mirror every morning and tell myself that so-and-so is president?

Don't start there. Start smaller. Ask what it would mean to reduce the resistance to something that is a minor annoyance, then to something moderately nagging at you. Work up to the big stuff. The good thing about reality is that it isn't going anywhere.

It can also help to remind ourselves of the things we all have to accept, without the weight of specific stakes from our own lives. The

Buddhist-inspired "Five Givens," articulated by author and *The One You Feed* guest David Richo, are life's equivalent of the Terms and Conditions we all click "agree" on without reading:

1. **EVERYTHING CHANGES AND ENDS.** (Including the wi-fi connection when you need it most.)

2. **THINGS DO NOT ALWAYS GO ACCORDING TO PLAN.** (Or, let's be real, even remotely close to plan.)

3. **LIFE IS NOT FAIR.** (Fairness is a kindergarten myth, like Santa, or paste being nontoxic.)

4. **PAIN IS PART OF LIFE.** (You're not special; even billionaires stub their toes.)

5. **PEOPLE ARE NOT LOVING AND LOYAL ALL THE TIME.** (I think we can do without an example here.)

These truths are both obvious and irritating. They're the life lessons we already know but wish weren't true. Embracing them isn't about resigning ourselves to a joyless existence; it's about tempering our expectations to match reality. And remembering them in moments when we're not struggling can help strengthen our resilience the next time they come to call.

From Let It Go to Let It Be

A phrase used in both recovery and spiritual circles is *let it go*, or sometimes *let go of what is not serving you*. I feel that phrase promising me that if I just set the right intention in this candlelit yoga class, whatever is plaguing me will drift off into the incense. The reality is that letting go is hard. I mean no disrespect to yoga or intention-setting (or candles), all of which can be part of an ongoing process. It's just that on any given day we try to let it go, the feeling may not seem to be mutual.

Another way that "letting go" is often referenced is with ". . . and let God" added to the end of it. I had to find a way to reckon with this quote in recovery. I wasn't sure there was a God out there doing anything, so who was going to pick up my burdens? Would it be like running a relay and handing the baton to . . . no one? Would the things I let go just drop to the track? In the immortal words of Anne Lamott: "People might say, jovially, 'Let go and let God.' Believe me, if I could, I would, and in the meantime, I feel like stabbing you in the forehead."

What I finally realized is that it does not matter whether anyone or anything is there to take over. It's the clinging, gripping, and resisting that is making me sick. It's the acceptance that frees my heart and frees up my energy for something life-giving. To get there I've found it useful to think of this idea as, instead of letting go, *letting be*.

Letting go assumes that something actually goes away. Letting be is an act of noninterference. I let all of it be. My feelings, my resistance to letting it be, the situation. No divine intervention or disappearing-into-smoke required.

The Beatles are one of my five favorite bands of all time and I can't use the phrase "Let It Be" without thinking of their song (although for my alternative friends out there I also can't hear that title without thinking of the name of the classic '80s record by my spiritual alter ego, the Replacements). I don't mind the association at all. When I hear Paul McCartney sing about waking up to music, it speaks to what happens when I am able to let go, or be.

I can hear something outside my own head. I can hear the music of the world.

Switch to "I'd Prefer"

Continuing with language, let's talk about "should" and "shouldn't." They're the verbal equivalent of trying to put a cat in a sweater: guaranteed to provoke resistance. "I should be thinner." "They shouldn't have done that." It's a battle cry for a war with reality that you're never going to win, mostly because reality is indifferent to your outrage.

Instead, what if we took the pressure down a notch? Replace "should" with "I'd prefer." "I'd prefer to weigh less." "I'd prefer they hadn't acted that way." See? Still aspirational, but without the emotional blowback of demanding the universe rearrange itself for your convenience.

It may seem like a superficial change, but remember that our inner monologue is made of words. Whether or not we speak it aloud, our language shapes our deepest thoughts and innermost perceptions, and vice versa. There's a reason I've been recommending simple rewordings throughout this book, from changing "don't want to" for "don't feel like it," to exchanging "never" and "always" for "sometimes," to swapping "or" for "and." When we accept that even the most prosaic words have power, we can start making them work for us.

Saying Yes to the Moment

We know acceptance doesn't mean approval—but it does mean saying *yes* to the moment. Yes means agreeing that "what's happening is happening." As David Richo has written, "Yes is the brave ally of serenity; no is the scared accomplice of anxiety."

"Yes, and" is the first rule of improvisational theater because to build anything with another person, you first have to accept whatever they bring to the table. If your scene partner comes on stage and says, "I'm a dragon" and you say, "No you're not, you're an aspiring comedian," you might get a quick laugh, but after that things are going nowhere fast. You've refused their premise, so now the audience doesn't know what to believe and you have nothing to build on. Whether this resonates or whether no one could pay you to attempt improv, the real world works the same way. Your scene partner is the universe, and when it says there's a dragon, your first words better be "Yes, and [I'm going to start running? Alert the media? Or, maybe I'll learn to speak dragon]."

Once you stop investing in the idea that you might achieve peace of mind by only letting in what is peaceful, it becomes easier to actually find peace in the middle of life's wilderness. At the end of the chapter is a still point exercise to practice saying *yes* to each moment, dragons or not.

Open Hand

The spiritual teacher Adyashanti once shared with me a lesson conveyed not through words but through a powerful visual metaphor. He demonstrated two states: first, holding up a clenched fist while saying, "Less of this," and then revealing his open palm, adding, "More of this." This simple yet profound gesture encapsulated an entire philosophy of acceptance and surrender.

Right now, clench your fist as tightly as possible. Feel the tension, the constriction. Now release it. Let your hand open naturally, without force—just ease. Notice the stark contrast. That shift—from tightness to openness—mirrors the practice we're inviting our hearts and minds into.

It's a physical embodiment of what it means to let go of control and soften into life's natural flow. Whether we're resisting an uncomfortable truth, gripping tightly to an outcome, or lost in the churn of our own thoughts, the simple prompt of an open palm can nudge our minds toward being a little more open, with grace and curiosity.

A DOOR TO BEING

We'll get into what it looks like to truly be in the moment in the next chapter. For now I'll leave you with one of the most profound experiences of acceptance I've ever had.

I was on a meditation retreat at the Omega Institute in New York, eating dinner in the Institute's meeting hall and thinking about the grand, wise ideas my teacher had imparted that day about letting things be the way they are and learning to say yes to life.

The thing is, I was sitting near a door that led to outdoor seating, and on this nice fall evening that door was getting a lot of action. It was one of those screen doors on a tight spring. Every time anyone went in or out, the spring would seize up and slam the door shut if it hadn't been closed slowly. Whack! Whack! Whack! Over and over again.

Anyone who knows me will tell you that I am noise sensitive, so my irritation level was growing by the minute. Between my salad and entrée, I went from irritated to enraged. Why can't these **morons** just hold the door? Don't they know we are on a **silent** retreat? Whack! Whack! Whack!

Then, begrudgingly, I remembered the teacher's guidance to try to say yes to life. I began to mentally say **yes** every time the door slammed. Whack! **Yes!** Whack! **Yes!** It became a "fake it till you make it" experience. First I was saying **yes** despite feeling

hell no, but eventually I found my anger and irritation genuinely relaxing.

I decided I would keep trying this internal yes-ing throughout the rest of the retreat. Whenever anything unpleasant came up, I would say **yes** to it. The next day, in one of the meditation sessions, I was struggling extra hard: My mind was racing when I wasn't busy dozing off or getting distracted by my aching back. In other sessions I had gotten into a loop of frustration with myself, but in this one I decided to allow everything to be what it would be. Every time I noticed my mind was wandering, I mentally said **yes**. Whenever I felt pain or tightness in my back or shoulders, I said nothing but **yes**.

Over and over, **yes, yes, yes**. And then it started. I felt this energy, this joy rising up in me. And I said **yes** to that. The sensation of back pain, **yes**. The feeling of joy, **yes**. The feeling of joy kept growing. The meditation session ended, and I walked outside, and then, Boom! The entire world opened up to me. I had what is often called a mystical experience. In Buddhism, it is called satori: sudden enlightenment.

The nature of these experiences is that they are ineffable, meaning you can't really put it into words, but I'll do my best. I suddenly saw and deeply felt that I was one with everything. It wasn't so much that I thought the tree over there was me, but in a deeply experienced sense, it also wasn't not me. There was an underlying unity to things, and I was part of that and could never not be a part of it. It sounds trite and clichéd, but the experience of it was freedom and peace beyond measure.

Do I wish that the spark for my enlightenment experience was something a little more cinematic than a screen door? A little part of me says, sure.

The rest of me is more than happy to let it all be.

ONE LITTLE THING YOU CAN DO RIGHT NOW

Whatever you're experiencing in this moment (yes, this one)—physical sensations, emotions, sounds around you, even resistance to this exercise—mentally say yes to it. Not "I like this" or "This is good," just "Yes, this is happening." Practice saying yes to what's already here instead of fighting reality. It's not approval—it's acknowledgment.

When you're ready to go a little deeper, flip to the appendix for extra exercises—or download the companion worksheets anytime at oneyoufeed.net/resources.

TEN

The Gift of Presence

> To pay attention, this is our endless and proper work.
> —MARY OLIVER

WE'VE BEGUN EVERY CHAPTER IN THIS BOOK WITH A STORY, AND FOR GOOD reason. Stories are how we connect the stars above us and the events around us and the relationships that contain us into tapestries of meaning. A story requires change, but it also requires resolution: somewhere meaningful to leave the reader or listener, perhaps with a cracked-open door through which to imagine a sequel.

The main character in this chapter's story is you, and the setting is right here, right now. The moment you're reading these words. I could have picked anyone else at any other time, but you and your world, in the moment you're reading this, are too interesting to pass up. There's just so much going on. Your lungs are circulating air; your heart is pumping blood, your neurons are firing. Light particles are hitting this page and then hitting your retinas, triggering a miraculous complex of cells to translate those photon signals into the black-and-white image of text, which your brain is then interpreting, drawing on the rules of language and literacy you learned as a child, in another place and time, when just as many stories were happening.

That's not even getting to where you are! Everything around you has layers to notice. Maybe you're sitting on a battle-scarred old couch; maybe you're leaning against the kitchen counter as you wait for pasta water to boil. Maybe you're on the subway headed to work, and in your peripheral vision are a dozen people in the middle of their own stories. Maybe you're listening to this as an audiobook, walking or driving around your neighborhood, and later you'll pass this tree again and you'll remember listening to this same passage, and the world will be hung a little more richly with the ornaments of your thoughts.

Even if you were in a monk's cell, with just a concrete floor and a single chair—you might look at that dust mote, navigating imperceptible currents of air that started somewhere far away with great movements of tides and temperature.

Wherever you are, and whenever you are, your present hosts a miracle box of forces and entities and incidents. Change is a constant; it's the thing that makes it so that each moment is unlike any before or after it. It's also not all there is to focus on.

Look around. Listen. Breathe deeply. Tell a story that starts and ends with noticing all the tales the world is already telling you, right here and now.

・・・

Where is real happiness? I can tell you where it's not. It's not in the past, no matter how many "Wish You Were Here" postcards you send via Nostalgia Express. It's not in the future, no matter how much hypothetical success you're going to have. It's not right around the corner when you get that thing you think you need. It's not one less wrinkle, one less pound, or one more friend on Facebook.

It's not the next sale, the next shirt, or the next promotion. It's not in the way it was, the way it could be, or the way it should be.

It's in the bird dancing on the limb, the beat coming out of your speakers, the tone of a friend's hello, the taste of your morning coffee. It's where your feet meet the ground and your eyes meet the light. It's nowhere if you look hard and everywhere if you just let yourself see.

Put simply, if we want a deeper experience of being alive, we need to learn to be present. It's just a core truth. Ram Dass said it best with *Be Here Now* back in 1971, and Eckhart Tolle gave us *The Power of Now* in 1997. Heck, even Marcus Aurelius was preaching the virtues of present-moment awareness in *Meditations* almost two thousand years ago.

Being present is about waking up to the moment as it's actually happening. In a strip of my beloved Calvin and Hobbes that begins with the two characters admiring the vista from a hill, little Calvin articulates this truth over a series of panels:

We assume it's Calvin who says "It's like *some*thing . . ." in the strip's last panel, though all we see are the two plumes of smoke from where he and Hobbes have crashed after careening down the hill during Calvin's entire speech. The joke, of course, is that the perfect metaphor Calvin "just can't think of" for the experience of going through life "watching out for what's ahead" except when we're forced to stop . . . is what we've just seen unfold. When Calvin talks about life becoming a "blur," the characters are blurs, and when they finally have a weightless, blue-sky moment, with Calvin able to look back toward the cliff they've just sailed off of, we all know it's "too late" to avoid the calamity to come.

Mr. Watterson, you've done it again.

As Calvin was getting at before he crashed: We tend to treat the ordinary moments of our lives as something we need to get through to get to the good stuff. The problem with this is that most moments of our lives are, as seen through one lens, ordinary, so we end up speeding through them in a comic-book blur. And once the habit of always looking forward (or back) is fully established, we may find ourselves unable to be present for even the special moments.

In the last chapter we talked about accepting that whatever is happening in the moment is, in fact, happening—and also about how this mindset is most obviously challenging when we don't like what reality has to say. But when we prioritize having and getting over simply being, experiencing the present as *enough* may be the greatest challenge of all.

This chapter, like the last, is about balancing possibilities for growth and change with an awareness that change isn't, and can't be, the whole story of a wise and happy life. If acceptance is about coming to terms with reality, presence is about expanding our experience of those terms—creating space, even in the middle of the mundane, for clarity and wonder. Or to put it in language familiar from earlier in the book: Acceptance is about framing. Presence is about attention—the most essential building block of being anywhere at all.

What is it that we can bring to any moment? Attention. What turns the ordinary into the extraordinary? Attention. This is the gift that great artists and poets bring to their work—a profound, unwavering focus on what is truly present.

In the following pages we'll discuss the art of attention as not only a cognitive tool, but an end in itself. We'll discuss the obstacles to exercising the kind of attention of which presence is made; and we'll go through various practices designed to foster a deeper sense of presence. The goal is not to live in the moment 100 percent of the time, because to do that would also be to miss out on the richest version of your life's story (not to mention that it's simply impossible). But right now most of us are somewhere else, mentally, 95 percent of the time, and only experiencing the wonder of being fully present 5 percent of the time. We can improve those percentages and watch the *now* unfold itself to us as we do.

ATTENTION REVISITED

Attention is a strange thing. Like breathing, it is one of those human processes that's both automatic and something we can consciously control. Think about it—I can alter my breathing, taking deep, deliberate inhales and exhales, or I can also forget about it completely and it will go on functioning all by itself. Attention works in much the same way. Imagine you're at a Fourth of July party and fireworks aren't your thing, so you've chosen to focus on chatting with other partygoers. But if I come up behind you at that party and set off a firecracker right behind your head (don't worry, I wouldn't actually do this . . . at least the adult version of me wouldn't), your attention would have no choice but to snap to it. Attention is both a passenger and a driver in the vehicle we call consciousness.

To describe this dual role cognitive researchers use two not-so-technical terms: **bottom-up** and **top-down** attention.

Bottom-up attention is our survival instinct in action. Bright lights, sudden movements, loud noises: These are the attention thieves that demand we look, listen, or act. Our brain yells, "Hey, pay attention to that!" when something new or different pops up. The only problem with this evolution-honed reflex is that what tugs at our attention isn't what often deserves it. A car horn may alert us to danger, or perhaps it is only an impatient driver. In either case, bottom-up attention doesn't ask any questions; it simply reacts.

Now, let's flip that around. **Top-down attention** is like a compass, pointing us toward what we've decided matters most. Slower, deliberate, rooted in choice: When you're searching for your keys in a messy drawer, or trying to read while someone's watching TikTok videos nearby (a feat I'm convinced is impossible), that's top-down attention at work. It's the architect, building your focus brick by brick.

The rub is that top-down attention takes real effort. The prefrontal cortex, the same part of your brain that helps with self-control, has to work overtime (along with something called the parietal lobe) to keep you focused in the face of a planet's worth of distractions. Just as with willpower, our capacity for sustained attention isn't infinite. In the same way we can burn out from resisting that plate of cookies or maintaining perfect gym attendance, we can exhaust our ability to stay focused.

Attention as Its Own Reward

With that bit of science in mind, let's shift the lens.

Discussions about attention often focus on what it can do for us—

how it fuels productivity, helps us survive, or optimizes performance. But there is also a place for thinking about the immense value of attention as a state of being in and of itself, given that it is the very fabric from which our experience is made.

Attention is not just a tool we use to make things happen. It's the light that illuminates our lives. It's how we connect to the world and, ultimately, to ourselves. William James, in *The Principles of Psychology*, put it simply yet profoundly: "My experience is what I agree to attend to."

I remember one summer evening a friend and I took a walk after dinner, as we often do. It was always a lovely time, the sunset, the sounds of birds singing in the trees. But that evening was different. Early in the walk, they said something that upset me. (True to form, it took me the whole walk to mention it.) To this day, I don't remember what was said, but I clearly remember how it changed the experience. The usual pleasures of our walk—the trees, the birds, the warm breeze—vanished because my attention was stuck on the frustration bubbling inside me. What could have been a lovely shared moment became a solitary struggle in my head.

To be clear, the external reality of our nightly walk was the same as ever. The trees, the birds, our winding route, the murmuring breeze. That's the power of attention. It doesn't just determine what we notice, it shapes how we feel—for better or worse.

For centuries, contemplative traditions have connected the virtue of presence with the practice of attention. Thich Nhat Hanh writes about this with humble profundity:

> *If while washing dishes, we think only of the cup of tea that awaits us, thus hurrying to get the dishes out of the way as if they were a nuisance, then we are not alive during the time we are washing the dishes. If we can't wash the dishes, chances are we won't be able to drink our tea either. While drinking the cup of tea, we will only be thinking of other*

things, barely aware of the cup in our hands. Thus, we are sucked away into the future—and we are incapable of actually living one minute of life.

Attention, fully given, brings intimacy not just with others, but with life itself. In this line of thinking, enlightenment becomes not some far-off peak to scale, but something that can be worked toward in our relationship to the mundane. Wisdom is to be found in listening fully, paying attention to the teacup, the dishes, the walk, the person beside us, and letting go of the endless chatter in our minds.

What we consistently notice and value becomes the essence of who we are. Attention doesn't just shape our experience; it shapes us.

OBSTACLES TO PRESENCE

We can hopefully all agree at this point that it's worth paying closer attention to the present moment a little more often. So what's standing in our way?

The first hurdle is what we covered in the last chapter: that it's impossible to be present while locked in a battle against reality. But while acceptance is necessary, it's not always sufficient to ground us in the moment. Three other all-but-universal roadblocks are *busyness*, *distraction*, and a *problem-focused mentality*.

Busyness

Busyness needs no introduction; it is the patron saint of modern life. And for most people, this is not going to change drastically. Life isn't slowing down, and no one's handing us any extra time. As we work to live a life that aligns with our values, we may gradually triage where we do and don't want to commit our time and energy—and if we're very lucky, at some point this may open up new swaths of time for reflection. But in the meantime what we need is a way to be more present amidst it all.

So before we retreat to the woods, what can we do to stop every moment from being a blur?

Rushing, it turns out, isn't about speed—it's about mindset. It's a constant leaning forward, a restless anticipation that becomes our default gear. And there are ways to change how we move through our days without changing what's on the schedule.

Picture me in my car. (Look, not all stories are riveting.) One version of me is running errands with the windows down, humming along to some Belle and Sebastian. I'm moving quickly, but I'm actually enjoying myself. The sun's out, there's a coffee in the cupholder, and I might even wave a thank-you to another driver. Life feels oddly pleasant considering I'm in stop-and-go traffic with a trunk full of grocery bags.

Then there's the other version of me: gripping the wheel like I'm navigating an asteroid field, leaning forward so aggressively that my face might as well be stuck to the windshield. I'm muttering under my breath about the "idiot" in front of me who has the audacity to go the speed limit. Every red light feels like a personal attack. Same route. Same errands. A completely different experience.

Why the difference? When I let my thoughts marinate in awareness of busyness, I get into a loop of *I don't have time for this*, which is also a loop of *I'd rather be anywhere else*. I trick myself into believing that what matters is always the next errand, the next meeting, the next milestone. And I keep tumbling forward, thinking, *I'll feel calm and present as soon as I finish this list*. But guess what? That moment rarely comes, because there's always another list.

Easing out of this cycle starts with noticing when we're in that frantic, leaning-forward mode—when the to-do list feels heavier than it really is. And then asking ourselves: Can I still get everything done, but with a little more ease? *Can I go fast without rushing?*

ER doctors, whose day-to-day business actually is imbued with life-or-death urgency, have been shown to move slower and more deliberately in crisis situations than the average person. This is because they are trained to know how much can actually get done in five minutes, one minute, ten seconds. (It's more than most of us think.) ER doctors know that the way to do their best work quickly is, paradoxically, to stop hurrying long enough to do it right.

Busyness doesn't have to be the enemy. It's just a state of doing. And if we can untangle it from the false urgency we so often attach to it, we can find peace even in high gear.

Distraction

Distraction comes in as many flavors as there are reasons to HEY, LOOK OVER THERE! But I want to focus on a source of distraction that's both ubiquitous and also, in the grand evolutionary scheme of things, brand new to human life: our phones.

We've all heard the reasons we should spend less time on them. Experts have weighed in. Articles have been written. Podcasts have made their cases. And yet, here we are, scrolling, swiping, tapping. I'm not going to add to that pile; another scolding about being addicted to screens or wasting our lives staring at the "black mirror" isn't a productive way forward. Instead, I invite you to take a few moments to notice your relationship to your devices and ask whether, just maybe, you'd rather pay more attention to other things.

Look at your phone—really look. What feelings come up as you regard it? If a notification comes in while you're looking, what reaction(s) do you experience? Mental, emotional, physical? Now turn the phone off and weigh it in your hand. Leave it on a table and walk into another room. Try finding a similarly sized rock; feel the weight of it in your hand instead. Imagine carrying the rock around all day and looking at it as often as you look at your phone. Imagine, instead of putting the rock back where you found it, leaving your phone in its place. How do you feel?

I'm not expecting a one-size-fits-all experience with these thought exercises; all that matters is your personal relationship with your phone, and maybe no unsettling feelings will come up as you explore it. But for a lot of us (me included) our phones have become the default escape whenever we have a spare moment, and we'd rather things were different. Instead of being present in the life happening around us, we vanish into a screen. Ask yourself: Does being glued to my phone feel good, or is it just . . . a thing I do? And what about the opportunity cost?

Opportunity cost is one of those concepts that's as simple to learn as it is hard to forget.

It's the idea that every time you choose to do one thing, you're automatically choosing not to do something else. Every choice comes with a trade-off—the cost of the opportunity you didn't take. Remember me and my nightly TV habit? The issue wasn't the TV-watching itself, it was the opportunity cost of not doing other things. For every hour I spent watching TV, the opportunity cost was the book I didn't read, the guitar I didn't play, or the conversation I could have had with a friend. The trade-off isn't always a bad thing, but it's always worth considering.

When it comes to our phones, presence is an opportunity cost. Every moment spent scrolling, swiping, or texting is a moment we choose to check out from the world around us. Even taking a photo requires putting a layer of distance between ourselves and our experience of the present—which can certainly be worth it, to create a lasting memory, but this doesn't mean that the opportunity cost of inserting a screen between us and the moment we're preserving isn't also real.

Of course, we often use our phones when we're pretty sure that there is nothing worth being present for. What's wrong with scrolling while we stand in the grocery line, after all? The answer is nothing. Except that with each choice to do so, we train ourselves, little by little, to be anywhere but where we are.

Problem-Focused Mentality

A final obstacle that consistently pulls us out of the present is what I call a problem-focused mentality. This is the tendency to see life as a series of problems to be solved rather than moments to be experienced. We introduced this mindset with the "problems versus puzzles" reframing technique in chapter 6, and it was present throughout the last chapter's discussions of what it means to accept any reality we identify, rightly or wrongly, as a "problem."

A problem-focused mentality is an inheritance from our evolutionary history. Our mind is wired to look for threats on the horizon—not just big-picture ones that require complex solutions, but all the little questions that need answers as we map our days: "Okay, I'll do this, then I'll handle that, and after that, maybe I'll tackle this." On my podcast, the author Mary O'Malley described our minds as "problem factories," which perfectly describes it. The moment we solve one, another rolls right off the conveyor belt and demands our attention.

For me, the problem-focused mentality feels like second nature, which makes sense considering my background as a project manager for software start-ups. In that world, it's all about anticipating obstacles, creating solutions, and keeping the moving parts in motion. That mindset was essential for my work, but over time it became the way I approached everything. Even on vacation my brain operated like a project manager, constantly scanning for what needed to be done, optimized, or fixed.

The problem-focused mentality can be helpful—it keeps things running smoothly and helps us tackle what matters—but like the above roadblocks, indeed in concert with them (busyness and the problem-focused mentality are a match made in bureaucratic heaven), it also robs us of something precious: the ability to simply *be*. We see life less as a collection of experiences and more as a series of levels of *Tetris*.

How should we be instead? There is a Buddhist story about a woman chased by a tiger. She clings to a vine hanging over a cliff, with the tiger above her and another below. Then two mice begin gnawing at the vine. In that precarious moment, she notices a wild strawberry growing nearby. Without hesitation, she plucks it and eats it. *How sweet it tasted.* That's what life often is: tigers above, tigers below, and a fragile vine in between. We can't escape the tigers, but we can still learn to taste the strawberries.

DOORS TO THE PRESENT

Presence isn't something you master overnight. Life's chaos sidelines our intentions, and when we do remember to take a beat our brains often rebel, because staying in the moment is hard. It's a skill we build slowly and steadily. (Imagine that, for this book!) Setbacks and detours are a given, but that's fine—no matter where we go, after all, there we'll be.

Two ideas are core to the practices I've found most useful in cultivating a sense of presence. The first is a variation on "Little by little, a little becomes a lot," articulated by the mediation teacher

Loch Kelly as "small glimpses many times." The idea is to focus on being present for just a moment or two—again and again. Being present for hours on end is unrealistic. But Kelly fully embraces the principle that has underscored this whole book: that small successes compound. String enough instances of deep presence and you'll notice a profound shift in how connected you feel to your life.

The second key idea is that our senses are the portal to the now. No surprise here; they are the fundamental building blocks of attention and, by extension, experience. Later in this chapter we will explore practices grounded in nature's original toolkit for stopping to smell the roses.

Training Attention

The two kinds of attention discussed earlier, bottom-up and top-down, are constantly being managed by something researchers call a *priority map*. Think of it as your brain's dynamic blueprint for deciding what's worth paying attention to. This map blends bottom-up signals (the shiny, the loud, the unexpected) and top-down directives (your goals and intentions) to help you steer through a world rife with competing stimuli.

In essence, the priority map reflects your ongoing negotiations with reality, balancing the urge to react with the capacity to choose. The bad news is that it's susceptible to being skewed by all the obstacles discussed above: by the gas-pedal adrenaline of busyness, the shiny red herrings of distraction, the *Tetris*-leveling of the problem-focused mentality. But the good news is that like any habit of mind we've explored, your priority map isn't fixed. You can train it.

Countless exercises, hailing from spirituality, psychology, sports, and the arts (not to mention driver's ed) focus on sharpening our experience through sensory awareness. Any of the practices included below can be used as still point exercises, inserted into your everyday patterns in a loop of **When** and **Then**. Each practice will become another "small glimpse" of the infinite, wondrous now.

The Art of Noticing What's Already There

Our brains tend to ignore much that is familiar. They are excellent energy savers: "Seen it, cataloged it, moving on." It's like living in a house where we stop seeing that weird paint chip on the wall or the family photos we walk past every day. This autopilot mode combines with our built-in novelty-seeking system to create a perfect storm of missing what's right in front of us.

This practice is a way to hack both tendencies at once. Choose a route you take regularly (maybe your daily walk, your commute, or even just the path from your bedroom to the kitchen). As you move through this space, set yourself this simple challenge: find something you've never noticed before. Maybe it's:

- A particular tree and the way its branches reach
- An interesting architectural detail on a building
- The sound your feet make on different surfaces
- A neighbor's garden ornament
- The way light falls at a certain time of day

The beauty of this practice is that it turns our novelty-seeking impulse—usually the thing pulling us away from the present—into a tool for becoming more present. Instead of reaching for your phone to scratch that "show me something new" itch, you're training yourself to find novelty in what's already there.

What often happens is fascinating: Once you start really looking, you realize how much you've been missing. That one new detail leads to another, and another. Suddenly your "boring" daily walk becomes an expedition of discovery.

I learned this lesson recently on my regular evening walk route. I've taken this same path hundreds of times, but one day I decided to play this game. Know what I found? A little free library that I swear must have been placed by neighborhood wizards because there's no way I could have missed it before. Except, of course, I had—probably hundreds of times.

This practice isn't just about becoming more observant (though that's a nice side effect). It's about retraining our relationship with familiar settings. It shows us that we don't need new experiences or constant stimulation to feel engaged and alive; we just need to look at what's already here with fresh eyes.

Think of it as a kind of treasure hunt where the treasure is your own attention. Each new discovery is proof that the world is more interesting, more detailed, and more worthy of our presence than our habitual minds would have us believe.

Sacred Ordinary: The Art of Mindful Work

In Zen monasteries, there is a common practice called *samu*: turning everyday tasks into meditation. It's about choosing one routine activity and making it your anchor to the present moment.

Samu serves a specific purpose in Zen training: It's designed to be a bridge between sitting meditation and the rest of our lives. You might be able to find some peace and presence while sitting quietly on a cushion, and you might even have moments of natural presence during peak experiences like watching a sunset. But what about all the time in between?

That's where *samu* comes in. It's like training wheels for bringing mindfulness off the cushion and into the real world. By choosing just one routine activity to practice with, you're creating a kind of laboratory for presence—more challenging than sitting meditation, but more contained than trying to be mindful all day long. It's the middle way between formal practice and daily life.

Thich Nhat Hanh, with his meditation on mindfully washing dishes, was evoking *samu* big-time. How it works:

1. First, pick your practice ground. Choose something you do pretty much every day—making your bed, walking the dog, washing dishes, folding laundry. (Warning: Don't pick something that requires a lot of problem-solving or complex decisions. Your taxes are not great mindfulness material.)

2. Make a clear commitment. This is going to be your daily mindfulness ritual. Not "whenever I remember" but "every time I do this specific thing."

3. When you're doing your chosen activity, make it the star of the show. Notice everything about it: the physical sensations, the sounds, the movements of your body. What does the soap feel like on your hands? How does your weight shift as you walk? What's the texture of the sheets as you smooth them?

4. When your mind wanders (and trust me, it will), just notice that happening and gently bring your attention back to what you're doing. No drama, no self-criticism—just return to the task at hand.

I learned this one the hard way. For years, I treated basic household tasks like they were stealing time from my "real" life. Then one day, while actually paying attention to washing dishes (instead of mentally rehearsing podcast interviews), I had this moment of realizing: This IS my real life. Certain tasks that used to feel like annoying obligations shifted into moments of peace. I found myself doing little things more carefully, more completely, and becoming more curious about their details. These small moments are what most of life is made of.

NO ORDINARY MOMENTS

A former student of mine, Joe, once shared with me a story I'll never forget. It's about the last conversation he ever had with his grandfather.

Joe drove two and a half hours from his home in Philadelphia to a hospital in Connecticut, knowing that his grandfather was nearing the end of his life and that the afternoon's visit might be their last chance to be together. "My intention was clear," he writes. "I wanted to be completely present, and to remain open to whatever my time with him would bring."

It turned out to be a good instinct. Here's how Joe tells the story of that afternoon:

> *When we were alone in the room, he asked me how work was. I assured him that I didn't want to talk about work and my focus was only HIM. He asked about my girlfriend, and I hesitated. I shared with him that although we had talked about marriage, I had a great deal of fear about making that commitment. He wanted to know why and I hesitated again. "Talk to me!" he said.*
>
> *... [So] I shared my fears about repeating the unhealthy, destructive patterns I had witnessed in my parents while I was growing up. I mentioned yelling and my grandfather said that came from him. He was a yeller and likely unfortunately set that example for my father to*

follow. "*How long have you lived with her and have you yelled at her?*" *he asked.* "*Six months and no, I haven't yelled at her,*" *I answered. He looked at me as if to say,* "*See? Nothing to worry about there.*"

I shared more of my fears and he asked a question about each that obliterated them one by one.

My grandfather had never been a particularly touchy-feely guy, never insisting on hugs or much physical contact, but during our visit he asked me to hold his hand. Though he was paralyzed, he could feel my hand in his. In one extraordinary moment, I looked down and saw our knuckles side by side and they looked exactly alike. I visualized my hand covering my father's and my father's covering my grandfather's. There was a remarkable sense of traveling through time and across generations and a feeling of being deeply, deeply connected to each other.

. . . For much of my life, my interactions with my grandfather were awkward and stilted because of a family rift, but that afternoon there was an openness about him that allowed me to see a part of him that I never had. My impression of the man was blown wide open.

Every single moment that day was extraordinary. It was pure presence . . . and I never wanted it to end.

Joe's singular experience of being fully open to the moment and to his grandfather may only have lasted an hour or two, but he says that the reverberations, as well as the cherished memory, have echoed through his life every day since. His grandfather's prompting about his relationship helped him shake off a fear of replicating old patterns, which led to an openness to new chapters in his own life and to the gradual softening of his relationship with his father. That relatively brief experience of deep, intergenerational connection bred seeds of empathy that grew over weeks, months, and years. Little by little.

Of course, not every time you find yourself fully, vividly awake to the moment will be something as obviously consequential as Joe's conversation with his grandfather. Then again, part of the wisdom of presence is that every moment has the capacity to be extraordinary.

When I was eighteen I read a book called *Way of the Peaceful Warrior* by Dan Millman, for the first time, but far from the last—I've revisited it so many times that it feels like catching up with an old friend. The book is a semi-autobiographical novel in which Dan, a gymnast of near Olympic caliber, crosses paths with an eccentric gas station attendant named Socrates. Socrates, as you'd guess, isn't your run-of-the-mill gas station worker—he's the classic wise-guru archetype, with a little "tough love" drill sergeant thrown in.

In one pivotal scene, Dan comes to an epiphany that makes him recall an earlier conversation with his mentor.

> *Several years before, Socrates had insisted, "Walking, sitting, breathing, or taking out the trash deserve as much attention as a triple somersault." "That may be true," I had argued, "but when I do a triple somersault, my life is on the line." "Yes," he replied, "but in every moment, the quality of your life is on the line. Life is a series of moments. In each, you are either awake or you are asleep—fully alive, or relatively dead."*

Dan vows "never again to treat any moment as ordinary," and then goes on to utter the line that pulls it all together: "I've learned that the quality of each moment depends not on what we get from it, but on what we bring to it."

The truest wisdom, indeed the only wisdom, is found right here, right where you are.

Presence is not about perfection or being mindful every second of every day—it's about shifting the balance. Whether it's practicing mindfulness in the shower, seeing the ordinary with fresh eyes, or pausing to truly notice the world around us, the invitation is the same: to wake up to life as it is happening. Small, consistent acts of attention can transform the mundane into the meaningful.

There are no ordinary moments. Because it's not, finally, the moment that makes the difference—it's you.

ONE LITTLE THING YOU CAN DO RIGHT NOW

Wherever you are, notice five things you can see that you haven't paid attention to in the last hour. Really look at them—the texture, color, shape, the way light hits them. You're not trying to find anything profound, just practicing the simple act of seeing what's already here. Presence starts with paying attention to what's in front of you.

When you're ready to go a little deeper, flip to the appendix for extra exercises—or download the companion worksheets anytime at oneyoufeed.net/resources.

CONCLUSION

I'D LOVE TO END THIS BOOK WITH A TIDY FIVE-STEP FRAMEWORK FOR changing your life and becoming happier. I really would. Part of me is still waiting for the meaning of life to arrive via FedEx, and if it does I'll pass it along. But the rest of me knows life doesn't lend itself to easy summaries.

So much of what's in this book is double-edged. Change is good. So is acceptance. Sticking to your plan is good—right up until it's not, and flexibility becomes the wiser move. The thing about double-edged swords is that you have to be careful how you handle them, or you'll end up wondering why self-improvement hurts so much.

What I've tried to give you here is something honest. Something that acknowledges the complexity of being alive, but still points toward ways of living in that complexity a little more wisely. Because just shrugging and saying "well, life is complicated" might be true, but it's not exactly helpful.

There's a metaphor I use all the time that somehow didn't make it into the earlier parts of this book, so let's sneak it in now. Picture yourself at the edge of a forest. A trail disappears into the trees, and about ten feet in, it bends hard to the right. You want to know what's around that corner. You want some kind of cosmic Yelp review before you start walking. But there's no preview button. You can theorize all you want from the trailhead, but you won't know what's ahead until you start walking. Here's the real challenge, though: Not only is the trail changing, *you're* changing too. Every step alters the person taking it. It's like trying to hike while shape-shifting.

That's part of why this book resists simplification. Because I'm hoping the version of you reading this now is a little different from the person who began it. And I'm hoping your path looks a little different too.

・・・

This book is ultimately about changing our relationship to change itself. Instead of seeing change as this thing that we have to do in order to become something or someone else, my hope is that you'll start to see change as already and always happening.

We began by talking about homeostasis—the system in our bodies and minds that tries to keep things the same. It's a survival system to help us stay balanced, to resist disruption, to maintain what we know. But when we're trying to change, it can feel like we're fighting gravity. Every little change we try to make gets pulled back toward the familiar. Even when the familiar isn't in our best interests.

I want to bookend things with a complementary idea: *allostasis*. Where homeostasis is about keeping things the same, allostasis is a biological term that describes *adapting to change in order to stay well*. It's the body learning what tomorrow might demand and making adjustments today. Not digging in its heels, but shifting, anticipating, preparing. It offers a different way to think about long-term change.

Like so many other ideas in this book, allostasis is something ancient wisdom understood long before modern biology caught up.

The Taoist tradition reminds us that we are not things, we are events. Not solid objects, but shifting, breathing, becoming processes. The "self" is not some finished product to defend. It's a constellation of relationships, moving and reshaping in every moment.

In that light, change isn't something we do to ourselves. It's something we *allow*. Something we *join*. Every time we show up to a still point, or start again with a small habit, or bring a little more kindness to the conversation in our heads, we're not imposing something new on ourselves. We're becoming more ourselves. Not in spite of the changes around us, but through them.

That's the kind of system we're trying to build when we commit to wise habits. Not a perfect schedule we never miss. Not a new self we finally "lock in." What we're trying to build is a mindset, a life that can move with the world instead of always trying to fight against it.

This is the paradox of real growth: that we become more whole not by standing apart, but by entering more fully into relationships—with our desires, our patterns, our people, our time on this earth.

That's what your life can be too. Not static. Not rigid. But steady in its own way—a steady that's flexible. This is what wise habits offer us: a way to stay connected to who we want to be, even as everything around us shifts.

· · ·

Another way to think about the kind of change this book has been exploring—slow, steady, sometimes frustrating, sometimes beautiful—is through the image of an upward spiral. Sue Monk Kidd has called the process of letting go a "winding, spiraling process," a description that has always stuck with me. When I interviewed her, she added: "You just go round and round, but you're always going in the right direction, hopefully." We loop back. We fall down. We try again. We learn something new. We forget it.

We relearn it, but a little more deeply this time. And slowly, quietly, things change.

Picture a spiral staircase with photos on the wall. You keep passing by some of the same images—your patterns, your memories, your old stories—but each time, you're seeing them from a slightly different angle, slightly higher up. With a little more light. With a little more distance. You notice something new in the frame. Maybe you understand something in the background you couldn't before. The pictures don't change, but you do.

The metaphor of the spiral shows up all over the place: Jungian psychology, 12-step wisdom, ancient mysticism, modern biology. Neuroscientist Alex Korb, in his book *The Upward Spiral*, describes how small positive actions—like getting good sleep or taking a walk—can rewire our brains toward more clarity and resilience over time. With wise habits, you don't just "get them" one day. You return to them again and again. And if you keep returning—if you keep showing up—you find yourself becoming someone new, even as you're still wrestling with familiar things.

An upward spiral is the long view. It's the lived experience of "little by little, a little becomes a lot." And it's an invitation—not to be perfect, not to "nail it," but to stay in the dance. To be willing to revisit old ground with fresh eyes. To treat setbacks not as proof you've failed, but as signs that you're in it for real. Because real change isn't about never coming back to your old patterns. It's about who you are when you meet them again.

• • •

When I was in AA, every meeting ended the same way. We'd stand in a circle, hold hands, say a prayer—and then, together: "Keep coming back." Sometimes we'd add, "It works if you work it."

If you've read through this book without working through any of the exercises, first: Thank you. Truly. And now, I'd encourage you to *try* the book. Choose one small action and do it. Right now, even. Or right after you finish this sentence. One of my core beliefs is that there's almost always *something* we can do—some small step we can take to nudge our life in a better direction. And small steps, those little things you can do right now, are not nothing. They're motion.

I believe in the spirit of "keep coming back," for recovery and for life. Keep coming back to your values. Keep coming back to the belief that you *can* make the changes you want to make.

Keep trying. Keep learning.

Keep coming back to yourself. Because that's, finally, the kind of change I believe in.

That little by little, we become who we are.

APPENDIX

End-of-Chapter Exercises

TO ACCESS ALL END-OF-CHAPTER EXERCISES AND OTHER RESOURCES, VISIT:

oneyoufeed.net/resources

Chapter 2: What Is Worth Wanting?

First up are several different exercises related to discovering and clarifying your values. Different exercises seem to work best for different people, so I've given you a wide range to choose from. As always with this book it's better to do one then none at all and it's better to give it ten to fifteen minutes than to wait until you have hours free.

WHAT MAKES ME HAPPIEST, PROUDEST, AND MOST FULFILLED?

This exercise emerges from concepts in humanistic psychology like Abraham Maslow's work on self-actualization and peak experiences. Take some time to reflect on the following questions. You may want to write down your thoughts as you go.

STEP 1: *Identify three times when you were happiest.*

Think back on moments, days, or periods in your life when you felt a deep sense of happiness, joy, or contentment. What was happening? Who were you with? What were you doing? Describe these experiences in detail.

STEP 2: *Identify three times when you were most proud.*

Recall situations where you felt a profound sense of pride, achievement, or self-respect. What had you accomplished? What challenges had you overcome? What principles or standards were you upholding? Describe these experiences.

STEP 3: *Identify three times when you were most fulfilled and satisfied.*

Consider the periods when you felt a strong sense of fulfillment, satisfaction, or sense of purpose. What needs were being met? What were you contributing to? How were you growing or expressing your potential? Describe these experiences.

STEP 4: *Determine your top values, based on your experiences of happiness, pride, and fulfillment.*

Once you have done this, look back over the experiences you described. What themes emerge? What qualities, principles, or motivators seem to be sources of happiness, pride, and fulfillment for you? This will give you an idea of some of the things you value.

You can go back to chapter 2 to see how I used this exercise to identify some of my values.

THE FIVE WHYS

This exercise actually begins with choosing your values—but the trick is, don't think too hard about it. Just quickly write down the first three to five things that occur to you as being important.

After you've done that, I'd like you to look at the first item on your list and ask yourself: Why is that important to you?

The Five Whys is a problem-solving technique used to identify the root cause of an issue by asking "Why?" five times in succession. It was developed by Sakichi Toyoda, the founder of Toyota Industries. But we are going to use it to get deeper into our values.

Here's how you might adapt it to identify and better understand your core values:

1. Start with one of the values or beliefs you just wrote down. For example, "I believe in honesty."

2. Ask yourself, "Why is honesty important to me?"
   Answer: "Because honesty builds trust in relationships."

3. Ask "Why?" again: "Why is building trust in relationships important to me?"
   Answer: "Because trust is essential for strong, healthy connections with others."

4. Continue with the next "Why?": "Why are strong, healthy connections with others important to me?"
   Answer: "Because having meaningful relationships enriches my life and brings me happiness."

Now you could ask "why" again, but happiness is a pretty deep emotional desire. We don't always need to go to all Five Whys; often a couple will lead us to a surprisingly foundational place. As we discuss in chapter 4, emotion is not the enemy of interior work but is foundational to it. The deeper the emotion you bring to this, the more life will feel in alignment, and you will have a big enough "Why" to help with motivation.

PICK A GUIDE

I've had the great fortune to talk to many founders of modern schools of psychological thought. Acceptance and commitment therapy (ACT) is a richly evidence-based approach known for its focus on acting according to our values regardless of how we are feeling. Several years ago I asked the two cofounders of ACT what their favorite exercise is for determining values. They each came back to me with the next exercise, which is called "Pick a Guide":

STEP 1: *Select Your Guide*

Start by choosing a person whom you deeply admire. This could be someone from your personal life, a historical figure, or even a fictional character. The key is to pick someone whose qualities and life decisions resonate with you on a profound level.

STEP 2: *Reflect on Qualities*

Take a moment to write down the qualities and attributes of this person that you admire the most. What is it about them that inspires you? Are they kind, brave, wise, or resilient? List as many qualities as you can think of that draw you to this person.

STEP 3: *Imagine a Conversation*

Close your eyes and imagine sitting down in a quiet place with this guide. Visualize yourself discussing a current dilemma or decision you are facing in your life. Ask them for advice. What would they say? How would they handle the situation?

STEP 4: *Listen for Values*

During this imagined conversation, pay close attention to the underlying values that inform the advice and perspective offered by your guide. What principles are they drawing on to guide their advice? For example, if they suggest being honest and transparent in a difficult situation, values such as integrity and honesty are likely important.

STEP 5: *Identify Your Core Values*

Reflect on the conversation and extract the values that were highlighted. Write these down. Consider whether these values align with how you currently live your life and how you make decisions. Are these values you want to embrace more fully?

THE FUNERAL

This exercise I first encountered in Stephen Covey's classic book *The 7 Habits of Highly Effective People*, but it has its origins in both Stoicism and Buddhism, which encourage practitioners to reflect on our own death in order to better understand what is important to us in life. (That said, if picturing your own funeral is a little too dark, your eightieth birthday bash will work just fine.)

STEP 1: *Prepare Your Mind and Environment*

Find a quiet space where you won't be disturbed. Make the space as comfortable as possible, perhaps turning off the light or finding a comfortable seat. Close your eyes and breathe slowly a few times to center yourself and quiet your mind.

STEP 2: *Imagine Your Funeral*

Visualize that you are attending your own funeral. Try to imagine all the details:

> Who is attending?
>
> What kind of setting is it?
>
> What music is playing?
>
> What emotions do you sense in the room?

STEP 3: *Listen to the Eulogies*

Imagine four people from different areas of your life giving eulogies at your funeral:

1. A family member
2. A close friend
3. A work colleague
4. A member of your community or an organization you belong to

For each person, visualize what you hope they would say about you. Consider the following:

What impact did you have on their lives?

What qualities would they highlight about your character?

What achievements or contributions would they mention?

STEP 4: *Reflect on Your Values*

Open your eyes and take some time to reflect on the eulogies you just imagined. What values were highlighted in these imagined speeches?

Many people find this exercise difficult because it shows the gap between what they wish people would say and what they might actually say today. The key here is to imagine this is in the future and that they are saying what you **hope** they will say about you then, not what they will say about you now. Everyone who looks deeply into values finds the ways that they are coming up short, and that's okay. Our goal here is to understand what is important to us.

VALUE-CONFLICT MAPPING

The purpose of this exercise is to help you quickly spot everyday situations where you feel torn between a short-term desire and a long-term value, then consider more harmonious alternatives.

Instructions

1. Recall a Recent Conflict
   - Think of a moment in the past few days where you felt pulled in two directions.
   - Maybe you wanted to watch TV instead of going for a run,

or you felt torn between saying yes to doing a favor versus protecting your own time.

2. **List the Two Forces**
   - On one side of a sheet of paper, write down your immediate want—the impulse you felt in that moment (e.g., comfort, relaxation, or avoiding difficulty).
   - On the other side, write the value that was making you hesitate or feel guilty (e.g., health, learning, integrity).

3. **Identify the Core Tension**
   - Briefly note why the tension existed: What benefit did each side promise you? (e.g., "TV = quick relaxation," versus "Going for a run = sticking to my fitness goal.")

4. **Envision a Healthier Response**
   - Considering both the short-term need (or want) and the long-term value, how might you respond differently if this scenario happened again?
   - For instance, "Maybe I compromise by running for just ten minutes and then watching my show," or "I say no to the favor but offer a smaller way to help."

5. **Reflect on Feelings and Outcomes**
   - Ask: How did I actually feel afterward, and did it align with who I want to be?
   - If there's a mismatch, note one small shift you could make next time to better honor your value.

Reflection Prompt:

When I see the push and pull between what I wanted in the moment and the deeper value I care about, what new insights do I gain about how to handle similar situations?

For worksheets for these exercises and additional exercises visit oneyoufeed.net/resources.

Chapter 3: Changing Plans

Focus: Creating specific, actionable steps toward change, harnessing the SPAR method (specificity, prompts, alignment, resilience), and preparing for obstacles.

PERSONAL SPAR BLUEPRINT

Purpose

Create a personalized action plan using the SPAR framework (specificity, prompts, alignment, resilience) to implement one meaningful change in your life.

Instructions

1. Specificity

    Choose one habit or change you want to implement in your life. Be precise about:
    - **What** exactly you'll do
    - **Where** you'll do it
    - **When** you'll do it
    - **How** long or how much you'll do

2. Prompts

    Select a reliable cue that will prompt your new behavior:
    - A specific time of day
    - A location
    - After completing another routine activity
    - Other people
    - Random
    - Emotional state

3. Alignment

    Modify your environment to support your new habit:
    - **PHYSICAL ENVIRONMENT:** What objects can you add, remove, or rearrange?

- **SOCIAL ENVIRONMENT:** Who can support or join you?
- **DIGITAL ENVIRONMENT:** What apps, reminders, or tools might help?

4. Resilience

Prepare for obstacles by creating backup plans:
- Identify one or two likely challenges that might derail your habit.
- Create an if-then plan for each obstacle.

Example: "If I oversleep, then I'll still meditate for at least two minutes. If I'm traveling, then I'll use a meditation app on my phone wherever I am."

For worksheets for these exercises, and additional exercises visit oneyoufeed.net/resources.

Chapter 4: Moments of Action

CHOICE POINT AWARENESS EXERCISE

Instructions

1. **GET A SMALL NOTEBOOK OR CREATE A NOTE ON YOUR PHONE** that you can easily access throughout the day.

2. **FOR THE NEXT TWO DAYS, NOTICE MOMENTS OF DECISION** in your daily life—those brief pauses where you have to choose between two options (work out or watch TV, healthy lunch or fast food, reply to that email now or later).

3. **WHEN YOU NOTICE A CHOICE POINT, IMMEDIATELY WRITE IT DOWN** as simply as possible:
   - "Choice: TV or workout"
   - "Choice: Healthy lunch or burger"
   - "Choice: Respond to email now or later"

4. **AFTER MAKING YOUR DECISION, ADD A BRIEF NOTE ABOUT:**
   - What you chose
   - Why you chose it
   - How you felt about the choice

5. **BE HONEST BUT CONCISE.** Examples:
   - Watched television. Needed some stress relief. Afterward, I felt guilty.
   - Worked out despite not wanting to. Later felt proud.
   - Delayed text response. Needed mental space. Worried until I finally responded.

6. **REVIEW YOUR NOTES AT THE END OF THE SECOND DAY AND LOOK FOR PATTERNS:**
   - What are the most common feelings or reasons?

- What decisions made you feel good about yourself?
- What decisions do you tend to regret?
- Are there certain times of the day that make decision-making more difficult?

7. **ANSWER THIS REFLECTION PROMPT:** Did simply paying attention to those choice points in the moment change your reaction to them or your feelings later on?

HALT STATE CHECK

This exercise will allow you to identify and work more skillfully with difficult states (HALT: Hungry, Angry, Lonely, or Tired) that can impair self-control.

Instructions

1. Do a midday and end-of-day "temperature check" over the course of a week: Just rate each of the four states on a 1–5 scale (low to high).

2. When the rating is high (such as "lonely: 4"), note what you did—did you comfort-eat, call a friend, or just tough it out?

3. At the week's end, consider: When were high HALT states resulting in unhelpful decisions, and when was I working with them in a way that honored my values?

Reflection Prompt:

Which HALT state, when it rises, tends to derail me the most—and what new strategies might I use next time?

For worksheets for these exercises and additional exercises visit oneyoufeed.net/resources.

Chapter 5: Be a Friend to Yourself

INNER CRITIC DIALOGUE EXERCISE

This exercise helps you practice the three-step process for engaging with your inner critic in a healthier, more productive way. It's important to remember that the inner critic has been around a long time. Don't expect to do this exercise once and see a massive improvement. This is a way of relating to your critic that will cause a shift over time. Little by little ...

Step 1: Meet Your Critic

1. **NAME YOUR CRITIC:** Provide a name to this voice. Is it a cartoon character (Eeyore), a fictional villain (the Evil Queen), someone in your past, or something else? List their name and a brief description.

2. **SET THE SCENE:** Imagine sitting down with your critic for a conversation. Where would this meeting take place? It should be somewhere comfortable but with enough distance to maintain perspective (a coffee shop, a park bench, across a desk).

3. **WELCOME THEM:** On paper, write a brief greeting to your critic: "Hello, [name]. I see you're here again. I'm willing to listen to what you have to say."

Step 2: Listen with Compassionate Distance

1. **RECORD THEIR MESSAGE:** Write down what your critic typically says to you. Don't censor or soften it—let the full force of their usual commentary come through.

2. **FIND THE FEAR:** For each critical statement, ask yourself: "What is this voice afraid might happen?" Write down what you discover. For example:

- "You'll never finish this project" might mask a fear of failure or disappointment.
- "Nobody finds you interesting" might hide a fear of rejection or abandonment.

3. **NOTE THE PATTERN:** Read over what you've written. What is the pattern or theme you see in your critic's objections? Is there a specific area of weakness that they target?

Step 3: Respond Wisely

1. **RECOGNIZE THE TRUTH:** Is there something to what your critic is saying? Not the scathing judgments, but is there a kernel of truth in it? Note this briefly.

2. **PROVIDE INSIGHT:** Give your critic a reply that:
    a. Acknowledges without consenting to their strict characterization
    b. Speaks with compassion and self-understanding
    c. Gives practical guidance or a fresh outlook
        i. For example: "I know you're worried about this presentation. Thank you for not wanting to see me humiliated. I'm thankful you're concerned about my reputation. And you're right that I should be better prepared. I don't have to be perfect to be respected. I'm going to practice twice again before tomorrow, and then have faith that I've done my best."

3. **CLOSE THE CONVERSATION:** End your conversation with a compassionate yet firm statement that creates boundaries with your critic and honors their protective intentions.
    a. For example: "I will consider what you've said; however, I will decide what I do next. I'm responsible here, not my fear."

Reflection Prompt:

After you've completed the exercise, stop and observe:
- How do you feel now compared to when you started?
- What was the biggest challenge of this conversation?
- Did you experience any change in perspective or insight?

REFRAME WITH KINDNESS

PURPOSE: Practice transforming harsh self-criticism into supportive self-talk.

1. **LOOK BACK AT YOUR NOTES** from the first exercise (or recall a specific self-critical thought from recent days).

2. **IDENTIFY ONE CRITICAL PHRASE**—e.g., "I can't believe I messed that up again. I'm so lazy."

3. **ASK:** If a close friend said these words about themselves, how would I respond?

4. **REWRITE** the statement in a supportive, constructive voice. For instance, "I made a mistake, but it's something I can learn from. I'm capable of doing better next time."

5. **COMPARE:** Read the new statement out loud. Notice how it feels different from the original.

Tip: *This exercise helps you see that a more compassionate tone can still be realistic and motivating. It is also much easier to respond to that inner voice when we have decided how and what we want to say instead.*

For a worksheet to walk you through these exercises visit oneyoufeed.net/resources.

Chapter 6: Perspective

STILL POINTS: PRACTICING PERSPECTIVE

In this chapter, we explored how our interpretations shape our experience—and how shifting perspective can change everything. These still points are designed to help you do just that: Step back, widen your view, and see things with more clarity and ease.

PROACTIVE STILL POINTS

These are short, planned mental interruptions built into your day.

You choose the "When"—a regular, everyday cue—and I'll suggest a "Then"—a reflection to practice.

Choose a When from these prompt types:

- Time-based (e.g., when I check the time, when I brush my teeth)
- Location-based (e.g., entering my kitchen, getting into my car)
- Preceding event (e.g., after a meeting ends, after sending an email)
- Other people (e.g., when someone interrupts me, when I greet a colleague)
- Random (e.g., using a reminder app that pings you unpredictably)

Pair it with one of these Then reflections:

    When _____, Then I will ask:

        "What am I making this mean?"

        "What else could it mean?"

        "What meaning would be most useful?"

When _____, **Then I will ask:**

"Am I taking this personally, permanently, or pervasively?"

Then I'll remind myself: Most things are temporary, not personal, and limited in scope.

When _____, **Then I will ask:**

"Will this still bother me in five hours? Five days? Five weeks?"

Tip: Choose one prompt and practice it consistently for a few days before switching or adding more.

RESPONSIVE STILL POINTS

These happen in real time—right in the middle of an emotional reaction.

You choose the "When"—a specific emotion—and the "Then" can be any of the perspective-shifting reflections above.

Choose a When (emotion):

- When I feel **frustrated**, Then...
- When I feel **anxious**, Then...
- When I feel **overwhelmed**, Then...

Create your own:

When I feel _____, Then I will _____

Example: When I feel anxious, Then I will pause and ask, "What story am I telling myself right now—and is there a kinder version?"

Example: Practicing Perspective with a Random Reminder

Set a reminder app to ping you four to five times a day with this still point: When my app notifies me, Then I will ask: "Is there a way to zoom out and see this more clearly?"

A Day in the Life with This Practice

10:30 a.m. Scrolling social media, feeling envy → Zoom out: "Everyone has ups and downs."

2:15 p.m. Dreading a family event → Zoom out: "These events are mixed bags, not all bad."

6:45 p.m. Minor disagreement with a partner → Zoom out: "One bump in an otherwise strong relationship."

9:20 p.m. Feeling unproductive → Zoom out: "A single off day doesn't define my overall rhythm."

Why This Works

Proactive still points build your default mindset. Responsive still points help you use that mindset when emotions flare up. Practicing both helps rewire how you interpret challenges—bit by bit, shift by shift.

OTHER EXERCISES

The "What Am I Making This Mean?" Journal

Choose three situations from your past week that triggered strong emotions or reactions. For each situation:

1. Describe the factual events as objectively as possible (just what a camera would capture).

2. Write down your initial interpretation: "What I made this mean was..."

3. Generate at least three alternative interpretations: "What else could this mean?"

4. Reflect on which interpretation feels most useful or constructive for moving forward.

Example:

- **FACTUAL EVENT:** My friend didn't respond to my text for two days.
- **INITIAL INTERPRETATION:** "They're mad at me or don't value our friendship."
- **ALTERNATIVE MEANINGS:** "They might be overwhelmed with work." "Their phone could be broken." "When I get too many texts I tend to lose track of them and forget to reply."
- **MOST USEFUL PERSPECTIVE:** Assuming they're busy rather than upset preserves the relationship while I wait to hear from them.

The Three P's Check-In

Bring to mind a scenario that has been upsetting or worrying you this week. Take five minutes and look at it through the lens of the Three P's.

Three P's:

1. **PERMANENT:** Am I seeing this situation as unchangeable and eternal? How might it evolve or shift over time?

2. **PERSONAL:** Am I taking this too personally, as if it's uniquely about or directed at me? How might others be experiencing similar challenges?

3. **PERVASIVE:** Am I letting this situation color my entire view of life? What areas remain unaffected and positive?

Create a simple chart with three columns for the P's and use check marks or brief notes to track how your thinking might be trending toward these patterns.

For a worksheet to walk you through the Three P's Tracker or The "What Am I Making This Mean?" Journal visit oneyoufeed.net/resources.

Chapter 7: The Middle Way

STILL POINTS

This chapter focused on embracing nuance, holding tension, and stepping away from extremes. The still points below are designed to help you soften polarized thinking, reframe either-or dilemmas, and settle into wiser, more balanced ground.

PROACTIVE STILL POINTS

These are short, intentional check-ins you build into your daily life.

You choose the **"When"**—a regular, everyday cue—and I'll suggest a **"Then"**—a reflection or practice to try.

Choose a When from these prompt types:

- Time-based (e.g., when I check the time, when I start the kettle)
- Location-based (e.g., entering the bathroom, sitting at my desk)
- Preceding Event (e.g., after sending an email, after finishing a meeting)
- Other people (e.g., when someone disagrees with me, when I'm interrupted)
- Random (e.g., using a reminder app that pings you unpredictably)

Pair it with one of these Then practices or reflections:

- **When** _____, **Then** I will take a deep breath and rephrase my most recent thought using more balanced language—replacing any extreme words like "always," "never," or "terrible" with something more moderate.
- **When** _____, **Then** I will pause and ask: "Is there a third path I'm not seeing yet?"
- **When** _____, **Then** I will ask: "Can I make space for both/and thinking in this moment?"

RESPONSIVE STILL POINTS

These happen in real time—right in the middle of an emotional reaction.

You choose the "When"—a specific emotion—and the "Then" can be any of the perspective-shifting reflections above.

Choose a When (emotion):

- When I feel **frustrated**, Then...
- When I feel **anxious**, Then...
- When I feel **overwhelmed**, Then...

Create your own:

When I feel _____,
Then I will _____.

OTHER EXERCISES

Finding Your Personal Middle Ways

Take some time to reflect on areas in your life where you might be veering toward extremes. For each area below, identify:

1. What the extreme positions look like for you.
2. What a middle way approach might involve.

Comfort and Discomfort

- Too much comfort might look like: _____
- Too much discomfort might look like: _____
- A balanced middle way could be: _____

Optimism and Pessimism

- When I'm overly optimistic, I tend to: _____
- When I'm overly pessimistic, I tend to: _____
- A more balanced approach would be: _____

Ordinary and Extraordinary

- When I pressure myself to be extraordinary, it shows up as:
  _____
- When I settle for less than I'm capable of, it looks like:
  _____
- A middle way that honors both contentment and growth might be:
  _____

Choice and Acceptance

- Areas where I try to control too much: _____
- Areas where I've given up agency unnecessarily: _____
  _____
- A balanced approach that respects both my influence and its limits:
  _____

Language Moderation Practice

This exercise helps you identify and moderate extreme language patterns that reinforce black-and-white thinking.

1. Make a list of your personal red-flag words—extreme modifiers, absolutes, and judgments you frequently use:
    - Adverbs (*always*, *never*, *completely*, etc.): _____
    - Adjectives (*terrible*, *perfect*, *horrific*, etc.): _____
    - Pronouns (*everyone*, *no one*, etc.): _____

2. For each word, write a more moderate alternative:
   Example: "always" → "sometimes" or "often" _____
   _____

3. Practice rewriting these sentences using your moderate alternatives:
    - "I always mess up when I try something new." _____
      _____
    - "That meeting was a complete disaster." _____

- "Everyone thinks my idea is stupid." _____

- "Nothing ever works out for me." _____

The Third Thing Exploration

Choose a situation in your life where you feel caught between two options or perspectives:

1. Describe the situation and the binary choice you perceive: _____

2. Now, challenge yourself to identify at least three alternatives that don't fit neatly into either category:
    - Alternative 1: _____
    - Alternative 2: _____
    - Alternative 3: _____

3. Reflect: What insights emerged when you looked beyond the either-or thinking? How might this "third-thing" approach create new possibilities?

For a worksheet to walk you through the middle-way exercises please visit oneyoufeed.net/resources.

Chapter 8: All Together Now

STILL POINTS

This chapter focused on the essential role of community in personal change—the way connection, contribution, and vulnerability deepen and sustain transformation. The still points below are designed to help you stay open to others, reach out even when it's uncomfortable, and remember that you're not in this alone.

PROACTIVE STILL POINTS

These are short, intentional check-ins you build into your daily life.

You choose the **When**—a regular, everyday cue—and pair it with a **Then**—a reflection or practice to try.

Choose a When from these prompt types:

- **TIME-BASED:** (e.g., when I make coffee, when I check the time)
- **LOCATION-BASED:** (e.g., entering a shared space, getting into my car)
- **PRECEDING EVENT:** (e.g., after sending a text, before logging into a meeting)
- **OTHER PEOPLE:** (e.g., when I see a neighbor, when a friend pops into my mind)
- **RANDOM:** (e.g., using a reminder app that pings you unpredictably)

Pair it with one of these Then reflections or practices:

- **When** _____, **Then** I will ask: "Is there someone I could check in on or send a quick message to today?"
- **When** _____, **Then** I will take a breath and remember: I don't have to do this alone.
- **When** _____, **Then** I will bring to mind someone I'm grateful for—and silently wish them well.
- **When** _____, **Then** I will ask: "What's one way I can be more open or available to others right now?"

- **When** _____, **Then** I will remind myself: Mutual support means letting myself receive too.

RESPONSIVE STILL POINTS

These happen in real time—right in the middle of an emotional reaction.

You choose the **When** (a specific emotion), and the **Then** can be any connection-oriented reflection or action.

Choose a When (emotion):

- **When** I feel isolated, **Then** I will text one person I trust—even just to say hi.
- **When** I feel reluctant to ask for help, **Then** I will remind myself: Connection isn't weakness. It's wisdom.
- **When** I feel resentful, **Then** I will ask: "Is there a need I haven't voiced yet?"
- **When** I feel like I don't belong, **Then** I will remember: Belonging isn't about fitting in—it's about showing up as I am.

Create your own:

When I feel _____,
Then I will _____.

OTHER EXERCISES

The "Lost Touch" Reach Out

This is an exercise that I try to do about once per week and it has been very useful in keeping connected to many friends. I'm always amazed at how easy it is to let a long time go by between contacts. This helps me minimize that.

As suggested in the chapter:

1. Take out your phone and scroll through recent text conversations.

2. Identify someone you haven't connected with in a while but who matters to you.

3. Send them a simple message: "Hi, I was thinking about you and wanted to connect."

4. Note how it feels to take this small step toward strengthening a connection.

Afterward, reflect: What hesitation, if any, did you feel before reaching out? What emotions came up after sending the message?

Community Exploration Map

Identify potential ways to deepen existing connections or find new communities:

1. List places you already go regularly (work, gym, coffee shop, online forums, etc.)

2. For each place, note:
   - Current level of connection (stranger, acquaintance, building friendship)
   - One small step you could take to deepen connection (introduce yourself, join a conversation, suggest coffee)
   - Potential barriers to connection and how you might address them

3. Identify two to three new places aligned with your interests where you might find community:
   - What values or interests would you like to share with others?
   - What organizations, groups, or places cater to these interests?
   - What's one small step you could take in the next week to explore this potential community?

For worksheets for these exercises and additional exercises visit oneyoufeed.net/resources.

Chapter 9: Allowing Everything to Be Exactly as It Is

STILL POINTS

This chapter focused on the radical power of acceptance—learning to stop resisting reality and instead allow things to be as they are, even when we wish they were different. The still points below are designed to help you soften resistance, step out of the struggle, and make peace with the present moment.

PROACTIVE STILL POINTS

These are short, intentional check-ins you build into your daily life.

You choose the **When**—a regular, everyday cue—and pair it with a **Then**—a reflection or practice to try.

Choose a When from these prompt types:

- **TIME-BASED:** (e.g., when my alarm goes off, when my calendar gives me an alert, when I turn off a light)
- **LOCATION-BASED:** (e.g., stepping into the shower, getting into bed)
- **PRECEDING EVENT:** (e.g., after finishing a task, when I pour my morning coffee)
- **OTHER PEOPLE:** (e.g., when I feel irritated by someone, when I feel unseen)
- **RANDOM:** (e.g., using a reminder app that pings you unpredictably)

Pair it with one of these Then reflections or practices:

- **When** _____, **Then** I will take a deep breath and say: "Yes."
- **When** _____, **Then** I will ask: "What if nothing needs to change in this moment?"
- **When** _____, **Then** I will soften my body and say gently: "Let it be."

- **When** _____, **Then** I will place a hand over my heart and silently affirm: "I can be with this."
- **When** _____, **Then** I will remind myself: Acceptance isn't giving up—it's the beginning of freedom.

RESPONSIVE STILL POINTS

These happen in real time—right in the middle of an emotional reaction.

You choose the **When** (a specific emotion), and the **Then** can be any grounded, accepting response.

Choose a When (emotion):

- **When I feel frustrated**, **Then** I will pause and whisper: "It's okay to feel this."
- **When I feel disappointed**, **Then** I will take a breath and say: "This belongs too."
- **When I feel tense**, **Then** I will relax my shoulders and repeat: "Let go, just for now."
- **When I feel like controlling everything**, **Then** I will ask: "Can I allow this to be imperfect?"

OTHER EXERCISES

Mapping Your Circle of Control

Following the Covey/Epictetus models mentioned in the chapter:

1. Draw three concentric circles on a piece of paper.
   - Inner circle: Label this "Direct Control" (thoughts, choices, actions)
   - Middle circle: Label this "Influence" (outcomes you can influence but not control)
   - Outer circle: Label this "No Control" (weather, others' actions, past events)

2. Consider a current challenge in your life and list specific elements of this situation that belong in each circle.

3. Reflect on where you're investing most of your energy:
    - Are you exhausting yourself fighting elements in the "No Control" circle?
    - Are there aspects in your "Direct Control" circle you've been ignoring?
    - How might shifting your focus inward change your experience?

The Resistance Inventory

Following the Suffering = Pain x Resistance" equation from the chapter:

1. Identify something causing discomfort in your life right now.

2. On a scale of 1–10, rate:
    - The actual pain or discomfort itself
    - Your level of resistance to this reality (fighting, denying, ruminating)

3. Multiply these numbers to get your "suffering score."

4. Now, imagine reducing your resistance by just 2 points. Calculate your new suffering score.

5. Write down specific ways you might lower your resistance even while the situation remains unchanged:
    - What mental stories could you let go of?
    - What physical tension could you release?
    - What expectations might you need to adjust?

The Practice: Wide Horizon Vision

1. **PREPARE THE SPACE:** Find a comfortable place to sit or stand. Ensure you are in a space where you can relax without distraction.

2. **START WITH A GENTLE GAZE:** Look straight ahead, allowing your eyes to focus softly on the room's center. Do not fixate on any specific object.

3. **EXPAND YOUR VISION:** Without moving your eyes, gradually broaden your gaze to include the edges of the room. Notice how the whole space comes into view without needing to "look" at any one thing.

4. **ENGAGE PERIPHERAL AWARENESS:** Extend your arms behind your head, out of sight, and slowly bring them forward until you can just barely see your fingers at the edges of your vision. Keep your gaze relaxed as you do this. The goal is to find the outermost limit of your peripheral field.

5. **STRETCH THE HORIZON:** Drop your arms but maintain the awareness of your peripheral field. Imagine your vision stretching to encompass everything from the farthest edges inward. Notice how you're not looking at anything, but rather seeing everything at once.

6. **SOFTEN AND SUSTAIN:** Hold this expansive awareness for a few moments or as long as you feel comfortable. Allow yourself to notice how your thoughts quiet and your body relaxes.

For a worksheet to walk you through the Allowing Everything to Be Exactly as It Is exercises visit oneyoufeed.net/resources.

Chapter 10: The Gift of Presence

STILL POINTS

This chapter focused on presence—our capacity to be in the here and now, rather than pulled into the past or future. Presence allows us to experience life more fully, access joy in the ordinary, and respond with greater clarity. The still points below are designed to help you return to this moment again and again, with curiosity and care.

PROACTIVE STILL POINTS

These are short, intentional check-ins you build into your daily life.

You choose the **When**—a regular, everyday cue—and pair it with a **Then**—a reflection or practice to try.

Choose a When from these prompt types:

- **TIME-BASED:** (e.g., when I sip my morning drink, when I glance at the clock)
- **LOCATION-BASED:** (e.g., stepping outside, entering a doorway)
- **PRECEDING EVENT:** (e.g., after checking email, before starting a task)
- **OTHER PEOPLE:** (e.g., when talking to someone, when interrupted)
- **RANDOM:** (e.g., using a reminder app that pings you unpredictably)

Pair it with one of these Then reflections or practices:

- **When** _____, **Then** I will pause and name three things I can see, hear, and feel.
- **When** _____, **Then** I will take a slow breath and say: "This is the moment I'm in."
- **When** _____, **Then** I will ask: "What am I noticing right now?"
- **When** _____, **Then** I will bring awareness to my body—my posture, my breath, my feet on the ground.
- **When** _____, **Then** I will remind myself: I don't have to be anywhere else.

- **When** I find myself waiting (in line, at a stoplight, for an appointment), **Then** I will scan my surroundings and notice as many things as I can that are red, then blue, then green.

RESPONSIVE STILL POINTS

These happen in real time—right in the middle of an emotional reaction.

You choose the **When** (a specific emotion), and the **Then** can be any presence-restoring reflection or action.

Choose a When (emotion):

- **When I feel scattered, Then** I will take one slow breath and focus on one sensory detail.
- **When I feel rushed, Then** I will whisper: "I can go fast without rushing."
- **When I feel disconnected, Then** I will bring my full attention to what is in front of me.
- **When I feel like I'm missing life, Then** I will pause and say: "Come back, just for now."
- **When I find myself waiting** (in line, at a traffic light, for an appointment), **Then** I will scan my surroundings and notice as many things as I can that are red, then blue, then green.

OTHER EXERCISES

Grounding in the Senses

We encountered this simple and effective sensory exercise in our introduction to still points. As a refresher, it's a three-part task:

1. Name five things you can see.
2. Name four things you can hear.
3. Name three things you can physically feel.

These three questions pull your brain into the moment. They work because they're concrete, structured, and—let's be honest—our minds like having something to chew on, even when we're "just" reflecting. This exercise also helps us sidestep the brain's habit of running the same old noticing patterns. By prompting ourselves to list multiple details for each sense, we start to stretch the boundaries of what we typically pay attention to. Bit by bit, we train ourselves to widen the circle of our awareness.

The Mindful Shower Practice

Do you know what is harder than it appears? Trying to tune in to what's happening in your body when you're just sitting totally still on a meditation cushion. Half the time I'm wondering if I'm actually perceiving something or imagining it because I'm so focused on detecting it. (The other half I'm choosing what I'm going to have for lunch.)

The shower, on the other hand, is something else entirely. You're surrounded by sensory experience: water hitting your scalp, dripping off your back, steam surrounding you, temperature shifting as you come in and out of the spray. It's a perfect mindfulness laboratory, and chances are you're already doing it every day.

How to Practice

1. Start at your head or your feet.

2. Feel every sensation as the water hits various parts of your body.

3. Become aware of the sensations: Is the pressure stronger or softer in some places? How does the temperature feel when the water is flowing over your skin? Do you perceive any sounds?

4. When your mind does wander (which it will), just bring your attention back to the next area of your body and whatever sensations you're having there.

The beauty of this exercise is that it doesn't involve any extra time in your day. You're already in the shower—you might as well get the most out of those minutes to train your attention muscles rather than rehearsing arguments in your head or composing emails you won't send.

In addition, beginning with an environment full of physical sensations makes it simpler to tune in to what's going on in your body at other times. Consider it training wheels for becoming aware of your body. Practice shower mindfulness, and before you know it you might be more attuned to how you're actually experiencing yourself throughout the day.

Seeing with Fresh Eyes

How to do it

1. **FIND A PLACE TO SIT OR STAND COMFORTABLY:** Choose a spot where you can look around without rushing—this could be indoors or outdoors. Anywhere with a variety of visual stimuli works well.

2. **ZOOM IN ON COLOR VARIATIONS:** Start by focusing on colors around you. Look closely at objects and notice how many shades you can identify. For example, a single leaf might have greens, yellows, or even browns.

3. **SQUINT AND JOIN OBJECTS TOGETHER:** Partially close your eyes and notice how objects blend together. This blurring effect helps you see forms and patterns instead of individual items, creating a new way of looking at the space.

4. **LOOK FOR THE NEGATIVE SPACE:** Shift your focus to the empty areas between objects. For example, the gaps between tree branches or the space around a coffee mug on a table.

5. **EXAMINE EDGES:** Trace the outline of objects with your eyes. Notice how edges meet and define the forms of things. Pay attention to where one thing ends, and another begins.

6. **OBSERVE SHADOWS AND LIGHT:** Look at how light falls across surfaces, creating highlights and shadows. Notice how they interact and shift, revealing depth and texture.

By shifting your focus to details like color, edges, and negative space, you challenge the brain's tendency to overlook what it has already categorized as "known." It's a way of seeing familiar things in a new way.

The Sound of Now: Finding Your "Sticky Anchor"

I struggled for years with standard breath meditation. I just couldn't seem to remain focused on it. But then I stumbled into trying something different.

Listening. Not just casual listening, but really listening. To everything.

I noticed that if instead of trying to focus on my breath, I just listened to whatever sounds were around me, I was better able to "settle in" to meditation.

That moment changed my entire relationship with meditation. Instead of fighting with my attention, I had found what I now call a "sticky anchor"—something that naturally holds attention because it's constantly changing and doesn't require effort to notice.

The Sound Meditation Practice (for a guided version of this, visit oneyoufeed.net/resources)

1. **FIND A PLACE TO SIT COMFORTABLY.** (Don't worry about making it perfectly quiet—that's actually missing the point.)

2. **CLOSE YOUR EYES IF THAT FEELS COMFORTABLE.** If not, soften your gaze.

3. **BEGIN TO NOTICE SOUNDS. ALL OF THEM.** The obvious ones, the subtle ones, the ones far away and the ones nearby. Try your best to let all sounds be neutral.

4. **WHEN YOU NOTICE YOUR MIND WANDERING (BECAUSE IT WILL),** gently bring your attention back to any sound you can hear in that moment.

What makes this practice special

- You don't have to create anything or force anything—sounds are already happening.
- There's no "wrong" sound to notice.
- The ever-changing nature of sounds makes them naturally interesting to your mind.
- You can do this practically anywhere: in a park, at your desk, even in a busy coffee shop.

A few tips from my experience

- Try not to rank sounds as "good" or "bad"—that bird isn't more meditation-worthy than that car alarm. However, you will notice that you naturally prefer certain sounds. Don't try to fight this, just notice.
- Notice how sounds arise and fade naturally.
- Pay attention to the spaces between sounds too.
- If you find yourself naming sounds ("That's a car," "That's my neighbor's dog"), see if you can listen to them as pure sound instead.

I recommend this practice especially if:

- Traditional meditation has felt frustrating.
- You're new to mindfulness.
- You tend to get caught up in thoughts.
- You want a practice you can do anywhere.

The real magic of sound meditation isn't just that it's easier than watching your breath. It's that it trains you to be present in the world as it actually is, not as you wish it was. That truck backing up? It's not interrupting your meditation—it is your meditation. The kids screaming next door? Also meditation. Your own stomach growling? You guessed it.

You might find yourself more able to be with experiences as they are, rather than as you think they should be. And that, it turns out, is what meditation was trying to teach us all along.

Start with just five minutes. That's it. See what it's like to simply listen, without needing to change anything at all about what you hear.

Reflection Prompt:

After practicing sound meditation for a week, what shifts do you notice in how you relate to distractions in other areas of your life?

For a worksheet to walk you through these exercises visit oneyoufeed.net/resources.

ACKNOWLEDGMENTS

I WAS NEVER MUCH INTERESTED IN THE ACKNOWLEDGMENTS SECTION OF books until I began to understand what it actually takes to write one. At which point I started paying attention, and I noticed something: Writing a book seems to require a tremendous amount of help from other people. This book is no different.

Also, those of you who know me know I am forgetful. I'm sure I have missed many people in this. Don't take it personal. ☺

I never know what order these things should go in: Most important people first? Most important people last?

I'll start with the team most directly responsible for this book existing at all: my wonderful agent, Richard Pine; William Callahan at Inkwell for helping me create a proposal out of the mess I dropped at his feet; my editor at Harvest Books, Sarah Pelz, for believing in this book and helping it find a home; and Meghan Houser, for her knowledge, skill, and dedication to this book.

To people who read early versions of this book and gave feedback: A. J. Jacobs, Carl Erik Fisher, and Andy J. Pizza. Your insights made this so much better.

Also Scott Edelstein for help when this was but a glimmer, and Todd Sattersen for guidance late in the journey.

This book wouldn't be possible without *The One You Feed* podcast, and the podcast wouldn't be possible without Nicole and Chris. Chris, whose enthusiasm, commitment, dedication, deep friendship, and help were critical to this podcast existing at all—none of this would have been worth doing if you weren't accompanying me the whole way. And we wouldn't be able to get anything done without Nicole's support, steering, and deep commitment.

To all *The One You Feed* guests, whose knowledge, wisdom, kindness, and generosity informed every page of this book. A particular shout-out to Andrew Solomon, Oliver Burkeman, Dan Millman, George Watsky, Lodro Rinzler, Frank Turner, and Mike Scott, who agreed to come on the show when it literally did not exist yet. Your willingness to do so helped me believe in it from the very beginning.

To all of our Patreon supporters over all the years—your belief in what we were doing made it possible to keep going. A special shout-out to John Britton.

To my friends further along the journey than I am: Rick Hanson, Henry Shukman, Krista Tippett, Lewis Howes, Dani Shapiro, Mirabai Starr, Cory Allen, Debbie Millman, Martha Beck, Rainn Wilson, Gabor Maté, Michael Bungay Stanier, Matthew Quick, Parker Palmer, Catherine Gray, Emma Gannon, Paul Gyodo Agostinelli, Adyshanti. You've shown me what's possible.

To Charles Fry for seeing something in me that I didn't and shaping my whole career.

To Jonathan Fields, whose advice, mentorship, and guidance have been helping me steer the ship for eleven years.

To Charlie Gilkey, my wise coach and friend.

To Susan Cain, for introducing me to Richard and for being my favorite person to nerd out about Leonard Cohen with.

To everyone who's had me on their podcast over the years—thank you for the platform and the conversation. I hope you'll have me back on your podcast to discuss this book. :)

To my family—my brother, Matt; my sisters, Joy and Mary; my mom for making me a reader; and my dad for teaching me how to work hard. (Maybe I should just say "family"—but then again, each of you has shown up in your own particular way.)

To all the people in 12-step programs who saved my life. Twice.

To all dogs everywhere, but to a few in particular. To Birdy for opening the door; to Sadie for teaching me about a different kind of love; and to Ralph, Beans, and Lola for deepening that love and giving me so many hours of joy. I miss you all.

To all the poets, writers, and musicians who have inspired and comforted me over the years.

To all the participants in my Spiritual Habits and Wise Habits programs, with extra thanks to those who have taken Circle of Connection. And to all the facilitators who have helped make that work possible in the world. To all my coaching clients—you've taught me as much as I've taught you.

To Jane Hamilton, for helping with reading this book and with the Tao Te Ching Project, and for being such a huge support to me and *The One You Feed* over the years in so many ways.

To my friends—Joe Russell, Steve Thompson, Bela Koe-Krompecher (thanks for the Sunday writing sessions), Ken Barker, Jon Mills. (And whoever I'm forgetting—you know who you are, and you know I'm grateful.)

How do you choose who gets the coveted last spot? I went with alphabetical order.

To Ginny, my partner, my adviser, my best friend, and the love of my life. Thank you for everything—which is both inadequate and exactly right.

To JRZ—writing this book is a big accomplishment, but it pales in comparison to the accomplishment of having a son as wonderful as you.

NOTES

Where there are attributed quotes in the text not cited below, they derive from interviews for *The One You Feed* or otherwise personal conversations.

Introduction

xiv The second was how rarely: I'm happy to say this has changed greatly in the eleven years since I started the podcast.

xv insights of this science narrowly focused: All these are worthwhile goals, but in their most lasting, consequential forms I believe they are always tied to deeper questions of meaning.

xix A favorite motto: Suetonius, John Carew Wolfe, *Lives of the Caesars*, vol. 1 (Harvard University Press, 1998).

Chapter 1: Little by Little

4 He became famous across India: "Dashrath Manjhi," *Wikipedia*, May 16, 2025, https://en.wikipedia.org/w/index.php?title=Dashrath_Manjhi&oldid=1290659826.

6 "The little decisions": C. S. Lewis, *Mere Christianity* (Geoffrey Bles, 1952), 132.

6 One answer to this cosmic question: When I say homeostasis is *one* explanation for our resistance to change, I mean just that. It's a useful starting point, but there are a lot of reasons that change is hard. The rest of this book will explore many others while offering paths forward.

6   a single word: homeostasis: While I have found homeostasis to be a useful model in describing resistance to change, it is worth noting that this is more metaphor than precise science when applied to behavior. Our brains are not consciously enforcing equilibrium like a thermostat. What could appear to be a "don't rock the boat" system is actually a complex dance of physiological processes (like hunger when we are dieting), psychological processes (status quo bias, whereby we like things to stay the same), and emotional attachments to our routine habits (habit inertia). When I attribute homeostasis as bringing on our "fuck-it" moments, I am simplifying a number of systems that interact to bring on resistance. Your body's automatic regulatory responses (temperature regulation, blood sugar, etc.) certainly do, but our resistance to changing behavior also encompasses comfort zones, habit loops, and how we respond to immediate versus long-term rewards. I use homeostasis as a metaphor throughout this book because it explains why change does feel like swimming upstream—our bodies and minds really do crave stability. But remember that we are also more than biological systems. Our attitudes, stress levels, and environments all get a vote in whether we push through discomfort or fall back into our old patterns.

7   If you are trying to lose weight: Venu Madhav Ganipisetti and Pratyusha Bollimunta, "Obesity and Set-Point Theory," in *StatPearls* (StatPearls Publishing, 2025), http://www.ncbi.nlm.nih.gov/books/NBK592402/.

12 First developed in the late 1970s and '80s: The Stages-of-Change framework has earned its place in the public lexicon because it gives people a simple, intuitive map for gauging "readiness." That clarity is why clinicians, coaches, and quitlines still reach for it, and why you'll see it referenced here. Yet the academic picture is more ambivalent. Since the mid-2000s, systematic reviews have struggled to show that stage-tailored interventions reliably outperform generic ones, and researchers have questioned whether the five stages are truly distinct or just arbitrary mile-markers (see West 2005; Riemsma et al. 2003). In other words, the model excels at describing how many of us *feel* while changing, but it is not a guarantee of *how* to change.

For that reason, treat the TTM as a conversation starter, not marching orders. If its language—precontemplation, contemplation, preparation, action, and maintenance—helps you locate yourself on the map and choose the next *low-resistance* step, use it. If you find your experience looping backward, skipping stages, or resisting neat labels, that is not failure; it is human complexity the model was never designed to capture. Pair the TTM's snapshots of motivation with other evidence-based tools (habit design, environmental tweaks, social support) and, above all, with your own lived feedback. Frameworks are scaffolding; real change is the building you erect around them.

13 The problem with large behaviors: Michelle Segar, "It's Time to Unhabit and Think Critically About Whether Habit Formation Has Been Over Valued as a Behavior Change Strategy Within Health Promotion," *American Journal of Health Promotion* 36, no. 8 (October 2022): 1418–20, https://doi.org/10.1177/08901171221125326f, as one example.

13 basic reward theory: Wolfram Schultz, "Neuronal Reward and Decision Signals: From Theories to Data," *Physiological Reviews* 95, no. 3 (June 2015): 853–951, https://doi.org/10.1152/physrev.00023.2014.

13 That balancing act considers all sorts of variables: Harold H. Lee, Jessica A. Emerson, and David M. Williams, "The Exercise–Affect–Adherence Pathway: An Evolutionary Perspective," *Frontiers in Psychology* 7 (August 2016), https://doi.org/10.3389/fpsyg.2016.01285.

14 "context" refers to the whole host: Wendy Wood, Leona Tam, and Melissa Guerrero Witt, "Changing Circumstances, Disrupting Habits," *Journal of Personality and Social Psychology* 88, no. 6 (June 2005): 918–33, https://doi.org/10.1037/0022-3514.88.6.918.

14 a high degree of "automaticity": Phillippa Lally et al., "How Are Habits Formed: Modelling Habit Formation in the Real World," *European Journal of Social Psychology* 40, no. 6 (July 2009): 998–1009, https://doi.org/10.1002/ejsp.674.

15 Matt Wilpers, a highly sought-after trainer: "Team Wilpers: Train Hard. Train Smart. Have Fun!," March 31, 2021, https://blog.teamwilpers.com/page/2/.

17 the voices that spoke to me: Jack Kornfield and Pema Chodron are Buddhist but not teachers of Zen Buddhism.

18 One of the most famous expressions: Laozi, *Tao Te Ching*, trans. Gia-fu Feng (Knopf, 1972), chap. 64.

18 "Drop by drop": Acharya Buddharakkhita, trans., *The Dhammapada: The Buddha's Path of Wisdom* (Buddhist Publication Society, 2008), Dhp 122.

18 As a user on the r/Buddhism subreddit wrote: Mayayana, "There are many stories . . . ," Reddit comment, R/Buddhism, November 1, 2022, https://www.reddit.com/r/Buddhism/comments/yj4knq/gradual_vs_sudden/iumftsu/.

18 a student named Gensha: Judith Ragir, "Gensha Stubbed His Toe," White Lotus Judith Ragir, judithragirr.org., https://www.judithragir.org/2017/04/gensha-stubbed-toe/.

18 There are also the meditative koans: In the Zen tradition, a koan is a teaching device—usually in the form of a question, dialogue, or short story—used to help students break free from habitual thought patterns and experience a more direct, intuitive insight into reality. While they often sound paradoxical ("Does a dog have Buddha-nature?" or "How do you stop the sound of a distant temple bell?"), their purpose isn't to confuse; it's to invite a different kind of knowing—a more direct, intuitive, and alive understanding than ordinary conceptual logic. Traditionally, a Zen student is given a koan to meditate with, not as a problem to figure out but as a gateway to deeper insight. Over time, the student brings their response to a teacher in one-on-one meetings called dokusan. The teacher's role is to discern whether the student's presentation expresses genuine insight. I've worked through about a hundred koans with my own teacher, and I can say from experience: It's an experience like no other. Not quite meditation, or therapy, or poetry workshop, not quite performance art, but something of all of them. The basic rhythm of our koan sessions was this: I'd go in, offer my best shot at interpretation, and my teacher would often say, kindly but firmly, "I think you just need to sit with that a little longer." Which is modern Zenspeak for: "Nope." Over time, though, something would change. It didn't feel like adding knowledge, but like wearing away something unnecessary. At some point, you stop trying to "get" the koan—and it gets you. Koans don't deliver answers in any conventional sense. But over time, if you keep showing up, they reveal a kind of clarity that doesn't rely on figuring anything out.

19 If there is someone out there: In a later chapter I will tell my own story of a "sudden awakening" that was, of course, preceded by years of practice.

20 scientific study after study shows: Aumyo Hassan and Sarah J. Barber, "The Effects of Repetition Frequency on the Illusory Truth Effect," *Cognitive Research Principles and Implications* 6, no. 1 (May 2021), https://doi.org/10.1186/s41235-021-00301-5.

21 "We are gripped by the moment": Gal Beckerman, *The Quiet Before: On the Unexpected Origins of Radical Ideas* (Crown, 2022), 3.

21 it took fourteen years: "Discovery and Development of Penicillin: International Historic Chemical Landmark," https://www.acs.org/education/whatischemistry/landmarks/flemingpenicillin.html.

Chapter 2: What Is Worth Wanting?

23 "You've got to get here right away": Dr. Michael Mosley, "Alien Hand Syndrome Sees Woman Attacked by Her Own Hand," BBC News, January 20, 2011, https://www.bbc.com/news/uk-12225163.

24 In 1981 Roger Sperry: Mosley, "Alien Hand Syndrome."

24 A concert pianist: Arantxa Alfaro et al., "When Playing Is a Problem: An Atypical Case of Alien Hand Syndrome in a Professional Pianist," *Frontiers in Human Neuroscience* 11 (April 24, 2017): 198, https://doi.org/10.3389/fnhum.2017.00198.

25 "It's such a pain": Hanna Rosin, "When Your Hand Has a Mind of Its Own," *Invisibilia*, July 29, 2017, NPR, https://www.npr.org/2017/07/29/540214710/when-your-hand-has-a-mind-of-its-own.

26 Religion, psychology, and philosophy: These are certainly oversimplifications, but I believe that directionally they are correct. It's also worth noting that in any faith tradition there are a multiplicity of views.

26 Among philosophers, Epicurus: In taking a philosopher's whole life and work and boiling it down to a sentence, I am, of course, vastly oversimplifying over a century of scholarly and public debate.

27 A more recent macro theory: Those needs come from self-determination theory (SDT). Developed by Edward Deci and Richard Ryan, SDT is a motivational theory emphasizing the universal psychological needs of autonomy, competence, and relatedness as foundational for intrinsic motivation.

27 I find parts of these theories relatable: Theories of human motivation broadly fall into five categories: (1) need-based theories (Maslow's Hierarchy, Alderfer's ERG, Herzberg's Two-Factor), emphasizing inherent human needs; (2) process-based theories (expectancy, equity, goal-setting), focusing on mental decision-making processes; (3) behavioral theories (operant conditioning, reinforcement theory), centered on external reinforcements; (4) cognitive theories (self-efficacy, self-determination theory), highlighting beliefs and cognitive evaluations; and (5) evolutionary/biological theories (evolutionary, drive reduction, arousal), stressing innate biological drivers. Then there are the theories that cross those boundaries. Suffice it to say that among psychology, philosophy, and theology the well of opinions is bottomless.

Chapter 3: The Architecture of Change

47 referred to as "self-regulation" or "self-control": These words tend to get mixed around a lot. However, there are certain times when self-regulation is used to mean the entire process that we cover in chapters 2, 3, and 4. Self-control is usually limited to what we do at the choice point when we feel temptation.

48 like an exhausted muscle: This theory of ego depletion has been questioned heavily in the intervening years since it was proposed and

has failed to replicate in many cases. Among psychology researchers there is ongoing debate about whether what gets depleted is actually willpower or something else, and whether it's simply biological fatigue in the way any part of our body gets fatigue. Some suggest that it's about motivation or our belief in our willpower. But the key here, I think, regardless of where the science ends up landing, is that the experience of us having less willpower after making more difficult choices or when we're tired is real. And the overall idea that we want to rely on willpower as little as possible remains a well-supported approach.

51 the flatline of a depressive episode: Depression has many ways of presenting, many causes, and many levels of severity. I am not making the case that exercise is better at treating depression than medication or other interventions.

53 trigger, routine, and reward: Charles Duhigg, *The Power of Habit: Why We Do What We Do in Life and Business* (Random House, 2012), 21.

53 B. F. Skinner's behavioral chain: B. F. Skinner, *Verbal Behavior* (Prentice Hall, 1957).

53 "antecedent-behavior-consequence": B. A. Iwata et al., "Toward a Functional Analysis of Self-Injury," *Journal of Applied Behavior Analysis* 27, no. 2 (1994): 197–209, https://doi.org/10.1901/jaba.1994.27-197.

58 "There is no more miserable": William James, "Habit," first published in *The Principles of Psychology* (1890).

62 There are a number of apps available: For a list of useful apps for this see oneyoufeed.net/stillpointapps.

63 "Rat Park" experiments: Bruce K. Alexander, Patricia F. Hadaway et al., "The Effect of Housing and Gender on Preference for Morphine-Sucrose Solutions in Rats," *Psychopharmacology* 66, no. 1 (November 1979): 87–91, https://doi.org/10.1007/bf00431995; Practical Recovery, "A Closer Look at the Rat Park Experiment, Part 3," August 2023, https://www.practicalrecovery.com/prblog/a-closer-look-at-the-rat-park-experiment-part-3/; "Rat Park," Stuart McMillen, stuartmcmillen.com, June 2023, https://www.stuartmcmillen.com/comic/rat-park/#page-11.

64 The results were striking: This is not to say that addiction is all environmental, or that all the rats suddenly stopped preferring the drug. What it shows is that environment is one important variable in the yet-to-be-solved equation of addiction.

64 proximity, convenience, and salience: James Clear, *Atomic Habits: Tiny Changes, Remarkable Results: An Easy & Proven Way to Build Good Habits & Break Bad Ones* (Avery, 2018), 63.

64 proximity to a fitness center: J. F. Sallis et al., "Distance Between Homes and Exercise Facilities Related to Frequency of Exercise Among San Diego Residents," *Public Health Reports* 105, no. 2 (April 1990): 179–85, https://pmc.ncbi.nlm.nih.gov/articles/PMC1580056/; Auriba Raza et al., "Distance to Sports Facilities and Low Frequency of Exercise and Obesity: A Cross-Sectional Study," *BMC Public Health* 22, no. 1 (November 2022), https://doi.org/10.1186/s12889-022-14444-7.

65 In 2011, students: iNudgeyou, "Green Nudge: Nudging Litter into the Bin," January 2021, iNudgeyou, https://inudgeyou.com/en/green-nudge-nudging-litter-into-the-bin/.

66 one of many such apps: For a list of useful apps go to http://oneyoufeed.net/resources.

66 A 2010 study: Kevin O. Hwang et al., "Measuring Social Support for Weight Loss in an Internet Weight Loss Community," *Journal of Health Communication* 16, no. 2 (January 31, 2011): 198–211, https://doi.org/10.1080/10810730.2010.535106.

Chapter 4: Moments of Action

74 Immanuel Kant viewed self-control: Marijana Vujošević, "Kant on Self-Control," *Elements in the Philosophy of Immanuel Kant*, May 2024, https://doi.org/10.1017/9781108885232.

74 Neuroscience has shown: Nicholas J. Kelley, Anna J. Finley, and Brandon J. Schmeichel, "Aftereffects of Self-Control: The Reward Responsivity Hypothesis," *Cognitive, Affective & Behavioral Neuroscience* 19, no. 3 (June 2019): 600–618, https://doi.org/10.3758/s13415-019-00694-3.

74 "hot" and "cool" cognitive systems: Janet Metcalfe and Walter Mischel, "A Hot/Cool-System Analysis of Delay of Gratification: Dynamics of Willpower," *Psychological Review* 106, no. 1 (January 1999): 3–19, https://doi.org/10.1037/0033-295x.106.1.3.

75 The drawback: Daniel Kahneman, *Thinking, Fast and Slow* (Farrar, Straus and Giroux, 2011).

76 strength model of self-control: Roy F. Baumeister, Kathleen D. Vohs, and Dianne M. Tice, "The Strength Model of Self-Control," *Current Directions in Psychological Science* 16, no. 6 (November 2007): 351–55, https://doi.org/10.1111/j.1467-8721.2007.00534.x

77 how we *feel* in the moment: Nadine Jung et al., "How Emotions Affect Logical Reasoning: Evidence from Experiments with Mood-Manipulated Participants, Spider Phobics, and People with Exam

Anxiety," *Frontiers in Psychology* 5 (June 10, 2014): 570, https://doi.org/10.3389/fpsyg.2014.00570.

78 like riding an elephant: Jonathan Haidt, *The Happiness Hypothesis* (Basic Books, 2005). Haidt himself credits the metaphor to Buddhist and Hindu sources as well. He also discusses Plato's metaphor in which the Rider is a chariot attached to two horses (the Elephant).

80 In a recent paper: Daniela Becker and Katharina Bernecker, "The Role of Hedonic Goal Pursuit in Self-Control and Self-Regulation: Is Pleasure the Problem or Part of the Solution?," *Affective Science* 4, no. 3 (June 2023): 470–74, https://doi.org/10.1007/s42761-023-00193-2.

85 These hormonal changes: Romain de Rivaz et al., "Associations Between Hunger and Psychological Outcomes: A Large-Scale Ecological Momentary Assessment Study," *Nutrients* 14, no. 23 (December 5, 2022): 5167, https://doi.org/10.3390/nu14235167.

86 a classic episode: *The Simpsons*, season 22, episode 3, "MoneyBART," October 10, 2010, Fox.

89 going through the motions: Nicholas A. Coles et al., "A Multi-Lab Test of the Facial Feedback Hypothesis by the Many Smiles Collaboration," *Nature Human Behaviour* 6, no. 12 (October 2022): 1731–42, https://doi.org/10.1038/s41562-022-01458-9; Emma Young, "Adopting a Smile Can Make You Feel Happier, Large Global Study Finds," British Psychological Society, January 2024, BPS.org.uk, https://www.bps.org.uk/research-digest/adopting-smile-can-make-you-feel-happier-large-global-study-finds.

Chapter 5: Be a Friend to Yourself

98 a harsh internal voice: And my father probably got it from his father.

99 four thousand words per minute: Rodney J. Korba, "The Rate of Inner Speech," *Perceptual and Motor Skills* 71, no. 3 (December 1990): 1043–52, https://doi.org/10.2466/pms.1990.71.3.1043. This study is the source of that number; however, exactly how fast we speak to ourselves is an area of much debate and discussion.

99 40 to 90 percent of our thoughts: The same caveat as above holds here for the exact number of thoughts that are repetitive. Claims as to the exact number vary widely; our own minds can confirm, in any case, that there is a LOT of repetition.

99 this default mode: Not to be confused with the "default mode network" used in neuroscience, although there is some commonality here.

100 Zen master Hakuin: "Blue Cliff Record Case 11, Huang Po's Gobblers

of Dregs," n.d., https://www.treetopzencenter.org/blue-cliff-record-case-11-huang-pos-gobblers-of-dregs/.

101 Theodore I. Rubin, MD, *Compassion and Self-Hate: An Alternative to Despair* (Touchstone, 1998).

102 "Each of you is perfect": David Chadwick, ed., *Zen Is Right Here: Teaching Stories and Anecdotes of Shunryu Suzuki* (Shambhala, 2007).

103 reduces the severity of PTSD: Katherine A. Dahm et al., "Mindfulness, Self-Compassion, Posttraumatic Stress Disorder Symptoms, and Functional Disability in U.S. Iraq and Afghanistan War Veterans," *Journal of Traumatic Stress* 28, no. 5 (October 2015): 460–64, https://doi.org/10.1002/jts.22045.

103 reduce depression and anxiety: Maria Hughes et al., "Self-Compassion and Anxiety and Depression in Chronic Physical Illness Populations: A Systematic Review," *Mindfulness* 12, no. 7 (March 2021): 1597–1610, https://doi.org/10.1007/s12671-021-01602-y.

103 situations including divorce: David A. Sbarra, Hillary L. Smith, and Matthias R. Mehl, "When Leaving Your Ex, Love Yourself," *Psychological Science* 23, no. 3 (January 2012): 261–69, https://doi.org/10.1177/0956797611429466.

103 domestic violence: Ashley Batts Allen, Emily Robertson, and Gail A. Patin, "Improving Emotional and Cognitive Outcomes for Domestic Violence Survivors: The Impact of Shelter Stay and Self-Compassion Support Groups," *Journal of Interpersonal Violence* 36, no. 1–2 (November 2017): NP598–624, https://doi.org/10.1177/0886260517734858.

103 even natural disasters: Joshua Yuhan et al., "Growth after Trauma: The Role of Self-Compassion Following Hurricane Harvey," *Trauma Care* 1, no. 2 (August 2021): 119–29, https://doi.org/10.3390/traumacare1020011.

103 People who have self-compassionate partners: Christine R. Lathren et al., "Self-Compassion and Current Close Interpersonal Relationships: A Scoping Literature Review," *Mindfulness* 12, no. 5 (January 2021): 1078–93, https://doi.org/10.1007/s12671-020-01566-5.

104 self-compassion was consistently effective: David D. Biber and Rebecca Ellis, "The Effect of Self-Compassion on the Self-Regulation of Health Behaviors: A Systematic Review," *Journal of Health Psychology* 24, no. 14 (June 2017): 2060–71, https://doi.org/10.1177/1359105317713361.

104 in helping people: Wendy J. Phillips and Donald W. Hine, "Self-Compassion, Physical Health, and Health Behaviour: A Meta-Analysis," *Health Psychology Review* 15, no. 1 (December 2019): 113–39, https://doi.org/10.1080/17437199.2019.1705872.

105 compassion-focused therapy (CFT): Paul Gilbert, "The Origins and Nature of Compassion Focused Therapy," *British Journal of Clinical Psychology* 53, no. 1 (March 2014): 6–41, https://doi.org/10.1111/bjc.12043.

105 In exploring how people change it's also important to look at the reasons they don't change, a topic into which Ross Ellenhorn's work has lent deep psychological insight. In *How We Change (And Ten Reasons Why We Don't)* (HarperCollins Publishers, 2020), Ellenhorn draws from his decades of experience working with people in mental health treatment to identify ten specific ways that the prospect of change can feel threatening. His insights reveal how seemingly self-sabotaging behaviors often make perfect psychological sense when viewed through the lens of someone who has learned to associate effort with pain.

107 Instead, Rubin suggests: Sometimes I find this way of approaching value to be transformative. Other times I just argue with the idea. We will discuss arguing with this inner voice later in this chapter.

107 "Better to live on a corner": Proverbs 21:9.

107 "the borrower is the slave to the lender": Proverbs 22:6–8.

108 In a 2015 study: Igor Grossmann and Ethan Kross, "Exploring Solomon's Paradox: Self-Distancing Eliminates the Self-Other Asymmetry in Wise Reasoning About Close Relationships in Younger and Older Adults," *Psychological Science* 25, no. 8 (June 2014): 1571–80, https://doi.org/10.1177/0956797614535400.

108 "People were much wiser": Ethan Kross, *Chatter: The Voice in Our Head, Why It Matters, and How to Harness It* (Crown, 2021), 57.

110 awareness as mindfulness: Dr. Kristin Neff, *Self-Compassion: The Proven Power of Being Kind to Yourself* (William Morrow, 2011).

116 a landmark book: Christopher G. Fairburn, *Cognitive Behavior Therapy and Eating Disorders* (Guilford Press, 2008).

Chapter 6: We Don't See the World as It Is, We See It as We Are

131 "Everything we hear is an opinion": Marcus Aurelius, *Meditations*.

131 "Facts is precisely": Friedrich Nietzsche, as translated from Notebooks, Summer 1886–Fall 1887, in Walter Kaufmann, ed., trans., *The Portable Nietzsche* (Viking Press, 1954), 458.

131 "We do not see things": *Seduction of the Minotaur* (Alan Swallow, 1961, 95). A slightly modified version, "We see the world not as it is, but as we are," has been falsely attributed to Stephen Covey.

132 Somewhere in that self-critical spiral: It's important to note that

sometimes when one door or window closes, it takes a while for the next to open. In the interim we are left in what I like to call "the dark hallway." Our job at these points is to keep walking.

133 The original *BuzzFeed* post: Cates Holderness, "What Colors Are This Dress?," *BuzzFeed*, February 26, 2015, https://www.buzzfeed.com/catesish/help-am-i-going-insane-its-definitely-blue.

139 "reality is subject": George Kelly, "A Mathematical Approach to Psychology," in Brendan Arnold Maher, ed., *Clinical Psychology and Personality: The Selected Papers of George Kelly* (John Wiley & Sons), 94–113.

144 Dr. Martin Seligman introduced: Martin E. P. Seligman, *Learned Optimism: How to Change Your Mind and Your Life* (Vintage Books, 2006).

147 "I don't have problems, I have puzzles": This quote is the stuff of anecdote, but Jones himself tweeted something similar on September 15, 2016: "The moment you see your challenges as a puzzle & not a problem . . . you've found your way out," Quincy Jones, X post, https://x.com/QuincyDJones/status/776447734454726656.

148 "The fundamental cause of the trouble": Bertrand Russell, "The Triumph of Stupidity," *New York American*, May 10, 1933.

149 "Doubt requires more courage": "John Patrick Shanley's Preface for *Doubt: A Parable*," commonwealtheatre.org, August 5, 2024, https://commonwealtheatre.org/john-patrick-shanleys-preface-to-doubt/.

150 "We 'Big Picture' people": Bill Watterson, *Calvin and Hobbes*, April 10, 1995.

151 five to ten times more stars: Our estimates of both stars and grains of sand are always changing but here's one reference: Phil Plait, "Do Stars Outnumber the Sands of Earth's Beaches?," August 2024, https://www.scientificamerican.com/article/do-stars-outnumber-the-sands-of-earths-beaches/.

Chapter 7: The Middle Way

159 Chapter 9 of the Tao: From the interpretation of the *Tao Te Ching* I did as part of the Rebind project. Eric Zimmer, "Selections from the *Tao Te Ching*," https://www.rebind.ai/library/selections-from-the-tao.

165 seem innocent enough: Once upon a time they did, anyway.

170 *Factfulness* by Hans Rosling: Hans Rosling, *Factfulness: Ten Reasons We're Wrong About the World—and Why Things Are Better Than You Think* (Flatiron Books, 2018).

170 The share of the human population: Joe Hasell et al., "Poverty," Our World in Data, October 2022, https://ourworldindata.org/poverty.

170　Maternal mortality: Max Roser, "Mortality in the Past: Every Second Child Died," April 2023, https://ourworldindata.org/child-mortality-in-the-past.

171　Rosling associated optimism: Rosling, *Factfulness*, 69.

Chapter 8: We Find Ourselves in Others

178　supposed to be a fifteen-minute conversation: "Dr. Bob's Nightmare," from *Alcoholics Anonymous, Big Book, Fourth Edition* (A. A. World Services, Inc., 2013).

178　the founding moment: Technically the founding happened a few weeks later when Dr. Bob had his last drink.

179　I've finally—gratefully—accepted: Why this was not obvious to me is slightly confusing given how much of my life had been shaped by 12-step programs and group therapies.

179　Surgeon General Vivek Murthy: Sarah Johnson, "WHO Declares Loneliness a 'Global Public Health Concern,'" *The Guardian*, November 16, 2023, https://www.theguardian.com/global-development/2023/nov/16/who-declares-loneliness-a-global-public-health-concern.

181　"the whole of the holy life": Upaddha Sutta (SN 45.2) in the Pāli Canon.

181　a study of privileged undergraduates: Robert Waldinger and Marc Schulz, *The Good Life: Lessons from the World's Longest Scientific Study of Happiness* (Simon & Schuster, 2023).

183　more people live alone: Daniel de Visé, "A Record Share of Americans Is Living Alone," *The Hill*, July 10, 2023, https://thehill.com/policy/healthcare/4085828-a-record-share-of-americans-are-living-alone/.

183　few to no close friends: Catherine Pearson, "Why Is It So Hard for Men to Make Close Friends?," *New York Times*, November 28, 2022, https://www.nytimes.com/2022/11/28/well/family/male-friendship-loneliness.html.

185　As Gershen Kaufman wrote: Gershen Kaufman, *The Psychology of Shame: Theory and Treatment of Shame-Based Syndromes* (Schenkman Books, 1992).

186　"a completely mutual thing": *Alcoholics Anonymous Comes of Age* (Alcoholics Anonymous Publishing, 1957).

186　One of the outcomes: What constitutes a sponsor is, let's just say, not an exact science. The word "sponsor" doesn't appear in the first 164 pages of the Big Book (AA's main text). Despite this, sponsors have become a foundational part of how the program is practiced today. For some, a sponsor is simply someone who walks you through the Twelve

Steps like a trail guide who's been up the mountain before and knows which turns tend to lead to poison ivy and existential dread. For others, a sponsor becomes something closer to a spiritual Swiss Army knife: mentor, therapist, life coach, surrogate parent, late-night voice of reason, occasional pain in the ass. And most of them fall somewhere in between. There's no one-size-fits-all definition, and maybe that's actually the point. It's a relationship, not a job description.

189 One of the most insightful studies: Rena R. Wing and Robert W. Jeffery, "Benefits of Recruiting Participants with Friends and Increasing Social Support for Weight Loss and Maintenance," *Journal of Consulting and Clinical Psychology* 67, no. 1 (January 1999): 132–38, https://doi.org/10.1037/0022-006x.67.1.132.

192 Becky and Jess: The inspiration for this story is drawn from two sources. The first is Amanda Rose's paper about co-rumination: Amanda J. Rose, Wendy Carlson, and Erika M. Waller, "Prospective Associations of Co-Rumination with Friendship and Emotional Adjustment: Considering the Socioemotional Trade-Offs of Co-Rumination," *Developmental Psychology* 43, no. 4 (January 2007): 1019–31, https://doi.org/10.1037/0012-1649.43.4.1019. The second is this web article: Shayla Love, "Rehashing Your Problems with Friends Can Turn into a Bad Habit," Psyche.co, June 27, 2024, https://psyche.co/ideas/rehashing-your-problems-with-friends-can-turn-into-a-bad-habit.

193 *a co-rumination cycle*: Ibid. Rose, "Prospective Associations of Co-Rumination."

193 cognitive reappraisal: Frédéric Nils and Bernard Rimé, "Beyond the Myth of Venting: Social Sharing Modes Determine the Benefits of Emotional Disclosure," *European Journal of Social Psychology* 42, no. 6 (April 2012): 672–81, https://doi.org/10.1002/ejsp.1880.

194 "Left to our own devices": Parker J. Palmer, *A Hidden Wholeness: The Journey Toward an Undivided Life* (John Wiley & Sons, 2009).

196 In a recent *Nature* article: Itai Yanai and Martin J. Lercher, "It Takes Two to Think," *Nature Biotechnology* 42, no. 1 (January 2024): 18–19, https://doi.org/10.1038/s41587-023-02074-2.

198 the Ferme Saint-Siméon scene: Phyllis Lee Levin, "An Inn Whose Setting Inspired Impressionists," *New York Times*, March 17, 1985, https://www.nytimes.com/1985/03/17/travel/an-inn-whose-setting-inspired-impressionists.html.

199 Research by Jeffrey Hall: Jeffrey A. Hall, "How Many Hours Does It Take to Make a Friend?," *Journal of Social and Personal Relationships* 36, no. 4 (March 2018): 1278–96, https://doi.org/10.1177/0265407518761225.

Chapter 9: Allowing Everything to Be Exactly as It Is

218 there was no mouth: This is a slight variation on Milarepa's story that I encountered here: Aura Glaser, "Into the Demon's Mouth: How to Face Our Fears like Milarepa," *Tricycle: The Buddhist Review* (blog), June 9, 2017, https://tricycle.org/magazine/milarepa-face-fears/.

219 the famous Serenity Prayer: The prayer was originally written—or a version of it—by Christian theologian Reinhold Niebuhr in the early 1930s.

221 It's a page in the AA Big Book: A quick note for AA sticklers: If you're looking for the old page 449—where the line "acceptance is the answer to all my problems today" lived in the third edition—you'll find it on page 417 in the current fourth edition. Same story, now titled *Acceptance Was the Answer*, just shifted a few pages earlier.

225 Suffering = Pain x Resistance: Shinzen Young, "A Pain-Processing Algorithm," Shinzen.org, December 7, 2016, https://www.shinzen.org/wp-content/uploads/2016/12/art_painprocessingalg.pdf.

226 Denmark and Finland: Benedict Carey, "Denmark's Secret to Happiness: Low Expectations," *New York Times*, January 8, 2007.

227 Expectations are premeditated resentments: I started hearing this phrase in recovery meetings in the 1990s. I have not been able to find an original source for it.

234 consider how hard it is: "Consider how hard it is to change yourself and you'll understand what little chance you have in trying to change others" has been attributed to Jacob M. Braude, a judge and author known for compiling collections of anecdotes and quotations.

234 "All parenting turns on a crucial question": Andrew Solomon, *Far from the Tree: Parents, Children and the Search for Identity* (Scribner, 2014).

238 The Buddhist-inspired "Five Givens": David Richo, *The Five Things We Cannot Change: And the Happiness We Find by Embracing Them* (Shambhala Publications, 2008).

Chapter 10: The Gift of Presence

247 little Calvin articulates this truth: Bill Watterson, *Calvin and Hobbes*, April 17, 1988.

250 bottom-up and top-down attention: Fumi Katsuki and Christos Constantinidis, "Bottom-Up and Top-Down Attention: Different Processes and Overlapping Neural Systems," *The Neuroscientist: Reviews at the Interface of Basic and Clinical Neurosciences* 20, no. 5 (October 2014): 509–21, https://doi.org/10.1177/1073858413514136.

250 we can exhaust our ability: As I've said before, there is still debate about what actually gets depleted when we talk about willpower, and the same goes for attention. Some argue it's a resource that runs low, others say it's more about shifts in motivation or priorities. Regardless of where the science lands, there's broad agreement that it becomes more difficult to maintain focus or self-control over time.

251 "If while washing dishes": Thich Nhat Hanh, *The Miracle of Mindfulness: An Introduction to the Practice of Meditation* (Beacon Press, 1996).

254 ER doctors, whose day-to-day business: Tobias Augenstein et al., "Multitasking Behaviors and Provider Outcomes in Emergency Department Physicians: Two Consecutive, Observational and Multi-Source Studies," *Scandinavian Journal of Trauma, Resuscitation and Emergency Medicine* 29, no. 1 (January 7, 2021): 14, https://doi.org/10.1186/s13049-020-00824-8.

257 We can't escape the tigers: To explore this idea and metaphor more, I highly recommend the poem "Relax," by Ellen Bass, from her book *Like a Beggar*. It is probably my favorite poem of all time.

258 "small glimpses many times": Loch Kelly, "Small Glimpses, Many Times," *Loch Kelly* (blog), September 20, 2017, https://lochkelly.org/small-glimpses-many-times.

258 a *priority map*: Jacob T. Fisher, Frederic R. Hopp, and René Weber, "Mapping Attention Across Multiple Media Tasks," *Media Psychology* 26, no. 5 (September 3, 2023): 505–29, https://doi.org/10.1080/15213269.2022.2161576.

264 capacity to be extraordinary: I am not saying that you can make all your moments extraordinary, because that would break the meaning of extraordinary. What I am saying is that the capacity to be extraordinary lies within each moment. I also think that feeling like every moment should be extraordinary is a recipe for strife. It's sort of the opposite of chapter 9's allowing things to be what they are.

264 "never again to treat any moment as ordinary": I love both this quote and Socrates's quote above it, as cited in Dan Millman's *Way of the Peaceful Warrior* (H. J. Kramer, 2006), but neither would pass a middle-way test ("every" and "never": red-flag words). Many moments are going to be just ordinary, rote and routine. Such is life, but a

greater attention to trying to be present will allow you to feel more alive more often.

Conclusion

268 a complementary idea: *allostasis*: Hat tip to Brad Stulberg and his excellent book *Master of Change* (HarperOne, 2023).

270 Neuroscientist Alex Korb: Alex Korb, *The Upward Spiral: Using Neuroscience to Reverse the Course of Depression, One Small Change at a Time* (New Harbinger Publications, 2025).

INDEX

ability, 8–9, 17–18, 60
acceptance, 102, 217–244, 248, 252
accountability, 190
action, 12, 21, 40–41, 71–94, 220, 227
addiction recovery, xix. *See also* Alcoholics Anonymous (AA)
adjectives, extreme, 164
adverbs, extreme, 164–165
Adyashanti, 241
alien hand syndrome (AHS), 23–25
akrasia, 46, 47, 73
Alcoholics Anonymous (AA), 16, 20, 178, 185, 186–187, 199, 219, 221–222, 270
Alexander, Bruce, 63–64
alignment, 56, 63–67
"all or nothing" thinking, 161, 165–166, 169
allostasis, 268–269
ambiguity, 58, 59
Ananda, 180–181
anchoring prompts, 62

"and," use of, 165–166
antecedent-behavior-consequence (ABC), 53
antecedents, 54
approval, acceptance versus, 223–224
Aristotle, 46, 158
Atomic Habits (Clear), 64
attention, 81–86, 89, 100, 249–252, 265
Aurelius, Marcus, 131, 247
autism, 235
automaticity, 34
autonomy, 27
autopilot pitfall, 84–85
availability heuristic, 143–144, 150
awareness, raising, 137–141

"bad faith," concept of, 34
balance, 80–81, 154, 155–156, 159
Balcetis, Emily, 65
Baumeister, Roy, 75–76, 85
Be Here Now (Ram Dass), 247
Beatles, 196, 239

Becker, Daniela, 80
Beckerman, Gal, 21
Behavior Design Lab, 7
behavior(s)
    choosing, 52–53
    combining with inner attitudes with outer, xv, xvii
    Fogg's model of, 8, 12, 60
    moving from values to, 40–43
    planning and, 54–55
    positive, 52–53, 55
    wise habits and, xvi
    See also individual behaviors
benchmarks, 57, 116
Bernecker, Katharina, 80
Bhagavad Gita, 159
biases, 135–136, 141–144, 149, 169
Big History, 151
binary thinking, 166–168
Blake, William, 152
body image, 114–115, 140
Borsheim, Sherry, 119–120
bottom-up attention, 250, 258
Boudin, Eugène, 197–198
Bowling Alone (Putnam), 183
Brahe, Tycho, 21–22
Buddha, 153–155, 180–181, 218, 221
Buddhism, 17–19, 149, 166, 166–167, 180–181, 223–224, 238, 243, 257, 260–261
Burgis, Luke, 31
Burkeman, Oliver, 227

Burns, Robert, 67
busyness, 252–254, 258
Byrne, Karen, 23–25, 27, 30

Calvin and Hobbes, 150–151, 247–248
celebration, 91, 124
certainty, 148–149
chance, 173–174
change
    acceptance and, 227
    architecture of, 45–70
    centering, 160–162
    changing relationship to, 268
    difficulty of, 6–7
    as spiral, 269–270
    stakes of, 211–212
Chatter (Kross), 108
choice, 173–174
choice points, 47
chosen family, 204–205
Christian, David, 151
Circle of Concern, 231–232
Circle of Control, 231–232
Circle of Influence, 231–232
Circles of Trust, 193–194
Civil Rights Movement, 21
Clear, James, 64
co-creation, 174
cognitive biases, 135–136, 141–144
cognitive reappraisal, 193
cognitive systems, "hot" and "cool," 74–75
comparison, 114–118

compartmentalization, 146
compassion, 102. *See also* self-compassion
Compassion and Self-Hate (Rubin), 106–107
compassionate breath, 124
compassion-focused therapy (CFT), 105
compensatory relationship between ability and motivation, 17–18
competence, 27
confidence, 10, 89–90
confirmation bias, 141–142, 143, 149
conflicts, values-based, 30
Confucius, 159
consistency, 5, 15–16
constructive alternativism, 139
contemplation, 12, 21, 40–41, 220
context, 14, 78
convenience, 64, 65
conversation, thoughts created during, 196–197
Copernicus, 136
co-ruination cycles, 193
Covey, Stephen, 231–232
critic, naming inner, 109–110
cues, 54

David, Susan, 32–33, 34, 41
decision-making, 51, 57–58
deep listening, 194
default thoughts, 99–100
delay discounting, 86–87
depression, 206–207, 223

desires
    mimetic, 31–34, 136
    motivation and, 39–40
    values and, 28–30, 38–40
detachment, 159
Dhammapada, 18
DiClemente, Carlo, 12
disappointment, paradox of, 105
discernment, 184, 191–195, 209
disordered eating, 116
distraction, 252, 254–255, 258
diversity, importance of, 187–188
Doctrine of the Mean, 159
Donne, John, 180
doubt, 148–149
Doubt (Shanley), 149
Dress (internet image), 133–134
Duhigg, Charles, 53

East of Eden (Steinbeck), 173, 174
80 percent rule, 213
elephant metaphor, 78–80
Ellenhorn, Ross, 105
emergence, 184, 195–198
Emotional Agility (David), 33
emotional containment, 89
emotional drama, 210
emotional escapism, 88–89
emotional volatility, 47
emotion-based/emotional state prompts, 63, 127
emotions, 77–80
empathy, 102, 113, 142–143, 192, 263

Enchiridion, The (The Handbook; Epictetus), 230
encouragement, 184, 188–191, 209
energy, conserving, 13–14
enlightenment, 18–19, 243, 252
environment, impact of, 63–66
environmental psychology, 64
envy, 31–32
Epictetus, 73–74, 229–231, 232
Epicurus, 26
episodic future thinking, 87–88
Epley, Nicholas, 182, 203–204
executive functions, 74
exercise, 51–52
expectations, 226–228, 238
external components, 48

Factfulness (Rosling), 170–171
Fairburn, Christopher, 116
faith in ourselves, loss of, 211–212
family, chosen, 204–205
Far from the Tree (Solomon), 234
fatigue fallout, 85–86
fault versus responsibility, 233
fear, inner critic and, 112–113, 114
Ferme Saint-Siméon, La, 197–198
Festina lente, xix–xx
fight-or-flight responses, 222
Fitzgerald, F. Scott, 160, 167
"Five Givens," 238
Fleming, Alexander, 21
flexibility, 81
Fogg, BJ, 7–8, 10, 12, 17, 60
Food Rescue US, 200
Ford, Henry, 90
fortitude, 211
four forty-nine, 221–222, 223, 229
framing, 81–83, 100
Freud, Sigmund, 26, 31
fulfillment, values and, 35–37
fundamental attribution error, 142–143

Gabirol, Solomon ibn, 229
Galileo, 136
Gazipura, Aziz, 112
Gilbert, Paul, 105
Golden Mean, 158
Gosho, Master, 166–167, 168
greatness, pressure to achieve, 171–173
Grossmann, Igor, 107–108

habit loop, 53–55
habits, "little by little" versus, 13–16
Haidt, Jonathan, 78
Hakuin, 100
Hall, Jeffrey, 199
HALT (hungry, angry, lonely, tired), 51, 85, 86
happiness
  reality and, 226–228
  study on, 181–182
  values and, 35–37
Happiness Hypothesis, The (Haidt), 78
"have-to" goals, 32–34, 78
have-to hassle, 31–34
"Hello, Stranger" study, 203
Hemingway, Ernest, 71–72, 83
Hendriksen, Ellen, 117

Hidden Wholeness, A (Palmer), 194
hierarchy of needs, 27
hindsight bias, 141
homeostasis, 6–7, 11, 13, 268
How to Be Enough (Hendriksen), 117
humanity, recognizing common, 117–118, 145

"I'd prefer," switch to, 240
identification, 184, 185–188
illusion of truth effect, 20
implementation instructions, 67–68
Impressionism, 197–198
improvement, 102
incremental goals, 91
indulgence, 104
inner attitudes, combining with outer behaviors, xv, xvii
inner monologue/critic, 99–101, 109–114, 136
insignificance trap, 91–93, 136
integrated interest, 32
interconnectedness, 159
internal components, 47
intrinsic interest, 32
Invisibilia (podcast), 25
Irvine, William, 232

Jacobs, A. J., 147–148
James, William, 58, 251
Jeffery, Robert, 189
Jobs, Steve, 171, 172
John and Paul (Leslie), 196
Jones, Quincy, 147

Jongkind, Johan, 197
Journal of Health Communication, The, 66
Journal of Medical Internet Research, 62–63

Kabat-Zinn, Jon, 73
Kahneman, Daniel, 75, 141
Kant, Immanuel, 74
Kaufman, Gershen, 185–186
Keats, John, 167
Kelly, George, 139, 163
Kelly, Loch, 258
Kepler, Johannes, 21
Kidd, Sue Monk, 269
kindness
    compassion and, 102
    daily intention for, 124
    with momentum, 118–120
    treating self with, 98, 100, 103, 105–107
King, Martin Luther, Jr., 228
Korb, Alex, 270
Kross, Ethan, 107–108

lagom, 157–158
Lamott, Anne, 239
language
    acceptance and, 240
    middle way and, 162–168
Lao Tzu, 159
learning, stress and, 104–105
Lennon, John, 196
Lercher, Martin, 196–197
Leslie, Ian, 196
"Let It Be," 239
letting be, 239–240

letting go, 238–239, 269–270
Lewis, C. S., 6
LGBTQ+ rights movement, 21
listening circles, 193–194
listening to inner critic, 110–113
"little by little"
    habits versus, 13–16
    impact of over time, 3–5
    meaning of, 5
    science of, 7–12
location-based prompts, 62, 123
loneliness, 179–180
low-resistance actions, 5

maintenance, 12, 21, 40–41, 220–221
Manjhi, Dashrath, 3–4
Marcus Aurelius, 131, 247
Maslow, Abraham, 27, 35
McCartney, Paul, 196, 239
Me Too movement, 185
meaning making, 137–141, 163, 225
meditation, 17–20, 125, 242–243, 260–261
Meditations (Marcus Aurelius), 247
middle way, 153–175, 228, 232, 233
Milarepa, 217–218, 220–221, 222
Millman, Dan, 264
mimetic desires, 31–34, 136
mindfulness, 110, 260–262, 264–265
Mitchell, Stephen, 37
moderation, 156–160

momentum, 13, 15
Monet, Claude, 197–198
motivation
    ability and, 17–18
    action and, 60
    complexity of, 25–28
    obligation and, 33
    resistance and, 15
    science of little by little and, 8–11
    self-control and, 77
    small wins and, 91
    values and desires and, 28–30
Mountain Man, 4
Murthy, Vivek, 179–180
mutuality, 199

naive realism, 135–136, 142
near enemies, 223–224
needs, hierarchy of, 27
Neff, Kristin, 110, 118, 185
negative capability, 167
negative stimuli, 39
negativity bias, 169
Newton, Isaac, 21–22
Nietzsche, Friedrich, 26, 131
Nin, Anaïs, 131
Nirvana, 18–19. *See also* enlightenment
novelty-seeking impulse, 259

observer's illusion of transparency, 141
obstacles, anticipating, 48–49
Old Man and the Sea, The

(Hemingway), 71–72, 83
O'Malley, Mary, 256
On My Own Side (Gazipura), 112
One You Feed, The (podcast), xiv, 30, 132, 178–179, 181, 226
open hands, 241–242
open-ended questions, 194
opportunity cost, 255–256
optimism, 169–171
ordinary/ordinariness
    embracing, 171–173
    as nonexistent, 262–265
    sacred, 260–262
outer behaviors, combining with inner attitudes, xv, xvii

pain, 225–226
Palmer, Parker, 193–194, 194
parenting, 234–235
parietal lobe, 250
Paris Syndrome, 226
patience, 211
Paul the Apostle, 46
peak experiences, 35
peer pressure, 190–191
people, as prompts, 62, 123
perception, pure, 134–135
permanence, 144–145, 146–147, 149–150
personal construct theory, 139, 163
perspective, 129–152, 209
perspectivism, 131
pervasiveness, 146, 149–150
pessimism, 169–171
phone use, 34, 41–42, 254–256

planning
    avoiding temptation and, 48–49
    changing behavior and, 54–55
    for when things go wrong, 67–68
Plato, 46, 73
"playing the tape all the way through," 87, 150
positive self-talk, 111
"possibilism," 171, 174
Power of Habit, The (Duhigg), 53
Power of Now, The (Tolle), 247
Practice of Groundedness, The (Stulberg), 41
practices, 123–124
preceding-event prompts, 62, 123
precontemplation, 12, 21, 40–41, 220
prefrontal cortex, 74, 105, 250
preparation, 12, 21, 40–41, 220
presence
    acceptance and, 221
    attention and, 246–252
    everyday life and, 245–246, 262–265
    obstacles to, 252–257
    techniques for, 257–262
    When-Then formula and, 122–123
pride, values and, 35–37
Principles of Psychology, The (James), 251
priority maps, 258
proactive still points, 125–127

problem-focused mentality, 252, 256–257, 258
problems, turning into puzzles, 147–148, 256
Prochaska, James O., 12
progress reminder, 124
prompts, 8, 54, 56, 60–63, 123–124
pronouns, extreme, 165
proximity, 64
psychology, motivation and, 26, 27
Psychology of Shame, The (Kaufman), 185–186
pure perception, 134–135
Putnam, Robert, 183
Puzzler, The (Jacobs), 147
puzzles, turning problems into, 147–148, 256

questions, open-ended, 194
Quiet Before, The (Beckerman), 21

radish experiment, 75–76, 85
Ram Dass, 247
random prompts, 62–63, 66, 123–124
Rat Park experiments, 63–64
reality, happiness and, 226–228
recalibration, 213–214
reciprocity, 199
reflections, 123–124
reframing techniques, 82–83, 87, 90, 92, 117–118, 256
relapses, 207–208
relatedness, 27

relationships/community
    chosen family and, 204–206
    developing, 198–204
    discernment and, 184, 191–195
    diversity in, 180–181
    emergence and, 184, 195–198
    encouragement and, 184, 188–191
    identification and, 184–188
    importance of, 177–180, 181–184
religion, motivation and, 26
RENEW framework, 209–211
repetition, 16–17, 19, 20
repression, 224
resets, 209, 213–214
resilience, 56, 67–68, 103, 228
resistance
    acceptance and, 227–228, 233
    alignment and, 56
    lowering, 9, 10–11, 60
    motivation and, 15
    overcoming, 73
    suffering and, 225–226, 235
responding wisely to inner critic, 113–114
responsibility, fault versus, 233
responsive still points, 125–127
reward theory, 13
rewards, 53–55, 74
Richo, David, 238, 240–241
Rimé, Bernard, 193
Rinzler, Lodro, 226
Rogers, Mister, 88

Rohn, Jim, 195
Rose, Amanda, 193
Rosling, Hans, 170–171
routines, 53–55
Rubin, Theodore, 101, 106–107
rushing, 253–254
Russell, Bertrand, 148

sacred ordinary, 260–262
salience, 64, 65
samu, 260–261
Sartre, Jean-Paul, 34
satori, 243
saying yes to the moment, 240–241, 242–243
Segar, Michelle, 51
self-acceptance, 102
self-actualization, 35
self-care, 85–86
self-care hierarchy, 51
self-compassion, 81, 101–106, 118–119, 145, 160–161, 185, 209
self-control, 47–48, 60, 73–76, 77, 80–81, 83–93, 136
Self-Control app, 66
self-criticism, xvi, 97–98, 100–101, 105, 108
self-directed calming, 89
self-doubt stalemate, 89–91
self-improvement, 102, 107
self-regulation, 47–48
self-soothing, 89
self-talk, 99–101, 111, 124. *See also* inner monologue/critic
self-trust, loss of, 211–212

Seligman, Martin, 144
Seneca, 73–74
sensory awareness, 258–260
Serenity Prayer, 219, 221, 229, 232
setbacks, 206–214
7 Habits of Highly Effective People, The (Covey), 231
Shakespeare, William, 167
shame-based syndromes, 186
Shanley, John Patrick, 149
shortsighted stumble, 86–88, 136
Simpsons, The, 86–87
Skinner, B. F., 53
slips, 207–208
small changes
    approach based on, 5–6
    effect of accumulation of, 4–5
    impact of over time, xii–xiii
"small glimpses many times," 258, 259
smiling, 89
Smith, Bob, 178, 179, 186
sobriety, author's path to, xi–xiv, 16–17, 20–21, 45–46, 49–50, 60–61
social contagion, 31
social fitness, 201
social media, 116, 190
social support, 66–67
Socrates, 34
Solomon, Andrew, 234–235
Solomon's paradox, 107–108, 191, 194
soup metaphor, 27–28
SPAR Method, 55–68

specificity, 56–60
Sperry, Roger, 24
spiral, upward, 269–270
"split brain" patients, 24
sponsors/mentors, 186–187, 197
Steinbeck, John, 173
still points, 100, 121–128, 259
stimuli, 53–54
Stoicism, 232
strength model of self-control, 76
stress
    learning and, 104–105
    relationships and, 182
structural components, 48–52
structural planning, 55
structure, as liberating, 49–50
Stulberg, Brad, 41–42
suffering, 225–226, 227, 228, 235
Sujata, 153–155, 172–173
Sun Tzu, 49
sunk cost fallacy, 141
support, 66–67, 177–180, 189–190, 209
surrender, 218
Suzuki, Shunryu, 102

Tao Te Ching, 18, 37, 159
Taoism, 130–131, 158–159, 166, 269
Terence, 118
Thich Nhat Hanh, 251–252, 261
third thing, 166–168
thought, habits of, xvi, 99
thought exercises, on values, 35–38
thoughts, generating new, 196–197

Three Essentials of Zen, 149
Three P's, 144–146
time-based prompts, 61–62, 123
timshel, 173
Tiny Habits (Fogg), 7
Tolle, Eckhart, 247
top-down attention, 250, 258
transparency, observer's illusion of, 141
Transtheoretical Model of Behavior Change (TTM), 12, 40–41, 49, 220
tribes, choosing, 200–202
triggers, 53–55, 60–61
trust, 211–212
Tversky, Amos, 141
twelve-step programs, 16, 103. *See also* Alcoholics Anonymous (AA)
Two Wolves, parable of, 28

unpredictability, 14
upward spiral, 269–270
Upward Spiral, The (Korb), 270

values
    desires and, 28–30
    exercise regarding, 35–38
    moving to behaviors from, 40–43
    naming, 35–38, 136
    reflection on, 34

Waldinger, Robert, 181–182, 201, 203, 206
"want-to" goals, 32–33, 78
wasatiyyah, 159

Way of the Peaceful Warrior (Millman), 264
weight loss programs, support and, 189
When-Then, 121–128, 259
Wherever You Go, There You Are (Kabat-Zinn), 73
willpower, 47–48
Wilpers, Matt, 15–16
Wilson, Bill, 16, 177–178, 179, 186
Wing, Rena, 189
wisdom, 228–233, 252
wise habits
    connection and, 269
    description of, xvi
    meaning of, 13
    returning to, 270
    See also individual habits
women's suffrage movement, 21
Wong, Carmen Rita, 125

Yanai, Itai, 196–197
Year of Living Biblically, The (Jacobs), 147
yin and yang, 158–159
Young, Shinzen, 225
yukta-vairagya, 159

Zen Buddhism. *See* Buddhism
Zhongyong, 159
zooming out, 149–152, 166, 209

ABOUT THE AUTHOR

ERIC ZIMMER is an author, teacher, a speaker, and the creator of *The One You Feed* podcast – an award-winning show with more than 50 million downloads. At twenty-four, Eric was homeless, addicted to heroin, and facing prison. His journey from those depths sparked his lifelong inquiry into human transformation and resilience. Over two decades into recovery, he has become a sought-after teacher and speaker on how to make profound change that leads to more meaning and fulfilment. Through his coaching practice and workshops, he's worked with thousands of people worldwide who want to stop fighting themselves and start moving forward. He lives in Columbus, OH, with his partner Ginny.

@one_you_feed
www.oneyoufeed.net